Patrick
Horsbrugh
Ex Libris

ÆGRE · DE · TRAMITE · RECTO

# LORD MOUNTBATTEN
# THE LAST VICEROY

In his study, Mountbatten and Campbell-Johnson had tidied the last paper into the last dispatch box and locked it.

'Is there anything else, sir?'

'No, Alan. Off you go.'

He looked at the clock on the wall. He had not thought about what he would do as midnight struck. He toyed with the idea of joining Edwina, but decided that he would prefer to be alone, here in the study, where so much of it had happened. He thought of Gandhi, who had left for Calcutta a week earlier to attempt to quell the rioting which had already broken out there. Some would rejoice but many would weep that night, the old man had told him. He smiled ruefully. Gandhi would be asleep now. Not even the dawn of Independence would shake him from his inexorable routine.

The last Viceroy crossed the room to the calendar. 'I DAY LEFT TO PREPARE FOR TRANSFER OF POWER,' it read. He tore the sheet off and dropped it neatly into a wastepaper basket. Below, the next sheet read simply, 'Friday 15 August 1947'. He moved over to the small drinks tray and poured himself a glass from the only bottle there, a vintage port. Then he turned and stood before the portrait of George VI that hung in the room. He raised his glass, and came to attention.

'The King-Emperor,' he said, for the last time.

DAVID BUTLER

# Lord Mountbatten
## The Last Viceroy

METHUEN

LORD MOUNTBATTEN THE LAST VICEROY

First published in Great Britain 1985
by Methuen London Ltd
11 New Fetter Lane, London EC4P 4EE
Copyright © 1985 David Butler

Printed in Great Britain by
Richard Clay (The Chaucer Press) Ltd,
Bungay, Suffolk

---

British Library Cataloguing in Publication Data

Butler, David, 1927–
    Lord Mountbatten: the last viceroy.
    1. Mountbatten, Louis Mountbatten, *Earl*
    2. Great Britain, *Royal Navy* – Biography
    3. Admirals – Great Britain – Biography
    4. Viceroys – India – Biography
    I. Title
    941.082′092′4        DA89.1.M59

    ISBN 0-413-59210-3
    ISBN 0-413-59220-0 Pbk

---

# Part One
# The Last Chukka

## ONE

Behind him on the rostrum, the green flags of the Muslim League were mixed with black flags of mourning. They hung without stirring in the stiflingly hot, humid air.

In the vast crowd gathered to hear him, he alone did not appear to feel the heat, and the roars of thousands of voices calling his name brought no flicker of response to his gaunt face with its high cheekbones and thin, almost bloodless lips. Tall and so spare he seemed nearly skeletal in his pin-striped, double-breasted suit and high collar, he stood at the microphone, his silver hair catching the light as his head lowered.

Mohammed Ali Jinnah, leader of the Muslim League, had just told his followers at this rally in Bombay that he had rejected the latest British plan for the granting of Independence and had withdrawn from active cooperation with the ruling Congress Party, dominated by Hindus. He would never compromise, he had promised them, nor swerve from his implacable aim, to force the Partition of India and the creation of a new sovereign Muslim state, Pakistan.

'*Pakistan Zindabad!*' the voices screamed. 'Long Live Pakistan!'

As Jinnah waited, he wondered how his followers would react to the call he was about to make. A lawyer himself, he had for years insisted on their strict obedience to the rule of law. By letting the Hindus invariably be the ones to start any violence, they would demonstrate to the British and to the world the dangers of handing political power to their opponents and the impossibility of allowing them to govern Muslims. Yet now he had been driven to the bitter

3

conclusion that the law-breakers were winning. It was clearly time for the Muslims to show that they, too, were able to strike, and strike hard, for their cause. He regretted the need for it and the bloodshed which might result; but one demonstration should be enough, one day of direct Muslim action.

The tumult died away as his head rose and his piercing eyes swept over the crowd. 'What we have done is the most significant act in our history,' he told them. 'Never in the whole history of the Muslim League have we done anything except by constitutional methods. But now we are obliged and forced into this position. This day we bid goodbye to constitutional methods!' He had to pause, interrupted again by cheering. 'Today we have forged a pistol – and are in a position to use it!' The cheering grew louder. 'If the Congress wants war, then we accept their offer! We shall have India divided – or we shall have India destroyed!'

The cheering and applause of the packed mass became deafening and he felt his heart swell at the chanting of the rallying cry he had sent echoing throughout the subcontinent. *'Pakistan Zindabad!* . . . *Pakistan Zindabad!'*

Although it was not quite daybreak and the air was still cool, it already had a density you would never sense in England. Arthur Lewis ran a finger round the neck of his shirt, and thanked God he had decided against wearing a celluloid collar for his first full day at the office. The sun had not yet broken the horizon, but the soft yellows and purples of the sky which had so impressed him by their beauty, more intense than any English dawn, were fading, and the pleasant coolness in which he had started his walk to work was giving way to a deep warmth. He felt the heat already under his arms and between his thighs. Perhaps after all he should have put on a lighter suit, though the one he was wearing was his best, for he wanted to make a good impression.

He had been in India for exactly fifteen days and much of that had been spent travelling up by train from Bombay.

4

Winning one of the few remaining places in the Indian Civil Service had been the fulfilment of a boyhood ambition. He had read everything he could and had thought himself well prepared, but nothing could have prepared him for the reality, the sheer immensity of the dusty plains stretching away on either side of the track, the glimpses of villages unchanged for millenia, where life moved at the speed of the bullock cart, the mountains and mountains beyond mountains, the great, slow rivers and the cities whose teeming masses filled the streets with an endless variety of costumes and races and languages, elephants dragging trailers piled with lumber through heavy motor traffic, a naked long-haired *saddhu* accepting alms gravely from a Hindu businessman in a white Congress cap and *kurta* and carrying a briefcase and a copy of *The Times*, bicycles and rickshaws and carriages, the cries of vendors of sweets and water and tea and ice and singingbirds, the brightly fluttering saris and the wide-eyed beggar children in rags, the cripples with their blackened stumps of legs and withered arms, the monkeys and ravens and kites and green parrots, the call of the muezzin to prayer and the garish, fearsome, tinselled Hindu shrines, all the myriad sights and sounds. The ever-present musty, spicy air and the smells that assaulted the senses, of food and excrement and perfume, the acrid stink of urine, the hot warm odour of human bodies and the cloyingly sweet scent of roses and musk and incense. And the heat, which they had assured him he would become used to, but which still left him panting and perspiring so much it embarrassed him.

He could understand now why the people among whom he had come to work and live retreated whenever possible to their compounds and private swimming pools and clubs, distancing themselves from the clamour and diversity of the life outside. If it had not been for the Club with its coolness and English newspapers and quiet conversation, he knew he might easily have been overwhelmed. Of course, the distancing from the native population and the everyday pursuits and interests of the country was wrong

5

and in the past had been overdone. Once he was acclimatized, and knew more of the customs and taboos of the various communities to avoid the pitfalls, he meant to mix more, himself. He did not, after all, have any of the prejudices of many of the older generation. It was all a question of approach and openness; that was how to bridge the historical gap between the Raj and those whose interests it served, he told himself sincerely, and a little smugly.

As he and his silent companion turned into the wide avenue, the sun was just beginning to shimmer through the dusty leaves of the eucalyptus trees that bordered it and a stray shaft touched a bed of scarlet salvias. It was as if they burst into sudden flame and for a moment Arthur caught his breath, ravished by the unexpected beauty of it. Other colours were beginning to stand out, but he was most conscious that the rising sun was making him perspire more freely. He faced another day of wet, slick hair and sodden clothes. He eased his back where already his shirt felt sticky. His so-called 'lightweight' flannel suit was stifling and he looked at his companion's white linen three-piece with envy.

'It's quite hot already, isn't it?' he said.

His companion grunted in agreement. George Cutler had spent thirty years of his life in the Indian Civil Service, most of them here, in Calcutta, though for a brief period he had been posted to Delhi, to supervise some of the administrative work involved in the building of the magnificent and vast new Viceroy's House there between the wars. Viceroy's House was larger even than Versailles.

Watching it rise from the dust of Raisina Hill, Cutler had felt more than a glimmer of pride, but also of foreboding. Had it been built as a sign of confidence, or as a memorial to the Empire? In his first few years of service in India, he had also been seconded as a secretary to the Hunter Committee of Enquiry into the notorious Amritsar massacre. On 13 April 1919, Brigadier General Dyer had ordered his detachment of Gurkha and Baluchi soldiers to

6

fire on an unarmed crowd of Hindus who were demonstrating against British rule. Ten minutes of rapid fire left 379 dead and 1,137 wounded. Dyer had justified his action in the name of law and order, but Cutler knew that that brutal ten minutes had gone deep into the Indian consciousness and had effectively rung the death knell of the British Empire in India.

'I daresay it'll get even hotter than this, before the monsoon comes,' Arthur said.

Cutler's reverie was broken. He glanced at the keen young man in his brand new suit walking alongside him and momentarily felt sorry for him. The boy had promise. It was, perhaps, a pity that he had opted for the ICS as a career at so late a date as this. He must have done very well in the examinations, for they were recruiting so few newcomers nowadays.

'Nothing like it'll be later on,' Cutler said. 'And Calcutta's so low-lying that the humidity can be even more unbearable than the heat. The worst of it is, there's no getting used to it. Whatever anyone may have told you.' Seeing the look of concern on the younger man's face, Cutler smiled. 'If it's any consolation, everyone feels like you do at first. You'll find that first thing in the morning's the only time you can have a decent stroll. You can get to the office and put in half a day's work before the first clerks arrive.'

'I must admit, I'm a bit nervous.'

'Why? You've been here a week.'

'Yes, but this is my first real day's work. I'm grateful to you for showing me the ropes, sir.'

Cutler looked at the young man again, appraisingly. He decided to be honest with him. 'I'm sorry for you, really. I can't pretend that it's the best time to come out here.'

'How's that, sir?'

'No chance of a long-term career. I mean, for chaps of my generation, the ICS has been our whole life. But this new Socialist Government back in England seems

7

determined to pull out some time in the next two or three years – say by 1949.'

'Well, we've been promising Home Rule to the Indians since before the war.'

'True enough, Arthur. But these things have to be very carefully prepared. Attlee and his bunch seem to want just to cut the lifeline and let the entire subcontinent sink or swim.'

Arthur had no wish to become involved in an argument, yet he could not let it pass. 'Surely that would be possible? There's a far larger percentage of Indians in the Service than ever before, many in very senior positions. And the army, the Police Force, the judiciary – and the Government in Delhi's wholly Indian now.'

Cutler nodded. 'Yes, indeed. Though you must remember that all the most senior, decision-making positions are held by us. In Delhi and the Provinces we control the administration. And the Government's more or less a token, a rubberstamp for the decisions of the Viceroy and his staff. We couldn't simply walk out and leave our Indian number twos to get on with it. There'd be utter chaos in a matter of days. Not to mention the fact that the various religious communities are split into separate political camps and would be at each other's throats in no time. They very much need us to keep the lid on the kettle, so to speak.'

'That's something I've been meaning to ask,' Arthur said. 'Back home I kept reading about riots and disturbances. I expected to find a lot of tension here, but I can't say I've noticed any.'

'Oh, it exists, make no mistake, yet considering the size of the population and the real antagonism among the various groups, it could be much worse. Here we have the usual Hindu-Muslim flare-ups in the poorer parts of the city, but the Governor has things well enough in hand.' Cutler spoke reassuringly, though privately he wondered just how well Sir Frederick Burrows *did* have things under control. An ex-railway trades union official, elevated to the Governorship of Bengal, a Labour Government appointee

8

who had only been in his post since February. He wondered. Still, at least the man had a sense of humour. Cutler smiled as he recalled Sir Fred's self-evaluation. 'All the rest of the Raj are good at huntin' and shootin' – me, I'm good at shuntin' and hootin'.' And there was no doubt that his Chief Minister, Shaheed Suhrawardy, was a capable chap, an old-fashioned political boss. Muslims generally seemed to be more able administrators than Hindus, less emotional somehow. And even if Suhrawardy was making a bit on the side – what then? Better to turn a blind eye to the devil you know . . . 'Anyway,' he said, 'there's certainly nothing to worry about today. It's been declared a general holiday. Since it's a Friday, and Suhrawardy and the Muslims are behind it, the Hindus will boycott it. For them it will be business as usual. But you can bet your bottom rupee none of our Muslim clerks will show up.'

The sun was just breaking over the roof-tops as the two Englishmen turned from the elegant, tree-lined avenue into Chowringhee Square and felt the first real hint of the broiling heat that was to come. In under two hours, the square would be like an oven, with every inch of shade occupied by people trying to avoid it and by the cream-coloured cows which freely wandered the streets everywhere.

One of these beasts crossed their path now, gazing at them reproachfully with its slanted, brown eyes as Cutler prodded the characteristic hump on its bony back to hurry it out of the way. 'Blasted animals. Get under your feet. Half of them are starving or diseased, but they'd never kill one. Against their religion. There's a fundamental difference you have to remember: Muslims eat cows, Hindus worship them. D'you know, there was an appalling famine here three years ago. Over two million people died of starvation, but not one Hindu killed a cow to save his own life.'

Arthur's attention had been caught by something else. 'Who are all these people?'

Cutler followed his gaze to where, in the shadows under

9

the walls and the gnarled, ivory trunks of the pipal trees, what looked like hundreds of tattered white sacks, of all shapes and sizes, were beginning to stir. 'Oh,' he said, 'they're the homeless, poor devils. They've nowhere else to go.'

'So many?'

'You'll find them all over Calcutta. They flood in from the countryside, and they multiply like rabbits.'

'Can't something be done for them?'

Cutler shrugged his shoulders. It was an old story to him.

'It's ghastly. Look at that child.' Arthur pointed to where a three-year-old sat playing in the dust by his still-sleeping mother. An open sore on his head was already infested with yellow flies.

The older man laid a hand on Arthur's arm. 'I know what you're thinking. It seems intolerable. I used to feel the same, until I realised they're used to it, that blessed fatalism of theirs. The truth is that there's simply nothing that anyone can – Hello, what's that noise?' They could hear a distant pattering, as of a heavy rainstorm approaching rapidly from beyond the other side of the great square. But it couldn't be rain. It was only August.

'Is it a train?' Arthur asked. Cutler had no time to answer. From the street directly opposite them across the square, a horde of men suddenly erupted. Raggedly dressed like the vagrants awakening from sleep at the sound of their cries, the men whirled iron bars, knives, and the cruel long bamboo truncheons called *lathis* about their heads. The two Englishmen watched, frozen with shock, as the men fanned out and a small group of five or six made for an old woman who was just rising from the ground to escape. They quickly formed a circle round her, tossing her from one to the other, taunting and laughing. One of the men, a giant with a thick black moustache, seized her round the waist. She twisted in his grip and bit him hard on the cheek. Screaming in fury, he hurled her to the ground, raised his *lathi* above her grovelling body and brought it smashing down. The other members of his gang followed his lead, but if their intention was to torture the old woman further, they were wasting their time. The first blow had crushed her skull like an egg.

Everywhere around the two Englishmen this scene of horror was repeating itself. Cutler winced as he saw a baby hurled high in the air and dealt a shattering blow with a crowbar as it fell to earth. Two other men stabbed and hacked at its mother as she wailed. A moment later, the men who had killed her ran towards them. Cutler placed his feet apart and gripped his walking-stick tighter, though he knew that if it came down to it, Lewis and he did not stand a chance. The group approached, fast. Then, to his astonishment, they nodded and smiled, touching their hearts and foreheads in the traditional greeting of *salaam*.

'Good day to you, sir,' the man holding the bloody crowbar said. 'Today we teach these stupid Hindus a thing or two, don't you think?' The men had bobbed past them and were gone before Cutler could reply.

Within two minutes the peaceful square had become a boiling hell which raged round Cutler and Arthur. Averting his eyes from a man plunging his dagger into the flank of a cow, Arthur saw two others wrenching the arms of a struggling young man, dislocating them. A maniacal cry rose from the throats of the slaughterers, settling into a rhythm to which the ferocity of the killing was matched. '*Lar ke linge Pakistan!* . . . *Pakistan Zindabad!*'

Seconds later, the square was deserted again. The engine of murder had moved on, to glut itself elsewhere, but there was no silence. The whimpers of the wounded and the dying penetrated the thick clouds of disturbed dust. Here, a stricken cow, its throat cut, tried to raise itself to its feet; there, an infant tugged in bewilderment at its dead mother's hand.

Seeking escape from what he could see, Arthur Lewis looked down.

And then stepped back, turning and falling to his knees, vomiting in the dust. An old man and a girl lay mangled at

11

his feet. The girl's head was nearly severed. Her light blue robe had been wrenched open and her breasts sliced off.

Cutler stood motionless in horror. He was looking at his suit. The immaculate white linen was drenched in blood, rapidly drying and caking in the heat of the risen sun. After what seemed an age he stumbled over to Arthur and helped him to his feet.

'Oh, God . . . Oh, God . . .' the younger man was muttering.

'Come on, lad,' Cutler urged.

The two of them picked their way across the square, hurrying towards the sanctuary of the Grand Hotel.

Two streets away, the chief reporter for *The Statesman* in Calcutta had finally got a line through to his news-desk.

'I've just seen the first response to Jinnah's Day of Direct Action,' he told the Duty News Editor. 'It's hideous. I'm filing copy now, and I'll ring back later – if I can. Dateline 16 August 1946, Calcutta. Headline it: "The Great Killing".' Despite the electric fan in his office, his hand was sweating so much that the telephone kept twisting round in his fingers.

Over a thousand miles away, on the opposite side of the subcontinent in Bombay, a sixty-nine-year-old Karachi-born lawyer lit his fiftieth cigarette of the day, poured himself a whisky and considered the results of his Day of Action. He polished his monocle and carefully slid it into his waistcoat pocket, then, just as carefully, smoothed out imaginary creases in his Savile Row suit before sitting down at his desk in the ugly but luxuriously appointed house he was occupying on Malabar Hill. So far, his agents' reports had been encouraging. And that morning he had been more than gratified at his meeting with Nehru, who had come to him – and he smiled at the thought – Congress cap in hand, when he had been able to make the Hindu leader sweat a little.

Mohammed Ali Jinnah sipped his whisky fastidiously.

He was, even now, sitting alone and in repose, a formidable figure. Totally and single-mindedly dedicated to his purpose, he was nevertheless a man of many contradictions. He was the undisputed head of the Muslim League and the champion fighter for the Partition of India after Independence into two states: Hindustan for the three hundred million Hindus, and Pakistan for the Muslims. Despite this, he was himself an atheist, and did two things that no Muslim would dream of doing. He ate pork and drank alcohol. He could not speak Urdu, the language of Indian Muslims, and even his name, Jinnah, was not Muslim but Hindu. His family were recent converts to Islam.

Jinnah was a widower. His first marriage had been arranged for him, and after his wife's death he had married again, in his forties. His second wife was an eighteen-year-old Parsi girl Rutten, the daughter of a friend and business associate, and he had married her against her family's wishes, but this mixed marriage of his own did not prevent him later from disowning his own daughter for marrying a Christian. His second marriage had not been successful. He had adored her, but she was like a butterfly caught in a net of steel. Rutten left him in 1929 and died soon afterwards. Since then, Jinnah had lived only for his burning political ambition. Outside that he was a dried husk, his frail body driven on for years by nothing but cigarettes, whisky and willpower. His sister Fatima, who looked like him, gave up her dental practice to become his nursemaid, housekeeper, and only friend.

At the outset of his political career, he had been a member of the predominantly but not exclusively Hindu Congress Party, fighting for Indian unity and Independence alongside Gandhi and Nehru. But his way was not their way. To him, progress could only be made by constitutional methods. Gandhi's increasing use of *satyagraha* – non-violent, passive resistance – struck him as futile and unrealistic. And he could see that Nehru was Gandhi's favourite. How he loathed Nehru! That superior, arty, Anglophile

Brahmin! Increasingly isolated, he had gone into the political wilderness, to return at the behest of Liaqat Ali Khan, now his right-hand man, fired with a new ideal which he had inherited from an obscure Muslim graduate student at Cambridge: Pakistan. To this end the Muslim League had been formed. Jinnah was unshakeably determined to use it to gain for him the creation of the new country, and his absolute leadership of it. Or to die in the attempt.

He settled in his chair, took another sip of whisky, removed the butt of his cigarette from its jade holder and immediately fitted and lit another. He would succeed. He knew it. Already they were calling him the *Qaid-i-Azam* – the Saviour of the People. And the battle-cries of his new nation's freedom – Fight for Pakistan! Long Live Pakistan – had been heard in Calcutta that very morning.

Jinnah reflected on the chain of events which had led him to declare his Day of Action. As always, Nehru and his Congress crew had tried to trick him, using that honourable fool of a Viceroy, Lord Wavell – about as politically astute as a mongoose – as a pawn in their game. But he had been one step ahead of them. The power play had been complex and tense.

Early in 1946 the new British Labour Government had sent a Cabinet Mission to India. Its three members were all old India hands: Sir Stafford Cripps, Lord Pethick-Lawrence – the Secretary of State for India – and the First Lord of the Admiralty. Their objective was to set up what the British Prime Minister, Clement Attlee, called a 'machinery of decision' to pave the way for a complete transfer of power to India. Home Rule at last, thought Jinnah bitterly remembering how the Mission had accepted Congress proposals for a unified India, and rejected the Muslim League's plan for a separate state of Pakistan, formed out of the six Muslim majority provinces: the Punjab, the North-West Frontier Province, Baluchistan, Sind, Bengal and Assam.

And yet at that point, back in May, the door had still been left open for those six provinces to be regarded as an administrative group. The Mission had at least recognized that British India naturally fell into two parts, Muslim and Hindu, and that these were roughly geographically separable. Congress didn't like it, and nor did its recently elected president, Pandit Nehru, but Jinnah saw his chance to strike a blow for the formation of Pakistan when the Viceroy invited individuals from the Congress Party and the Muslim League to form an Interim Government, on the basis of two separate major administrative groups of provinces.

Jinnah finished his whisky, stood up to refill his glass, and paced his study angrily in the gathering dusk as for the hundredth time he rehearsed in his mind the events of the past two months.

He had felt power to be well within his grasp. The Congress said they could not accept the Viceroy's invitation. He, Mohammed Ali Jinnah, would surely be asked to form an Interim Government without them. It was logical. It stood to reason. It was fair. Congress had been offered a chance and refused it. And then the blow fell. To his fury, on 26 June Lord Wavell announced that the Cabinet Mission plan was shelved, and that a Caretaker Government of permanent officials was to be created instead.

The elections to the Constituent Assembly out of which the Caretaker Government would be formed dealt Jinnah a trump card. The Muslim League gained seventy-four of the seventy-nine Muslim seats. But still Nehru insisted that there could be no separate grouping of provinces. Once more, Jinnah saw his way to Pakistan blocked. Baulked, but with the Muslim League indisputably a power in the land, Jinnah took the only line open to him. He withdrew support for the British plan for the hand-over of power, he set the Muslim League apart from any obligations to the British, and made his speech declaring 16 August a 'Direct Action Day'.

Jawaharlal Nehru had heard the news of the Calcutta slaughter with dismay. He had fatally underestimated Jinnah's power and now realized how dangerous an adversary he was. A gentle, sensitive man in many ways, Nehru was also an acute politician, and rapidly revised his strategy as he drove away from his meeting with Jinnah on 16 August, a hopeless attempt to win the Muslim leader round. The only way to avert civil war would be to set up an Interim Government as soon as possible, including Muslim representatives, albeit non-League members. By the time he had arrived back in Delhi on 17 August the Calcutta blood-bath showed no sign of abating, only now *both* communities were hacking each other to death. Nehru was in the greatest agony of mind.

At Viceroy's House, he and Lord Wavell swiftly prepared a list of proposed members for an Interim Government. A week later, the Government was announced and Wavell, broadcasting from Delhi on All-India Radio, appealed to the Muslim League to reconsider its decision, and join it. Jinnah's reaction was to declare 2 September, the day the new Government took office, a 'Black Day'. Muslim flags of mourning decorated every Islamic building in India. From Bombay, the *Qaid-i-Azam* announced: 'India is on the brink of ruinous civil war.' His cry of 'Pakistan or nothing' sent shockwaves of hate and terror across the country, and rioting and killing took place from Bombay to Dacca.

But civil war did not come, and Jinnah soon saw that if he were to press his advantage he would have to do so from within the Interim Government. Congress and Nehru had British backing and between them in time they could force the Muslim League out into the cold and shatter forever his dreams of Pakistan, if he remained aloof.

The Viceroy handed his visitor a drink.

'What is it?' asked Mohammed Ali Jinnah.

'Whisky. That's your tipple, isn't it?' said Lord Wavell.

'Thank you.'

Wavell glanced surreptitiously at his watch. He had a good deal of sympathy with the Muslim cause but there was something about this cold fish of a man that made him deeply uncomfortable. His three years as Viceroy had seemed like a lifetime, and yet it seemed to him too that he had been able to do little other than tread water. The two months that had passed since the outbreak of violence in August had unnerved him. He wondered how Attlee would respond to his contingency 'Operation Ebb-Tide', to evacuate the British from India, when he met the Prime Minister in London the following month.

But the Muslim League had finally agreed to join the Interim Government. That at least was a step in the right direction. And now, as soon as they'd had this courtesy drink together, he would get the insufferable Bombay lawyer out of his house and out of his hair. He raised his glass.

'To a free and unified India,' Wavell said firmly.

Mr Jinnah did not reply.

On 26 October, five representatives of the Muslim League, including Jinnah's right-hand man, Liaqat Ali Khan, joined the Interim Government. Keen to provoke the Hindus, and especially the high-caste Brahmin Nehru, in the smallest way, Jinnah had also included an Untouchable in his team. He was showing the coldness of his own spirit and underestimating the greatness of Nehru's.

A month later, when Lord Wavell was in London, Jinnah issued an *ukase* to his followers forbidding any of them to take his seat on the Constituent Assembly. It was the first step in his plan to paralyse government and cramp constitutional progress from within.

When news of this latest action was relayed by the India Office, it merely served to convince the British Prime Minister, Clement Attlee, of the correctness of the step he was about to take.

# TWO

She laid down her pen for a moment and flexed her fingers. The daunting task of writing letters of thanks after the marriage of her daughter Patricia to John Brabourne had to be finished today, but she simply had to rest her eyes for a minute. She could feel the all-too familiar signs of a headache coming on, something which the smell of her mother-in-law's cigarettes did little to help. The old lady sat behind her in the room, reading the *Manchester Guardian* and chain-smoking, as usual.

Her old Sealyham, lying on the floor at her feet by the escritoire, sensed the break in her concentration and looked up at her. She nuzzled the dog with the toe of her shoe.

'Sh-sh, Mizzen. You'll get your walk later.' Reassured, the animal laid its head on its paws again. She looked at the photograph in its silver frame on her writing table. Hard to imagine that it was already five years old. He'd just been promoted Commodore when it was taken, and it showed him, proud and handsome, in his new uniform. And in the short time since then, so much had happened. It was easy to see why the years had flown. Only a few months after the photograph, Churchill had made him Chief of Combined Operations, at the age of forty-one, and he had been accorded the acting ranks of Vice Admiral, Lieutenant General, and Air Marshal, with authority over men many years his seniors. They had both thought that was honour enough, and while she had shared his elation, she had also at the bottom of her heart envied him his achievement. But greater honours than this were in store. Barely two years later Churchill had again summoned him, to give him the position of Supreme Commander, South-East Asia Command. Between that time and the end of the war, he had turned a demoralized army into a force which swept the Japanese from the gates of India, out of Singapore and Burma, and into the sea.

Yet she herself had not done badly, she reflected. At this very moment she was wearing her own uniform, as Superintendent-in-Chief of the St John's Ambulance Brigade, and on her jacket she bore three rows of medals. No, at forty-five, she had not done badly at all. And their marriage . . .

She lifted her gaze through the window to the rolling lawns and bare trees outside, under a brooding December sky. Well, she considered, their marriage had had its ups and downs; perhaps more downs than ups, she thought ruefully, remembering Laddie Sandford, and how the Press had treated her over him, and the difficult times they had had in the late twenties. And Dickie had had affairs too, she knew. She also knew that it was her fault that he had had them, and from his love letters she knew, too, that it was she whom he had unwaveringly loved from the first. Now, with the approach of middle age, and with the hard work in which they had competed with each other during the war years, perhaps the lack of sexual fire mattered less. They had two beautiful daughters. They had money, and success. Besides, she thought, they had driven themselves, worked, far too hard for there to be room for anything but sleep when they went to bed. And now they had found peace of a sort with one another. She doubted if another man would ever again set her on fire. Certainly no man could make her more jealous. She acknowledged with something approaching shame the jealousy with which she regarded the closeness of his relationship with Patricia, their elder daughter.

She glanced around the room, settling back in her chair. The drawing-room at Broadlands, their Hampshire home, had been one of the first she had turned her attention to when redecorating the house after its wartime duty as a hospital. It reflected her. Light, bright, and businesslike, and by no means overpowering. Visitors had called it charming. Her gaze took in the many framed photographs, all signed, of King George and Queen Elizabeth, of Churchill, Roosevelt, General Eisenhower, Chiang Kai-Shek. On the chimney-piece were two of Patricia and Pamela as children, and on a side-table, one of the most recent, of Patricia's wedding.

It reminded her of the task in hand, but as she turned to it again her mother-in-law paused in the act of lighting yet another cigarette.

'Edwina, my dear, you look worn out.'

'I'm just a little tired after the wedding.'

'You ought to take more care of yourself. You're not getting any younger.'

'Thank you.'

Princess Victoria, Marchioness of Milford Haven, refused to be drawn. 'Was it really necessary to have a thousand guests? This is supposed to be a time of austerity.'

'Dickie and I wanted Patricia to have just as wonderful a wedding as we had.' Edwina forebore to mention that, time of austerity or not, as an heiress to millions she could well afford to push the boat out now and then. Broadlands itself had belonged to her father, and she had inherited much of her grandfather's fortune: Sir Ernest Cassel, a German-born Jewish banker, had left £7½ million when he died. But Edwina had left the giddy times of high society behind her long ago, and, having been born to it, money was not of the first importance to her. 'The only trouble is, now there're all these thank-you letters to get through.'

'I'd throw them in the bin.' Princess Victoria of Hesse had been born in 1863. Now in her eighties, her forceful personality was undiminished. Since her husband, Prince Louis of Battenberg, had died a broken man in 1921, following a vicious whispering campaign led by the gutter-press baron Horatio Bottomley, directed against him during the First World War, she had learnt to be tough and to

20

devote her energy and pride to the career of her youngest child. Prince Louis had been created First Sea Lord by Churchill in recognition of his having the British Fleet ready in time to oppose the Kaiser's forces. But he had been forced to resign because he was himself a German. He had changed his name from Battenberg to Mountbatten at the same time as King George V had changed his from Saxe-Coburg to Windsor. Since his death, all the ambitions of his younger son, Louis Francis Albert Victor Nicholas, had been directed to following in his footsteps, achieving his rank, and vindicating his memory.

'Throw them in the bin?' laughed Edwina. 'Nonsense. But I must finish them today. There's so much to clear up and get ready before we go off to Malta.'

'*If* you go,' said Princess Victoria. 'You'll hate Malta. You won't be queen of the ball there, you know. Dickie's not Supreme Commander any more. Just a plain naval officer again.' 'Dickie' was a family nickname: Louis Mountbatten had originally been called 'Nicky', but so many of his cousins shared the name in a family that spanned the aristocracy of Europe that it was confusing.

'He does realise that. Anyway, the Lords Commissioner have made him a Rear Admiral. I don't call that "just another naval officer".'

Princess Victoria brushed this aside. 'You won't be sharing any limelight there, either. It won't be like Burma. You'll have to take third or even fourth place to all those navy wives with husbands senior to him.'

'It'll be easier for me than him. Anyway, we've discussed it all. It's the right thing for him.'

Finally, against all Edwina's hopes, the old lady lit her cigarette. 'Why?'

'Because of the envy he generated when Churchill promoted him so fast. He's got to prove to the navy that he's still serious about his career with them. That's why he's on this Senior Officers' training course at Portsmouth at the moment. It's not easy for him to come down so many pegs, but if he doesn't – '

' – he won't ever get to be First Sea Lord?'

'That's what he wants.'

'Yes.' Princess Victoria looked at her daughter-in-law shrewdly. 'Or is it what you want?'

Edwina smiled. 'I have no influence over him. Mother, I really must get on with these letters.'

'Just a minute! Of course it's what you want. You've guided every step he's taken up the ladder so far.'

'I think you should give Mr Churchill and President Roosevelt some credit, too.'

Princess Victoria ignored this. 'You two have always got to compete with each other. Don't think I don't know what drives him! You both have to be best at whatever you do, and you both have to be the centre of attention. But it isn't the world you're trying to impress; it's each other!' The old lady softened, and puffed her cigarette for a moment. 'But the most sensible thing he ever did was to marry you.'

Outside, a car drew up, and Mizzen, instantly awake again, rushed from the room, barking happily. The two women looked at each other in surprise. Only one person would merit that kind of welcome from Mizzen. Now, they heard voices in the hall as the butler opened the front door, and moments later, preceded by Mizzen, who was fussing around him, Louis Mountbatten entered the room. He walked over and kissed first his wife, and then his mother, on the cheek.

Dickie Mountbatten's grandmother was Queen Victoria's third child, Princess Alice. Through her, and the mighty house of Saxe-Coburg and Gotha, he could trace relatives throughout the royal families of Europe. His uncle by marriage was Tsar Nicholas II, who died so tragically with his children, Mountbatten's cousins, in the Russian Revolution. He was the brother-in-law of Andrew of Greece, and Gustav VI of Sweden; the second cousin of Kings Edward VIII and George VI of England – known to him by their family names of 'David' and 'Bertie' – through their grandfather, his great-uncle Edward VII, who was also Edwina's godfather. Through his great-aunt Beatrice he could claim as relatives the Duke of Segovia and the Count of Barcelona, father of King Juan Carlos. He was as old as the century, and 1946 found him in the prime of life, poised, after a wartime career which would have crowded most men's existences, to resume the ambition of his lifetime.

Confident, athletic and handsome in his Rear Admiral's uniform, with looks that any film star might have envied, Mountbatten seemed to have found unfair favour with the gods. He had been born rich and an aristocrat, and his marriage had made him a man of fabulous wealth. His life had been so filled with travel and adventure that even by the time he was twenty-two he could praise the beauty of the Grand Canyon and qualify his praise by adding, 'and I know what I'm talking about when I call it one of the most beautiful places on earth, for I've seen eighty-five per cent of the world already.' At Dartmouth and at Cambridge he had formed a reputation for radical thinking, which had not gained him many friends among his hidebound colleagues, although Churchill had not been alone in recognizing its positive qualities.

'What are you doing here? Turning up like a bad penny,' said Princess Victoria, stubbing out her cigarette.

Edwina had returned to her letters. 'Don't pay any attention to her. This is her day for being cantankerous.'

'Just because I've been telling her to slow down a little. Not that she will as long as you don't.'

'I'm afraid you're right,' said Dickie, perching on the arm of a chair and tickling Mizzen's ears.

'Why doesn't she give up this St John's Ambulance business, at least? You'd have thought she'd have done her fair share by now. All that work in Burma.'

'I'll give it up if you give up smoking,' said Edwina, adding another completed letter to the pile on her right.

Princess Victoria bridled and promptly reached for another cigarette. 'By the way, Dickie, since you are here there's something I've been meaning to ask you. I couldn't help noticing Philip and Princess Elizabeth at Patricia's wedding. They seem almost inseparable.'

'Really?'

'Yes, really,' answered Princess Victoria. 'And I want to know what's going on.'

Mountbatten smiled. It was true that his nephew Philip, who had lived with him as his son for eighteen years, was seemingly now, at twenty-five, deeply drawn to Bertie's older daughter, the shy, pretty twenty-year-old who would one day be Queen of England. Philip's advances did not seem to be unwelcome, either.

He exchanged a quick look with Edwina. 'It's all highly confidential,' he began, cautiously.

'You can drop that diplomatic manner with me,' said Princess Victoria emphatically. 'Now, what is going on?'

'I gather the King and Queen Elizabeth know about it, and they seem to approve. In fact, I shouldn't be at all surprised if there isn't an announcement of an engagement quite soon. But for God's sake keep it under your hat.'

'And do you approve? You know what it will mean for Philip.'

'The fact that they love each other seems to be the main thing. And personally, I couldn't be more delighted.'

'Quite an addition to the family tree.'

'It's remarkable how it all links up. I can't wait to do some more work on it. If only there were more time.'

'I sometimes wonder if you don't spend too much on those genealogical tables of yours as it is,' put in Edwina. She closed an envelope and added it to the pile on the right-hand side of the escritoire. 'There. Only another dozen or so to do, and they're the least important of the lot. I should be able to polish them off after luncheon.' She stood up. 'How rude I've been to you, Dickie. I'll ring for some drinks, and you can tell us what brings you back home so unexpectedly. Or have you decided that there's nothing on your course at Portsmouth that you don't already know?'

Mountbatten became more serious. 'I've been summoned to Downing Street.'

Edwina frowned. 'By Mr Attlee? Do you know what for?'

'No idea, really. Some administrative mess-up in Burma, I think. I told them they should put old Dorman-Smith out to grass. As it is, I reckon we've just about lost all the influence we had there.' He broke off, glancing at his watch. 'As a matter of fact, I'd better get on. I just dropped in here *en route* to see you and to struggle into some civvies.'

'It's that urgent?'

'Apparently it is.'

'Well, I shall look forward to hearing about it all tomorrow.'

'Tomorrow?'

'Yes. I was going up to town in the morning anyway. I'll meet you at Chester Street.'

Mountbatten didn't take long to change. With the help of his valet he had got changing clothes down to a fine art, and had introduced various technical innovations into his wardrobe. Zips for trousers for one thing, which *London Life* had heralded in 1934 as 'one of the most important developments of men's trousers since knee breeches'. Always immaculate, he could nevertheless undress, bath and dress again in two minutes. By the time he was ready the drinks tray had been brought in, and although he was not a great drinker, he felt justified in taking a large whisky and soda before leaving to keep his appointment with the Prime Minister at Number 10, Downing Street.

Clement Attlee was worried. Since he had swept to power the previous year one of the election promises he had made which he most urgently wished to fulfil was that of granting Independence to India. The policy was not entirely altruistic: it was long overdue, and had in his view not been achieved earlier because of the extraordinarily old-fashioned and unenlightened attitudes of his predecessors in office, notably his immediate predecessor, the old war-horse, Winston Churchill. Churchill was half a century out of date at least, Attlee considered, and obviously the country felt the same way. He had been a great wartime Prime Minister, but no sooner was the war over than he and his Conservative Party had been swept from power and Attlee and the Labour Party had been brought in by a landslide. However, as Leader of the Opposition Churchill was still a power in the land and Attlee knew that he regarded any ateempt to give up India as a blow to the heart of British world supremacy.

Nevertheless, the deed must be done. The Indians were clamouring for Independence, which had in any case been more or less assured them in 1942; and what was more, the war had cost Britain dear. The old country could no longer afford to support the expense of administration in India.

Attlee took out his pocket watch and glanced at it before slipping it back into his ginger tweed waistcoat pocket. A foxy, donnish man of sixty-three, with one of the most agile intellects ever to occur in British politics, he was outwardly unprepossessing. Slightly built, stooping and bald, his appearance was not improved by clothes which seemed never to be pressed and always a size too big for him, and a small apology for a moustache. It was not until you became aware of the intelligent eyes and the wry cast of the mouth that you recognized the stature of the man you were dealing with. He sat at the large mahogany-and-leather Prime Ministerial desk, which Churchill had dominated, but which seemed to dwarf him, yet he could not settle. He rummaged in his pockets for his pipe and tobacco, filled and lit it, and settled back to review the situation in his mind.

Over two million Indians had volunteered to serve with the Allies during the war. Indeed even now Sikh battalions were still stationed abroad, one in particular guarding British oil interests at Basra in Iraq. India herself had not, however, aligned against the Axis Powers, thanks to Mr

26

Gandhi. Attlee admired Gandhi, but smiled at the recollection of Gandhi's advice to Britain to bare her neck to the Germans. Letting the Nazis in and then offering them passive resistance wouldn't have cut much ice with Hitler. Nevertheless, Gandhi and his disciple, Nehru, had been such thorns in the side of the British administration that with the advance of the Japanese, it became necessary to step in. The Coalition Government had sent over Sir Stafford Cripps, a man with deep experience of India, in 1942. Cripps, an austere socialist, and a vegetarian, with long-established friendships within the Congress Party, was sent to offer Independence after the defeat of Japan, in return for cooperation against the enemy now. However, the offer was conditional upon the formation of a separate Islamic state, Mr Jinnah's Pakistan. Such Partition was against the first principle of the then all-powerful Congress Party, and indeed, as Attlee now saw, the terms of the proposal were simply not generous enough for India to accept. The 1942 mission was a failure, and only a miracle had stopped the Japanese Imperial Army at the gates of India and driven them back to the sea.

Dickie Mountbatten. . . .

Attlee ran a hand over his bald head, tapped his pipe out in the heavy brass ashtray on his desk and glanced around the oak-panelled, book-lined room. It was hard, in this womblike power centre of the Empire, in cold, foggy London in mid-December, even to imagine the atmosphere of that vast subcontinent six thousand miles to the east. He pressed his fingers together and looked ahead.

His meetings with Lord Wavell had not given him much cause for celebration. The elderly soldier had seemed tired and dispirited. True, he had managed splendidly in conditions of increasing difficulty since taking over the Viceroyalty from the cold and reactionary Lord Linlithgow in 1943, but Attlee had to acknowledge that now the man had shot his bolt. What Wavell had told him about the situation in India also indicated that time was of the essence. Unless Independence were granted very soon,

Britain would find herself presiding over a bloody and anarchic civil war. Attlee closed his eyes at the thought of the damage that would do to the resources of his own country, emerging poor and tattered and grey after six years of battle. No, power must be handed over within the next two years. Barely time enough, especially if Britain were to leave without appearing to desert India. But it had to be done.

He became aware of a knock at the door. 'Come in.' The door opened and a lean, ascetic man entered briskly.

'Am I late?'

'On the contrary, you're early. And he hasn't arrived yet,' said Attlee.

Sir Stafford Cripps, ex-President of the Board of Trade, Leader of the House of Commons, and now, at fifty-seven, Chancellor of the Exchequer, crossed the room and threw himself down in a leather armchair by a low table. He picked a copy of *Punch* off the table, leafed through its pages impatiently, then flung it down, rose, and paced the room.

'The whole thing's such a damned mess.'

'Not irretrievably so, Stafford.'

'D'you think he'll say yes?'

'I expect him to make every effort to wriggle out of it,' smiled Attlee, 'but, handled the right way, I think he may agree.'

'If only I were free,' said Cripps, and there was a hint of a serious offer in what he said. He personally knew the Indians involved, and he had been out to negotiate in Delhi twice in the last four years.

'I think I need you here. Anyway, you agreed that we had to start off again with a clean slate.'

'Still a bit awkward. Especially with Wavell still in London.'

'We haven't time to observe niceties. Wavell leaves the day after tomorrow. We'll simply have to keep it under our hats until then.'

'If he agrees.'

'Quite so.'

There was another knock at the door. Attlee and Cripps glanced at each other, and Cripps moved round to the side of the desk.

'Lord Mountbatten, sir,' said the secretary who entered, making way for the Rear Admiral, now dressed in a formal, double-breasted pin-stripe suit.

'Good afternoon, Lord Louis,' said Attlee, as the secretary left.

Mountbatten's eyes were on Sir Stafford Cripps. He had nothing to do with Burma. What the devil was he doing here?

'Good afternoon, Prime Minister – Sir Stafford.'

Attlee reached for his pipe, indicating a chair to Mountbatten. 'Sorry to drag you away from Portsmouth,' he said, opening his tobacco pouch. 'All's going well there, I trust?'

'There's a lot to take in.' Mountbatten glanced again at Cripps, who had remained standing.

'I'll try not to keep you too long.' Attlee's manner was mild. He leant back in his chair. 'This shambles in Burma. Seems the Governor's to blame. Seems you were right all along about Aung San.'

Mountbatten relaxed slightly. 'Is that what you want my advice about? All right, here goes. Dorman-Smith's living in the past. By arresting the Nationalist leaders, all he's managed to do is convince them that our offer of Independence isn't worth the paper it's written on!'

'So what would you recommend?' Cripps wanted to know.

'Replace him! Replace him with someone the Burmese can trust. I suggest you get General Rance out of retirement, and send him over there as Military Administrator.'

Attlee glanced across at Cripps for a moment, who gave the faintest of nods. Reaching for a buff folder on the side of his desk, Attlee flipped it open and made a brief note.

'Rance. Very well. We accept your advice with gratitude.' He paused, then continued in a neutral tone of voice: 'Of

29

course, Burma isn't the only problem we have out in that part of the world at the moment. An even more pressing one is India. You know it quite well, I suppose?'

Mountbatten replied carefully: 'Most of the time I spent out there I had my HQ in Ceylon, of course.'

'But you must have been very aware of the situation in India,' put in Cripps impatiently. 'You must have met the Indian leaders.'

'Some of the ones we hadn't put in prison after 1942,' smiled Mountbatten. 'I did meet Jawaharlal Nehru. When he was released after VJ Day, he came to Singapore to visit his people there. I made a point of welcoming him.'

'No doubt he appreciated that,' said Attlee.

'He certainly appeared to. Especially when he found out how wholeheartedly I approve of our intention to give India full Independence.'

Attlee and Cripps exchanged another look.

'If you have a moment, Lord Louis, perhaps we could review the situation there. Stafford?'

So that's why Cripps is at this meeting, Mountbatten realized.

Cripps had already begun, running over the situation in British India from the rise of Jinnah and the Muslim League to the present, not sparing himself in his recollection of the failure of his own two missions. '. . . However, the Cabinet Mission Plan we tried to put across earlier this year still stands a chance as a basis for discussion with them,' he concluded.

'But speed is essential,' added Attlee. 'If the present Interim Government fails – and there's every chance that it will – then the bloodshed we've seen so far over Partition, and Hindu-Muslim tensions, will be as nothing. The whole of Northern India, at least, will become a slaughterhouse.'

'Is any of the violence aimed at us?' Mountbatten was sitting forward now, his hands clasped in front of him, entering the discussion with characteristic energy.

Cripps shook his head. 'No. For once it's not Gandhi's old cry of "British, quit India!" Actually, it's more sinister.

It's a deliberate campaign to show that Muslims and Hindus cannot live together, side by side.'

'Well,' said Mountbatten, 'why don't you discuss all this with Lord Wavell? And as he's an old friend, if you think my experience might be of any help, I'll gladly talk with him too.'

Attlee hesitated for a moment before answering, and then did so cautiously. 'Under the circumstances, that might not be a very good idea. You see . . . strictly between ourselves, we've come to the conclusion that an entirely new approach is needed – a new style of Viceroy, if you like. We are considering replacing Lord Wavell.'

In his enthusiasm for the discussion and his natural keen interest in all that had been said, Mountbatten had momentarily forgotten the premonition that had struck him when he had first entered the room to see Sir Stafford Cripps standing there. Now it returned in its full force. His collar felt tight.

'Good God, you're not thinking of me, are you?'

Again, Attlee paused for a fraction of a second before answering. 'Actually, we're offering you the job.'

Mountbatten was aghast. 'But I can't possibly accept!'

'Why not, Lord Louis?'

'Well, for one thing, Wavell's a friend of mine! And he's first class! He's a great soldier, with a brilliant mind – and frankly he hasn't had a lot of support from Whitehall. He's had his hands totally tied by London. Why, they wouldn't even let him have a meeting with Gandhi! He knows India far better than I do: look at his efforts in Bengal in '43 during that famine that Linlithgow chose to ignore!'

'Yes,' Cripps cut in, moving around the desk and sitting by Mountbatten, 'but the trouble is that the Indian leaders quite simply find him difficult to communicate with. It's not that they don't trust him – they just feel he's run out of ideas. And so, to be frank, do we.'

'We need you as Viceroy, Lord Louis,' said Attlee, simply. 'Under what conditions will you accept?'

Mountbatten's mind was racing. The one thing he was

sure of was that he didn't want the job. But he was used to being in tight corners and relying on quick thinking to get him out of them. Conditions, the Prime Minister had said. Well then, he would give him conditions which he couldn't possibly meet. And then he would be honourably free of the whole bloody business.

'I'll need all Wavell's staff kept on, for a start.'

Attlee looked bland. 'Naturally.'

'In addition to my own team. To be selected by myself alone. Maybe half a dozen men. And their wives and families, of course.' Attlee nodded. Mountbatten forced himself to think more coherently, not to let all the words out in a rush. 'I want my own aircraft, as well. The York I had in SEAC – MW 102. Totally at my disposal.' He continued more confidently, getting into the stride of his demands, half his mind registering interest in the job which the other half was doing its best to get out of. He asked for Lord 'Pug' Ismay, Churchill's old Chief-of-Staff, to be Chief of the Viceroy's Staff, and for Sir Eric Miéville to be Principal Secretary. These men had served as Military and Private Secretary respectively in the early thirties to the then Viceroy, Lord Willingdon. He asked for complete control of the Indian Honours List. To all of this Attlee assented without demur. Aware that he was backing himself into a corner rather than getting himself out of one, Mountbatten further insisted that, *if* he accepted the job, it should not be to the prejudice of his Naval career when he resumed it on his return from India. He asked for his appointment to command the First Cruiser Squadron, Mediterranean, a post his father had held on his way to becoming First Sea Lord, to be confirmed now, and not only by Attlee, but by the Admiralty.

To his dismay, all that he requested at this meeting was granted. There was only one possible bolt-hole left.

'Anything else?' Attlee wanted to know.

'Nothing I can think of. For the moment. But naturally I can't come to any decision until I've discussed it fully with my cousin, King George.'

32

'I've just come from the Prime Minister, Bertie. It's incredible, but he wants me to take over as Viceroy.'

His Imperial Majesty King George VI looked at his younger cousin and smiled. 'Yes, he told me last week he was planning to offer it to you. I think it's a splendid idea.'

To cover his confusion, Mountbatten turned and looked out of the tall windows of King George's private sitting-room. Beneath him, the splendid gardens of Buckingham Palace bent under the bleak December sky. Bertie *knew*! 'But the Viceroy is your representative. To all intents and purposes he *is* you! I'm sorry, Bertie, but you're not only my sovereign, but an old friend. Damn it, we were at Cambridge together. Do you realize what my job in India will involve?'

'Yes. You'll be ringing down the curtain on the Raj.' The King was sombre.

'The problems are enormous. Look how bad it will be for you and the Royal Family, if I fail.'

'But how good if you succeed. Dickie, we must accept the inevitable.' King George rose and joined Mountbatten at the window. His voice remained quiet, but there was no mistaking the firmness in it. 'I can't help a deep sadness that the end of the Empire should be coming in my time. India is the jewel in the imperial crown: can you imagine how much I regret that the war prevented me from going there? And now it will be given away without my ever having seen it. However, the job's got to be done.'

Mountbatten felt trapped. 'So you want me to take it on?'

'I want you to accept, Dickie. You're the only one who can do it. And I hope that somehow you will do it in a way which will ensure that not all our links with India will be severed.'

The following day a withdrawn and silent Mountbatten took his wife for a walk in St James's Park, not far from their London home, and close, too, to Buckingham Palace. Edwina shared the silence, and sensing their mood, Mizzen padded along close to them, head held low. The dog did not even bark at the pelicans, huddled morosely against the weather on their island in the lake. For Edwina, the news had not yet really sunk in. The possibilities of the job, and the idea of her becoming Vicereine, had immediately struck her as enormously exciting, but she kept her counsel, preferring that Dickie should make up his own mind. One thing was certain: there was no one else for him to consult but her. His old mentor, Churchill, would regard the move as a betrayal, but the King and the Government were for it, and the trust they reposed in him was a tremendous honour. She did not envy him his decision. Yet he was asking her to help him make it. Finally, as they turned back towards Chester Street, she broke the silence, weighing her words.

'I can't advise you on this. . . . You know how much I love India. I just have to think of it and I can't wait to be there. I'd be less than honest, too, if I didn't admit that these last few months have been, well, a bit of a let-down after the war. The excitement . . .' She remembered all the glamour of Ceylon, all the horror of Burma. The work she had done for the survivors – bitterly hard work, but she had revelled in it. There seemed to be so little to do in England, and Malta promised even less. 'You're the obvious choice for the job,' she continued.

Finally he spoke. 'But what if I can't bring it off?'

She smiled at him. 'That doesn't sound very like you. I don't know, Dickie. I haven't really taken it in yet. But how can I tell you not to accept the greatest challenge of your career?'

They had reached Birdcage Walk and she stooped to put Mizzen on the leash. As she rose, he put out his hand for hers, and held it tight.

The Prime Minister was a cautious man, and it was not without discussion that he had let Sir Stafford Cripps persuade him that Mountbatten was the right man for the job. Between the wars, and particularly after his marriage

34

to Edwina, the young naval officer had developed a reputation as a playboy. The couple had spent much time in what many had regarded as frivolous company; their friends had included Douglas Fairbanks, Mary Pickford, and Charlie Chaplin. Noel Coward, too, was a close friend. He had even made a feature film, a splendid piece of wartime propaganda, about Mountbatten's heroic action as Commander of the destroyer *HMS Kelly*. Mountbatten had shocked Rolls Royce by redesigning their bonnet in a more streamlined way for his own model. He raced speedboats. To the anger of the King, he had twice been rejected for membership of the Royal Yacht Squadron: some of the older members regarded him as rackety. And then there was the marriage. Of course, all marriages had their moments of tension, but didn't the Mountbattens seem to have more than their fair share, especially for such a public couple? What about that time when Edwina had stayed behind in America, and that awful scandal over the American polo player, Laddie Sandford? What about her politics? She was well known for her radicalism. How would the British Indian community react to her?

Against all this, Cripps set the fact that Lord Louis was capable of working at least as hard as he played. He pointed to the man's astonishing war record, where he had shown an administrative ability, and a skill in handling people and getting the best out of them, which were describable by no other word than phenomenal. And after Mountbatten had gone missing on the *Kelly*, Edwina had spent night after night on the quay at Newcastle, waiting with the other wives. She'd laid her life of spoilt little rich girl aside then, and thrown herself into nursing work with such dedication that she had ended up running the St John's Ambulance Brigade. Wasn't that proof of her integrity? The Mountbattens would make a perfect Viceroy and Vicereine. They had become engaged in India; they were known and respected there. 'Not only that,' Cripps concluded, 'but to the Indians Mountbatten is a victorious leader and a nobleman: he saved India from the Japanese. His appeal will be universal there, not only to Congress, and the Muslim League if he plays his cards right, but to all the rajahs and maharajahs who still run their own states independently of British India. To them, he'll be an equal, another aristocrat. With any luck, he might even be able to unify them under one central government before he leaves.'

'That would take a paragon,' Attlee sighed.

Mountbatten had been able to stall his decision until Christmas, but he had not returned to Portsmouth. Instead, he had hoped to buy a little more time by taking Edwina skiing at Davos. But it was not to be for long. The Indian situation was deteriorating faster than anyone had anticipated, and Mountbatten was summoned to return to London within forty-eight hours of his arrival in Switzerland. Still fighting what was fast becoming the inevitable, Mountbatten went home with one last card to play. He suggested that Sir Claude Auchinleck, the Commander-in-Chief of the Indian Army, should succeed Wavell. The suggestion was quickly stamped on by Attlee, who pointed out that Auchinleck's duty to keep the army united was too important to remove him from his present post. Besides, Auchinleck was another soldier, like Wavell. What was needed was a man with a gift for diplomacy.

As the discussions continued, and as he contributed increasingly to them, Mountbatten found that he was being placed irrevocably in a position of acceptance. He proposed that the transfer of power should be achieved by June 1948.

'But by the time that can be announced, it'll only be about fifteen months away!' protested Cripps. They were once more gathered together in Attlee's study.

'Well, I don't want to sit there twiddling my thumbs.'

Attlee pounced. '*You* don't want to? That means you accept – provided we approve the time limit!'

Mountbatten barely hesitated before replying: 'As Viceroy, I'd be answerable to the Secretary of State for India, wouldn't I?'

'Naturally.'

36

'Well, I can't have that, I'm afraid. There simply isn't time for me to have Pethick-Lawrence breathing down my neck. I've thought about this, and I have a solution. Billy Listowel's an old friend, and knows India backwards. If he were Secretary of State I could work with him. It's either that, or according the Viceroy full plenipotentiary powers – I do as I like without reference to London.'

'That's out of the question.'

'Then I cannot accept. If I can't make decisions on the spot.'

Attlee looked at the man sitting opposite him. By God, if there was ever a man who could sort Nehru and Jinnah out . . .!

'Very well,' Attlee said heavily. 'You have full plenipotentiary powers.'

It was February. The first few buds were beginning to appear on the trees at Broadlands, and for the first time that winter there was a faint promise of spring in the air. It did nothing to improve the atmosphere in the drawing-room. Mountbatten had accepted the Viceroyalty, and Princess Victoria was taking the news badly. She almost never swore, but now she did.

'Damn, damn, damn! How could you be such a fool, Dickie? You know they'll all say you only took it for the glamour of the thing!'

Mountbatten was soothing. 'Oh, I doubt that, Mama.'

Princess Victoria snorted in indignation. Couldn't he see that Attlee and his crew had boxed themselves in with their promise of Independence, and that they'd decided to use him as a scapegoat? He'd fail to transfer power, India would collapse into civil war, and he'd be ruined. It was in vain that Mountbatten and Edwina tried to comfort her; to convince her that what she foresaw was not the inevitable outcome. The old lady would listen to none of it. Her son would be sacrificed just as her husband had been. She left the room in fury.

Edwina looked at her husband. The doubt on his face

37

was an unfamiliar sight, and it had to be got rid of if he were to do as she wanted him to.

'Surely you wouldn't have accepted the job if you didn't think there was at least a chance of succeeding?' she asked gently. 'I'm sure you can do it, you know, Dickie.'

He looked up at her, his expression clearing. She could not be sure how much he was putting on an act, to reassure her in his turn. 'Attlee put the odds at six to four,' he said. 'Personally, I see them as nearer a thousand to one. But even so, I'm damned well going to have a go!'

Ismay had been persuaded out of retirement to become the new Viceroy's Chief-of-Staff. At first Mountbatten had hesitated to ask him, but Ismay told him, 'If you are going out to play the last chukka twelve goals down, count me in on your team.' Well, now the team was assembled. They were sitting round a table in one of the most dismal rooms Ismay had ever seen, one of a suite of four which Mountbatten had commandeered at the India Office. The room, with its high, grimy windows, its dark, funereal panelling and its uninspired official portraits of Victorian senior Indian Civil Servants, hardly visible beneath layers of ancient varnish, seemed to him to represent all that was worst about the old Raj and its hidebound attitude to India. It was ironic that the new men seated round the table were dedicated to writing its final chapter.

Eric Miéville of course he knew well. They had served together in Delhi in the thirties. It must have taken all Mountbatten's powers of persuasion to woo him away from his business interests in the City for this last tour of public duty, thought Ismay, wryly. The younger men he knew only slightly, if at all. Very young chaps, indeed, all under forty, and all closely allied with Dickie during the war in South-East Asia. Hence, Ismay supposed, that nickname they had earned themselves in certain circles, 'The Dickie Birds'. Ismay could not be sure in what spirit the name was meant. They were all good-looking, all highly competent, a fairly formidable bunch when working together as a team, he imagined. Captain Ronald Brockman, of course, he remembered. He would continue as Personal Secretary to the Viceroy, and Commander George Nicholls would be his deputy. Both Royal Navy, both good sound Navy Secretariat chaps.

Mountbatten was introducing the next. 'To be Conference Secretary, Lieutenant Colonel Vernon Erskine Crum.'

'Scots Guards,' Crum added, with a slight smile to his naval colleagues.

'Let us not forget the Scots Guards,' Mountbatten murmured and they laughed. 'And last, but far from least, Alan Campbell-Johnson. Alan will be in charge of Public Relations, publicity, Press liaison and so forth.'

Miéville had raised an eyebrow. 'There's never been a Press spokesman appointed to the Viceregal staff before.'

'No, this will be the first time,' Mountbatten said, 'but I feel it should have been done long ago – to interpret the Viceroy's views and lessen his remoteness from the public. I want the ordinary Indian, as well as his leaders, to know why I have come and what I am doing.'

'A very good move,' Ismay approved. He knew that Campbell-Johnson, an ex-Wing Commander, had been invaluable to Dickie in SEAC and his appointment as Press Attaché seemed such a good idea he could not understand why one had never been considered necessary up till now.

The men nodded and smiled to one another, glad to be functioning together again under their old chief, and arranged their notes in front of them, as Mountbatten, assisted by his principal ADC, another naval man, Lieutenant Commander Peter Howes, chased a couple of technicians from the room and took over the job of setting up a small cinema screen and projector. Ismay smiled. Mountbatten had always had a passion for films. He'd be pleased to learn that Viceroy's House had its own private cinema.

Brockman and Campbell-Johnson had drawn the blinds and Mountbatten had his double reel threaded. He called the meeting to order. 'In many cases, I believe one picture is worth a thousand words. To prevent us all becoming too cosy and to give us a better idea of what to expect, I've had these extracts of recent newsreels linked together. They show some of the rioting there's been over there – in Calcutta, Bombay and the Punjab. I've seen the film myself and I'd better warn you that it isn't pretty.'

He switched the projector on. From then on, there was silence in the room, apart from the clicking whirr of the projector. The faces of the men watching the screen became deeply serious, watching the frenzy of the rampaging mobs and the shots of the sickening aftermath of communal riots.

'Ye Gods . . . it's worse than a war,' Nicholls muttered.

The pianist sat in a corner of the Mountbattens' drawing room at 15, Chester Street, strumming chords quietly with his right hand. As he sipped his champagne, he watched the other guests, a pretty fair cross-section of *Who's Who*. He saw Edwina talking quietly with a shorter, brightly attractive young woman. By the fireplace, Dickie was heads-down with his nephew Philip and the conductor, Malcolm Sargent. Three guesses what they would be talking about. He looked back at Edwina. The short, vital woman with her said something and she laughed.

Edwina had all her old vivacity, yet he could see the signs of strain round her eyes and the lines which powder could not hide. Strictly speaking she had never been beautiful – more striking, with an animation that made you neglect other, lovelier women in her company. But she was not ageing too well. Dickie was still as handsome as ever, more handsome, lucky devil. Of course, she had just had an operation. When he rang to ask after her and find out what was wrong, she had told him dismissively, 'Oh, just women's trouble, Noel, very minor.' Seeing her, he was not so sure about the minor. He knew she was not nearly as strong as she looked, that frequently she drove herself on by sheer willpower. She was like Dickie, unable to refuse a challenge and always taking on more than one human being could feasibly manage.

She could not have recovered yet from the pressure of her commitment during the war, when she had seemed to be trying to make up for her previous butterfly existence by an orgy of work for the wounded, the auxiliary services, bomb victims, the homeless, first into Burma after the Japanese defeat, bullying the authorities into providing food and medical supplies for the Allied prisoners-of-war in the death camps, and not only for them, but for the starving and brutalized native population. She had unquestionably saved thousands of lives. Since then, she had concentrated on the relief of displaced persons and the medical care of returned prisoners. Poor little rich girl, she was not – or not any more. She seemed driven by a compulsion.

Perhaps it was to match Dickie. In one way or another, they had always been rivals. The ideal couple in public, in private they often went for each other like cat and dog. Of course, there were strains. The marriage, outwardly perfect, had barely survived at times, no doubt due to Dickie's absorption in the navy. Presumably, if Edwina had had something equally absorbing to occupy her, she wouldn't have become involved with other chaps. And yet, through-out the war when she was most busy, she was also engrossed in her most serious affair, the one that really could have destroyed the marriage. Socially, it was playing with dyna-mite. When Bunny Phillips had broken it off, ending it effectively by getting married himself, she had been prostrated. He had never seen anyone take the end of an affair so badly. And Dickie's concern for her and sympa-thetic understanding had been nothing short of phenom-enal. No reproaches, no conditions, no self-pity, just the offer of sympathy and healing companionship. And thank the Lord Harry, Edwina had responded. There was no doubt that Dickie and she loved each other very deeply, although in far from the conventional pattern.

Heigh-ho, if love were all. . . . He played a few bars of the song, almost unconsciously.

Because of it all, Dickie had developed his own closest

relationship, perhaps the most satisfying he had ever had. Not sexual, not with one of his girlfriends or one of the society women who threw themselves at him. With his daughter, Patricia. She had become the companion and confidante he desperately needed, in the absence of a devoted wife. A fearsome responsibility for a girl – young woman, he should say, now that she was married. That must have been a wrench for him, too. It was fortunate she was not only very attractive, but serious and highly intelligent. And her husband was a thoroughly likable, sensible fellow. He doubted that Patricia would allow the marriage to affect her special relationship with her father. With care, it could only make it more mature.

He saw that Edwina and the shorter woman had been joined by her younger daughter, Pamela, fair, very pretty, as serious as her elder sister, but still painfully shy. She must be very excited at the prospect of going to India.

The India business . . . He frowned and stopped playing. He knew what he thought about that. The government had backed itself into a messy corner over this Independence offer and had called on Dickie to get them out of it. He had less than a snowball's chance. Not that he could ever tell him so. When Dickie had accepted to do something, nothing would deflect him from getting it done and any suggestion that it was beyond human capability was brushed aside as 'adopting a negative attitude'. This time, though, he might have bitten off more than even he could chew. Yet he would get the blame, not the politicians. While, if he succeeded, they would grab the credit. Thus runs the world away. Enhancing or not for Dickie's career and reputation, it might however be the saving of Edwina. She needed taking out of herself, plunking down in a whole new environment with a fresh set of rules and challenges. She would certainly find that as Vicereine. He smiled as he remembered her exhilaration when she had broken the news to him. In spite of her genuinely sincere, if somewhat muddled, socialist outlook, she would accept all the trappings of pomp and circumstance to the manner born. And after all, what woman could resist the lure of sitting next to her husband on a gilded throne?

She was still profoundly unhappy, he knew, and had confessed herself to be in a sort of limbo. She had been prepared to follow Dickie to Malta, to accept the social and cultural exile for his sake. Not to mention setting aside her own work and career. That could have been a disaster for both of them, him off charging around the Med in his cruisers, while she was left twiddling her thumbs and feeling her age in Valetta. Yes, perhaps India would be the saving of her. He put down his champagne glass and began to play her favourite among his many songs.

The younger woman with Edwina was Elizabeth Ward, a former FANY officer, one of her two closest personal assistants during the war. Hearing the pianist play 'I'll Follow My Secret Heart', she glanced round. 'Oh, isn't that – ?' she began and stopped, not wishing to appear impressed.

'Yes, it's Noel Coward,' Edwina smiled. 'He's one of our oldest friends.'

They had interrupted Pamela who was eager to have her question answered. 'I mean, you've been to India already, Miss Ward,' she said, 'but just to be going there . . . What's it really like?'

'Heat and flies and dysentery and dust,' Elizabeth told her.

Seeing Pammie's face fall, Edwina smiled. 'I'm sure Elizabeth will agree that it is also unbearably beautiful and the people are absolutely delightful.'

Elizabeth had been teasing, and smiled. 'Absolutely.' She was concerned about Edwina, who had clearly still not fully recovered. 'Shouldn't you have stayed in hospital a day or two more, Lady Louis?' she asked.

Edwina shook her head. 'I couldn't. There was so much shopping to do. Besides, I was giving a dinner party for the Royal Family.' Seeing Pamela frown a warning to her, she smiled. 'Elizabeth and I have struggled through the jungle and waded crocodile-infested rivers together. WE don't

43

have any secrets from each other.' They laughed, and Edwina lowered her voice. 'It's all very hush-hush, you see, but it was really an engagement party for Elizabeth and Philip.'

Elizabeth Ward's mouth rounded at being let in on the secret. 'Engagement?' she whispered.

'Isn't it fun? They're so happy together. The official announcement won't be till some time in July. As you can imagine, Dickie's thrilled about it.'

Mountbatten had taken a bottle to the piano. It was not merely to refill his old friend's glass. Noel was often a very useful and impartial reporter of public opinion.

'The buzz when your appointment was made public could be heard all the way from Westminster to darkest Tooting,' Coward said.

Mountbatten chuckled. 'Yes, I thought it might ruffle a few feathers.'

'What does Winston say?'

Mountbatten tried to smile, but was obviously still hurt by the attitude of his former chief. 'I gather he ranks me now somewhere between Judas Iscariot and Lord Haw-Haw. Still, I expected that.'

'Par for the course, one might say.'

'What interests me more is what the rest of our friends think – and the man in the street. You have your ear to the ground, Noel. What are they saying?'

'The trouble with having one's ear to the ground,' Coward told him, 'is that it frequently gets filled up with mud. However, the average reaction seems to be in favour.'

Mountbatten was relieved. 'Of course, there are some who say you only took the job for the show and splendour. Others, that you should never have lent your name to a shameful abandonment of Britain's Empire.'

Mountbatten stiffened. 'It's a new world! We have to accept that colonialism is over. I want us to leave with honour and dignity, to have done the best we can for those people we have ruled – yes, and exploited – for so long.'

'You don't have to explain your reasons to me, Dickie,'

Coward said quietly. 'I knew you would take it on, the moment I heard it was in the wind.'

'Why were you so sure?'

Coward shrugged. 'Oh – because I realized your personal demon wouldn't let you turn down something everyone else says is impossible. Because of your sense of duty. And because . . . being what you are, you don't know any better.'

'What do you mean?'

Coward smiled and played a short introduction on the piano. When he began to sing, Mountbatten laughed and joined in. The other guests closed round them, laughing with Edwina as Coward and Mountbatten sang together, 'Mad Dogs and Englishmen Go Out in the Noonday Sun'.

Winston Churchill had reacted with predictable fury both to Attlee's proposals and Mountbatten's appointment. He said categorically that he never intended to speak to his protégé again. He was so angry that he could hardly speak to his friend and former chief of staff, Lord Ismay, who came to ask him not to sabotage whatever chances Mountbatten might have before he even reached India.

The old lion was still bitter at being rejected by the British people in the first election after the war. 'It's all changed, Pug,' he said, heavily. 'Nothing's the way I thought it would be – afterwards. We survived the war. But will we survive this Socialist Government? Everything we fought for is being destroyed.' They were walking in the grounds of his country home at Chartwell and he paused, looking out over the lake. 'And now this shameful abandonment of the Empire.'

'It's part of the historical process,' Ismay said. 'It had to come.'

'Perhaps. When the time was right. When India had proved able to govern herself democratically. Certainly not now, when we have not begun to recover from the financial drain of these past seven years. As a nation, the price of victory was to bankrupt ourselves. Before the war, with the exception of America, we were still the world's major power. Now . . .' He shook his head. 'If we give up India, we shall no longer even be able to claim to be in the second rank.' He looked at Ismay. 'You're not going to get any honours out of this, you know, Pug.'

Ismay had been sympathizing with him, but now had difficulty in keeping his temper. 'That is not why I am going.'

'Then why?'

'Because I am proud of our record there,' Ismay said stiffly. 'I'd hate to see it spoilt by the way we leave. And I can't let Dickie go into the lion's den alone.'

'I'm sorry you're having anything to do with it,' Churchill growled.

They turned back towards the house. It was a raw February day with no sign of the spring to come.

'He's hoping that you'll understand,' Ismay said, 'and that you'll have some word of encouragement for him.'

Churchill did not break his stride. 'Encouragement for someone whom I never intend to see again? You can tell him from me that I consider, by accepting this post, he is betraying his family, his King and the Empire. What I have to say will be said to the nation in its proper place, the House of Commons.'

There was total silence when Churchill rose in the House some weeks later. Standing by his seat on the Opposition Front Bench, he eyed the crowded Labour benches across from him and knew, with Attlee's vast majority, that the issue was already settled. He could only fight a rearguard action. He spoke long and eloquently, building to a grim plea for the House to reconsider. 'As for the new Viceroy, is he to make new efforts to restore the situation, or is it merely Operation Scuttle on which he and other distinguished officers have been dispatched? . . . Many have defended Britain against her foes, none can defend her against herself. But at least, let us not add – by shameful flight, by a premature and hurried scuttle – at least let us

46

not add to the pangs of sorrow so many of us feel, the taint and smear of shame.'

These were words which won loud approval in the House and in large sections of the Empire, but it was a speech which Clement Attlee in his reply was able to demolish. The Government carried the day by a majority of one hundred and fifty-two.

Two wartime York transports had been specially converted for civil use. MW 101 had been allocated to the King, MW 102 to Mountbatten. Both aircraft were used for the last Viceroy's flight to India. MW 101 left for Delhi on 19 March with Lord Ismay and Sir Eric Miéville on board, and the four young men who constituted Mountbatten's personal back-up team. Newsreel cameras, reporters and a small group of friends turned up in the early morning to see MW 102 leave a day later, carrying Mountbatten, Edwina, their younger daughter Pamela, Edwina's assistants, Muriel Watson and Elizabeth Ward, Peter Howes, Ronnie Brockman, Edwina's maid and Mountbatten's valet. Pamela carried on board the old Sealyham, Mizzen.

Turning from saying goodbye to his nephew Philip, Mountbatten helped Edwina up the steps to the plane. It was a cold, misty morning and they were glad at least to be leaving behind the bleakness of the appalling winter which, this year, had gone on and on. As they paused to wave one last time, he noticed with surprise that she was holding a battered old shoebox under her arm. 'What on earth have you brought that thing along for?' he asked.

Edwina opened the box and showed him that it contained the magnificent diamond tiara he had designed for her. 'I thought I might need it, so I got it out of storage yesterday. I was all packed and I couldn't think where else to put it.'

Mountbatten laughed. 'Just as long as you don't walk off the plane with it still under your arm. They might think we'd brought our sandwiches.'

The flight normally took three days, but Mountbatten

wanted to make up time, so they stopped only at Fayid in Egypt and at Karachi. They landed at Delhi's Palam Airport on the afternoon of 22 March.

# THREE

Edwina sat by the window of the Vicereine's bedroom and tried to collect her thoughts. For once her headaches, and her dislike of flying – which she fought so hard against – had been banished by the speed of events during the past few hours. There had been the formal introductions at the airport. Claude Auchinleck had presented Liaqat Ali Khan of the Muslim League, and Mr Nehru. She remembered Nehru with gratitude, a charming man whom she would like to get to know better. She had met him briefly with her husband in Singapore, but her chief memory of that meeting had been when Nehru and Mountbatten had had to rescue her from being trampled underfoot by an overenthusiastic welcoming crowd which had burst through the doors and windows at a reception held at the YMCA! Then there had been the drive in the open landau to Viceroy's House. Dickie was perhaps just a little disappointed that there were no great crowds to welcome them, but, as he'd said, they might equally well have turned up just to hurl abuse. They had arrived at Viceroy's House at 3.45 pm, where Lord and Lady Wavell stood waiting to welcome them at the top of the broad flight of sandstone steps. Poor Wavell, with his bandy legs and blind left eye. And yet she could gauge the sensitivity of the man from his poetry, and recognized his heroism as a soldier from the five rows of ribbons on his tunic. Looking at that tired, gnarled face, she had prayed that the difficulties confronting Dickie would not wear him out in the same way. Dickie was closeted with Wavell now: the Viceroy and his successor had only a few hours to confer, for Wavell would be returning home early the following morning. Even those few hours were a luxury, for Viceroys had never before overlapped; another break with tradition, for this last time. And how stupid so many of these traditions had been, she thought.

She looked across at Mizzen, lying on the bed, who mournfully returned her gaze.

'Don't worry, darling. I've asked them to bring you some food,' she smiled. Poor Mizzen. Never mind, there'd be plenty of exercise here. The house alone, she had learnt from Lady Wavell, had one and a half miles of corridors – no wonder some servants used bicycles! – and three hundred and seventy-seven rooms and state rooms. She wondered if she'd have time to visit every single one of them. At present, her one concern was not to get lost. Still, with five thousand servants to attend on her, there seemed to be small chance of remaining so for long.

A discreet knock on the door brought her to her feet. Two tall liveried and turbaned servants entered, bearing a silver salver covered with a napkin. Mizzen pricked up his ears. The servants placed the tray on a table, and stood to attention.

'It's your snack,' said Edwina to Mizzen, who by now was on the floor, wagging his tail and whining excitedly. She lifted a corner of the napkin, and gasped. Lying on the salver was a pile of cold roast chicken. 'Thank you very much,' she said to the servants, rapping Mizzen on the nose as the dog came too close to the food. 'Now, if you'll excuse me, I'm going to take a bath.' The men immediately crossed to the door of the adjoining bathroom, opened it and bowed. After a moment's hesitation, Edwina moved towards the bathroom herself, but seeing the servants about to follow her in, she turned and said firmly, 'I think I can manage by myself now, thank you.' To her relief the men retreated, bowing as they went, and disappeared.

'Sorry, Mizzen,' said Edwina, closing the bathroom door on her pet. Alone, delightedly, she began to eat the chicken. After years of rationing, her mouth tingled at the delicious taste.

She was not so selfish as to eat it all herself. Nor would she have had time to, for minutes after the servants had delivered their tray of 'scraps' for Mizzen, Mountbatten himself arrived, bringing with him two things which Wavell had given him. One was the Viceroy's diamond-encrusted badge of office as Grand Master of the Order of the Star of India. The other was a buff folder.

'"Operation Madhouse"?' said Edwina, reading the cover.

Mountbatten took another piece of chicken. 'It's an accurate description. It's one worse than "Operation Ebb-Tide". A plan for the British evacuation of India, city by city, province by province, first the women and children, then the civilians, and finally the last remaining British army units – leaving the country to chaos.'

'What will you do with it?'

'Hide it at the back of the safe and pray it'll never be needed.'

'Are you going to tell me your alternative plan?'

'It's a case of playing it by ear. I've written to Gandhi and Nehru and Jinnah and invited them to come and see me as soon as possible. Oh – and the leading princes of the independent states as well. There's no time to lose.'

Mizzen began to whine, looking up at them appealingly.

'Poor old Mizzy. Seems a bit unfair. It was supposed to be for you,' said Edwina.

'Just one piece then,' said Mountbatten, taking another for himself. 'What do you think of this place?'

'The house? I think it's hard to believe that it's barely twenty years old. It seems like a leftover from Kipling. But I'm taking stock of it with Pamela once I've recovered from the journey.'

'There's one thing I'd better tell you, Edwina. I think it's important that we revive all the pre-war pomp and panoply. Lots of ceremonial, all the old splendour of the Raj.'

'Whatever for?' Edwina asked, troubled. 'Your enemies are already saying that's all you care about.'

'It's for the people of India. I want them to know they have a real Viceroy, who speaks for the King, the Government and the British Nation. When we go out, we'll go with all flags flying.'

In the day left to them before the Swearing-In Ceremony, Mountbatten organized his staff, got to know George Abell, who had been Wavell's private secretary and whom Mountbatten had retained, and followed up his letters of invitation to the Indian leaders. To his relief, Jawaharlal Nehru had accepted with alacrity. Jinnah, he was sure, would follow – if only not to be left out of discussions – and as for Gandhi, well, Gandhi was a law unto himself, but see him he would, sooner or later.

Edwina, meanwhile, walked the length and breadth of Viceroy's House until her feet ached. She met Faiz Mohd, the Head Butler, whose Indian title she learnt, *Khansama*. The silent but superbly attentive servants were called *khitmatgars*, and their already imposing number was swelled by four hundred gardeners who worked tirelessly in the large formal Mogul Gardens behind the house and in the Viceregal estate beyond them, where the staff quarters and senior British officials' bungalows were situated. As she conducted her tour, accompanied by Pamela and her two personal assistants, Elizabeth Ward and Muriel Watson, she learnt more of the India for which her husband had assumed such awesome responsibility.

At the time the subcontinent contained one fifth of the world's population, divided roughly into two main religious groups, the three hundred million Hindus and the hundred million Muslims. Between them they spoke twenty-three different languages and over three hundred dialects, the main languages being Hindu and Urdu, but the *lingua franca* being English. British India covered about half of the subcontinent, the rest being divided into 565 independent princely states, the largest of which were as big as France or Germany, though the smallest might be no larger than a couple of hundred acres. The states were bound to the

Crown by independent treaty, and their fate when India gained self-rule would be one of Mountbatten's main headaches.

To complicate matters further, the Hindu population of India was rigidly divided by the caste system, an imposition of social order dating back to the time of the first Aryan invaders of India. The Hindu word for caste, Edwina learnt, was *varda* – meaning, literally, dark. The system was originally intended to suppress the dark-skinned aboriginal Dravidian population. Of the four castes, the Brahmins came first, forming the cream of Indian society. By the twentieth century being a Brahmin no longer had anything to do with social status. Nehru was one, but so were a host of minor officials and clerks. Next came the warrior caste, the Kshatriyas, said to have sprung from the biceps of the god Brahma. Thirdly came the caste to which both Gandhi and Jinnah had belonged, the traders and businessmen, the Vaisyas. Below them were the Sudras, artisans and craftsmen. But there was another social group, fifty million strong, the Untouchables, those who had not sprung from divine soil. Contact with these Untouchables meant defilement for a Brahmin which could only be cleansed by ritual ablution. Gandhi, in an attempt to integrate them into a modern Indian society, called them the *Harijan*, or children of God. As a deliberate policy, he lived and worked among them, and made their traditional task, latrine sweeping, his own. These five divisions were themselves subject to five thousand subdivisions of which 1,886 applied to the Brahmins alone.

Edwina could barely assimilate the complexity of it all. She wondered how Dickie could possibly rationalize so many centuries of tradition and prejudice and hand over power to a modern, twentieth-century government within the space of fifteen months.

'Mummie!' called Pamela. 'Look in here!'

They had arrived at the State Ballroom. It was so grand that even Edwina, dressed as she was in a simple cotton frock, hesitated for a moment before she entered it. On the

53

floor beneath the black-and-red marble ceiling, from which a dozen great chandeliers were suspended, lay a red Mogul carpet large enough to have covered the entire ground floor at Broadlands.

As the first sunlight struck the great dome of the Durbar Hall of Viceroy's House on 24 March, Edwina's maid helped place the diamond tiara on her head. Slim, elegant, her short, wavy, dark hair flanking a strong, lean face, Edwina looked at herself in the mirror, briefly checking. Well, she thought ironically, if it's the shadow of royalty that he wants, that's what he's got. In fact she looked both radiant and regal, in a long gown of parchment brocade over which she wore the dark sash and the star of the Order of St John, together with the Order of the Crown of India, and her war medals and decorations. She felt how dry her mouth was. She had not expected to be so nervous. Her maid arranged the train of her dress, and opened the door of her bedroom. Outside, flanking the high, immensely long corridor, stood lines of tall servants liveried in ceremonial white and gold.

Mountbatten himself was hurrying now. A last-minute conference with Alan Campbell-Johnson had delayed him fractionally, but as this was the first time photographers and film crews had been allowed to cover the Viceregal Swearing-In Ceremony, no item should be neglected. Mountbatten had a zest for detail, and, as he had said to Campbell-Johnson, 'After all, it's not every day a country gets its last Viceroy. History deserves a record of it.' He had another innovation in mind, too, which he did not doubt would come as a surprise to the Indian leaders who attended the ceremony, but which he wanted the Press to be fully aware of.

He walked briskly along the corridor to meet Edwina, feeling for the first time not exactly nervous, but tightly strung. His perception, he noted, was highly tuned that morning as he observed details which at another time might have escaped him. For example, the brass doorknobs of the house had been cast by Lutyens in the shape of British lions.

He wore his full-dress admiral's uniform, with the ribbon and star of the Garter, the badge of the Grand Master of the Order of the Star of India, his full medals, and his Coronation medal at his throat. His shoulders bore the full ermine-trimmed pale blue velvet mantle of the Grand Master of the Star of India. Its weight bore down on him slightly and he thanked God that the ceremony had been scheduled for early in the morning, that it was only fifteen minutes long, and that it took place in the high, black and white marble Durbar Hall. But these thoughts did not diminish his sense of the solemnity of the occasion.

As soon as he met Edwina he noticed how nervous she was, though he caught his breath at how beautiful she was looking. Hard to believe that this same woman, in her undress uniform, would think nothing of carrying a Burmese leper whom no one else would touch out of his hovel and into an ambulance.

'Edwina, my dear,' he said. 'I am sure no Viceroy has ever had a more beautiful consort.' She smiled quickly, tightly, at the compliment. He took her hand and together they walked on. He tried to think of something which would relax her, then he suddenly remembered what Lady Reading, the Vicereine when they had become engaged in 1921, had said to Edwina: 'My girl, you are a fool to think of marrying someone with so little of a career ahead of him.'

'If only Lady Reading could see you now,' he said, and saw her smile, and felt her hand relax in his. 'Is my hair all right?' he added. Now she nearly laughed out loud, her nerves cured. Ahead of them stood Lieutenant Commander Peter Howes and the junior ADCs, one drawn from each of the Indian armed services, another Mountbatten innovation. They looked resplendent in their dress uniforms, and beyond them the Viceroy's bodyguard, in scarlet and gold, stood to attention on either side of the entrance to the Durbar Hall. Howes and the other ADCs saluted briskly, spun smartly on their heels and preceded the new Viceroy and his consort into Lutyens' grand centrepiece, the hub of the Indian Empire.

For Edwina the ceremony passed like a dream: afterwards, she could remember every detail, but it did not seem as if it could have really happened. She remembered the blue-and-gold thrones on a dais, overhung by a vast crimson velvet baldachin. She could remember Sir Patrick Spens, the Lord Chief Justice of India, administering the Oath, and then the intentness on the faces of the Indian leaders as her husband, with the ceremony to all intents and purposes over, had risen to address the assembly, causing a buzz of excitement and heightened interest as they realized he meant to speak, something which no Viceroy, protected in the remote and semi-mystical panoply of State, had ever done before. She had seen how Mr Nehru's right hand had toyed with a rose he wore in one of the top buttons of his tunic as he listened. The speech itself had been short and to the point.

'Although I believe it is not usual for a speech to be made at the Swearing-In Ceremony, I should like to say a few words to you, and to India.

'This is not a normal Viceroyalty on which I am embarking. His Majesty's Government are resolved to transfer power by June 1948; and since new constitutional arrangements must be made, and many complicated questions of administration resolved – all of which will take time to put into effect – this means that a solution must be reached within the next few months. I believe that every Indian political leader feels, as I do, the urgency of the task before us. I hope soon to be in close consultation with them; and I will give them all the help I can.

'In the meanwhile, every one of us must do what he can to avoid any word or action which might lead to further bitterness or add to the toll of innocent victims. I am under no illusion about the difficulty of my task. I shall need the greatest goodwill of the greatest possible number – and I am asking India today for that goodwill.'

Pandit Jawaharlal Nehru had much to ponder on before his first meeting with the new Viceroy that same afternoon. Born in Allahabad in 1889, the son of an influential lawyer and political associate of Gandhi, Nehru had grown up in an Anglophile household, and at sixteen had been sent to complete his education in England. He had attended Harrow school, Trinity College, Cambridge, and the Inner Temple. On his return to India in 1912, he acknowledged that culturally he had become a split personality, half English and half Indian, which at first he had no idea how to resolve.

Finding the profession of law enervating, he quickly developed an interest in politics, sitting at the feet of Gandhi and espousing *swaraj*, the cause of Indian Independence. To do this, he remembered, he had had to go through the painful process of learning to be an Indian again. Even so, over thirty years later, a part of him still felt like a stranger in his own land. By 1929 he had succeeded his father as President of the Indian National Congress, having been instrumental in furthering Gandhi's campaign to ban cotton imports from Lancashire in England, and to encourage Indians to adopt once more their own homespun *khadi*. It was from this time that Gandhi discovered what were to become his own principal symbols. The great leader eschewed all dress but a cotton homespun *dhoti* and shawl and at the same time started to use the *charkha*, or spinning wheel, to make cotton himself. Nehru in his turn gave up European dress, adopted the long tunic buttoned to the neck known as an *achkhan*, and wore the plain white Indian cotton cap which became known as the Congress cap. But in his third buttonhole he almost always wore a rosebud.

By 1947 Nehru had spent nine years of his life in British prisons for his political activities: he was a hardened politician and undisputed leader of the Congress Party and of the Hindus of India. Only Gandhi enjoyed more influence, and Gandhi had withdrawn from direct political involvement. His toughness, however, was tempered by his charm. His handsome, gentle, expressive face might have been that of an artist, and though his political calculations might sometimes be cold, his emotions were warm. His susceptibility to flattery had been tempered by his wife and daughter, but Kamala had died eleven years earlier, and Indira was now married. Nehru barely had time to feel lonely, but there was an undeniable void in his life.

At the moment, however, his mind was on other things, as his car drove him past the row of innumerable stone lions that led up to the entrance of Viceroy's House.

He was surprised, but pleased, to see that both the Mountbattens were waiting to meet him, and that there was little formality either in their manner or their dress. The Viceroy himself was wearing a lightweight double-breasted suit instead of the white tropical admiral's uniform Nehru was expecting, and his wife was in a simple print frock. Another thing impressed Nehru: the speed with which the new Viceroy appeared to be getting down to work. After only a few minutes' conversation with the Mountbattens, Nehru found himself charmed and relaxed, the English half of him responding to the couple with warmth.

'It seemed to go very well this morning, Your Excellency,' he said. 'May I compliment you on your unexpected speech.' His voice was liquid, his English precise and cultured.

'Thank you.'

'Oh, it was very effective.' Nehru paused, then continued lightly. 'It also sounded as if you had the authority to make your own decisions.'

'I do,' replied the Viceroy. But Mountbatten was not to be drawn into a political conversation quite so quickly. 'However, let's not go into all that today. I just wanted to have an informal talk with you – so that we can get to know each other better.' He leant forward. 'Mr Nehru, I really do want you to regard me not as the last Viceroy, but as the first to lead the way to the new India.'

Nehru smiled. 'Now I know what they mean when they

58

speak of your charm being so dangerous.' It was his turn to switch the conversation. Looking round the long drawing-room, its walls decorated with ancient swords and halberds, its wooden floors covered with costly Persian rugs, he said to Edwina, 'How are you finding it here, so far?'

'Hot.'

'Ah, just wait until next month, or the month after. Last year it reached 115 degrees in the shade!'

'Then I'd better pray that the air-conditioning here won't break down!'

Nehru laughed: 'You are fortunate to have it. But I imagine that in any case you will shortly be moving up to Simla for the summer?'

'Not this year,' said Mountbatten. 'Too much to do.'

Edwina looked at him. She shouldn't have been surprised, but if that was the case, she certainly wasn't going to spend the summer cooped up in Viceroy's House with nothing to do but entertain. Plunging in, she asked Nehru about the possibility of her being able to help with the work of India's Nursing Council, and learnt to her dismay and his embarrassment that such an organization did not, as yet, exist. Legislation prepared for its creation had always encountered religious objections, and for the present it had been shelved to make way for more urgent matters. Edwina herself felt that there could hardly be more urgent matters than the creation of nationwide medical care, particularly in this country, beset as it so often was by famine and disease, and privately determined to press for it. At such an important time, she was the last person to sit back and let Dickie do all the driving – besides, there was more than enough for two people to do.

'Another thing I'd like to do as soon as possible is to get to know some Indian women – if you'll be good enough to introduce me?' This suggestion was not only inspired by genuine interest, but by the fact that the Mountbattens knew that – again, thanks to Gandhi's influence – Hindu women had more of a say and more of a share in power than almost anywhere else in the world at that time. She

59

knew that she should have to get to know at least three women well, and break down any barriers between them: Nehru's sister, who already represented India at the United Nations, Patel's daughter Maniben, and Jinnah's sister Fatima.

'I'm sure that would be mutually instructive,' said Nehru. He thought what a welcome change this was. Most memsahibs preferred to ignore the existence of their Indian counterparts. 'Speaking for my own family, I know that my sister and my daughter Indira will be only too delighted to see you. Unfortunately, as you know, my wife is dead . . .' Unable ever to hide his emotions, Nehru looked bleakly into space, remembering Kamala's long death, and how prison had so often separated him from her.

How soulful he looks, thought Pamela Mountbatten, as she came into the room to tell them that tea was being brought. She took off her glasses and popped them into the pocket of her dress as he looked up at her. She was seventeen, she had just left school, and this was her first time in India. She thought that the past three days had been the most exciting of her life. She wondered what she could say to Mr Nehru that could possibly interest him, but she told him about the young people's discussion group that Daddy had already arranged for her to join, to make contact with her own Indian contemporaries, and the sad-eyed politician seemed impressed. A lull in the conversation was broken by the appearance of tea.

'Ah,' said Mr Nehru, smiling broadly, 'tea. The one debt to India England will never be able to repay.'

Six hundred miles to the south-east lay the province of Bihar, a peasant farmland recently ravaged by clashes between its Hindu and Muslim communities. In the wake of the Calcutta killings of 1946, violence had spread to the neighbouring areas of Noakhali and Bihar, to the east and west. Mohandas Karamchand Gandhi, the father of India, whose friend the Bengali poet Tagore had conferred upon him the title of Mahatma, or Great Soul, had arrived in

Calcutta on 29 October, in preparation for a penitential pilgrimage to Noakhali, where in the course of four months he visited forty-nine villages on foot, bringing a message of peace and brotherhood to a fractured and confused society.

Now, instead of returning to Delhi immediately upon the arrival of the new Viceroy, the Mahatma had extended his mission to Bihar. 'Where Gandhi is, there is the capital of India,' Nehru had explained to Mountbatten.

In March 1947 Gandhi was seventy-seven years old. Barely five feet tall, he weighed no more than 114 pounds. To an outside observer there was much of a living caricature about this small, nut-brown man, dressed in nothing but white *khadi* – which had moved Churchill to describe him contemptuously as a 'half-naked fakir' – with his outsize steel-rimmed spectacles, his ready, gap-toothed smile, and his spidery arms and legs, as he flapped along the dusty trails between remote villages with his core of devoted followers – though in truth, all India followed him in spirit. Long ago, he had set aside not only material desire, but any influence the West might have. Married at thirteen, he had fathered four sons before undertaking the vow of *brahmacharya*, or celibacy, at the age of thirty-seven. Although he had allowed himself to be operated on by a British Surgeon-Major for appendicitis in 1924, so opposed had he become to accepting even Western medicine, and so strict was his adherence to his own principle of non-violence, that he allowed his wife Kasturbai to die in 1944 rather than allow her to have the hypodermic injections which might have saved her. His sole possession was an eight-shilling Ingersoll watch, and it was purely practical, for Gandhi held that every second of life was precious and should be put to good use – a view which led to obsessive punctuality. He had trained his body to subsist on the barest diet. He was regarded by all Hindus as a saviour and a saint. For all that, and for all his vast humanity, his private life bore traces of a heartlessness comparable to Jinnah's. His oldest son, Harilal, was to die in 1948 at the age of sixty, after years as a derelict alcoholic, racked with tuberculosis. When his youngest son Devedas expressed a desire to marry Lakshmi, daughter of Gandhi's first disciple Chakravarti Rajagopalachari, a difficulty arose: Devedas was a Vaisya, and Lakshmi a Brahmin. The young couple were enjoined by their fathers to wait for five years, after which they would be allowed to marry if they still wanted to. They did, in June 1933, when Devedas was thirty-three years old. In November of the same year Gandhi for the first time publicly denounced the evils inherent in the caste system.

But his personal shortcomings were drowned in the light of his charisma as a public man. He had denied himself all possessions and any status, and yet by teaching Indians the simple but universal means of revolution through non-cooperation and passive resistance, he had gained a stature which had dwarfed any other figure in Indian politics for fifty years. By his policy of gentleness, of turning the other cheek but never knuckling under, this man who would regard with horror the shedding of the life blood of any creature on earth had become the world's greatest revolutionary.

Now, as he walked, sometimes leaning on the shoulders of his two 'walking sticks', his great-nieces, Manu and Abha, his mind was appalled at what he had witnessed. He had restored peace where he could – but how long could it last? And the heart of India was in its villages. What hope was there for his beloved country if that heart were split?

He could see the smoke rising from the village before he reached it. Then he heard voices raised in anger. He knew what he would find: a Muslim family besieged in their home by their Hindu neighbours with whom they had lived in amity for years before this turmoil started.

Recognizing him, mouths agape, the villagers fell back at his approach. Children who had been placing bundles of kindling against the door of the besieged house in preparation to set light to it, moved aside shamefacedly. Motioning his secretary and constant companion Pyarelal Nayyar to wait, Gandhi proceeded alone.

'What madness is this?' he asked the village headman, sternly.

'Gandhiji! We are only returning blow for blow. Hindus have been attacked in the villages round us – their houses burned down!'

'Do you not see that by turning against your Muslim neighbours you are returning evil for evil? Hindu and Muslim have lived side by side in peace for centuries. Are your bellies suddenly so full that you can afford to burn each other's crops? Have the sun and rain stopped beating upon you, that you can afford to destroy each others' houses?' Gandhi turned to the door of the house, thrusting the kindling aside as he did so, and knocked. After a long moment the door was opened a fraction. Immediately the villagers started to mutter angrily, gripping the staves they were holding more tightly. The Mahatma quelled them with a look. Then he turned and spoke gently to the Muslims, asking them to come out. Assured of his protection, they did.

'Now,' said Gandhi, taking the village headman and the Muslim elder aside, 'what is happening here?' He knew the story already. It was nearly always the same: the Muslims would protect their innocence – rightly, for this family had done no harm. They would accuse the Hindus of singing and playing music at sunrise and sunset to desecrate the Muslim prayer-time. The Hindus would accuse the Muslims of slaughtering cows. The Muslims would point out that the cows, half-starved and disease-carrying, simply ate the heads of the young crops.

'You must understand each others' religions and tolerate them,' said Gandhi. 'The tree has many leaves, but only one trunk: thus it is with our religions and the one God we all pray to. I am a Hindu, but I am also a Muslim. You are shocked when I tell you this, but I am also a Sikh, a Christian, a Jew, a Buddhist, a Parsi.'

The Hindu and the Muslim looked at him, and then at the ground.

'Do you not see how much more important, how much

63

better it is for you to be friends than enemies? Your very survival depends upon it.' The Mahatma looked at them. 'And now I will ask you to do three things: to embrace, and to pray and eat a meal together with me.'

By the end of March Mountbatten had set the pace he meant to maintain. Over and above the administrative work, he and Edwina meant to set about wooing Indian society. The first matter to be attended to was that of inviting Indians to Viceroy's House. In itself this was nothing new, but now every week would see two garden parties, three or four luncheons for at least thirty guests, and two or three large dinner parties. The vast mahogany table in the State Dining-Room at Viceroy's House would seat over seventy, and Mountbatten made it a rule that never should less than fifty per cent of his guests be Indians. He imposed this rule throughout the provinces, and when one day Pamela overheard a memsahib guest remark to another, 'It makes me absolutely sick to see this house so full of dirty Indians,' Mountbatten repeated the remark to an assembled meeting of his provincial governors and invited their cooperation in sending home anyone who expressed similar sentiments.

The first garden party had gone well, and now that it was coming to a close Mountbatten found it easier to circulate. As he had hoped, Ismay, Abell and Campbell-Johnson had managed to detain guests to whom he wished to speak more fully. The brilliant display of flowers in the Round Pool Garden gave a heavy scent to the evening air. Neither Edwina nor the Viceroy had had much time to appreciate the atmosphere, but as Pamela drank it in, she thought it was the smell of India, as much as the sight, that made it irresistible.

Across the lawn, Mountbatten was talking to his Reforms Commissioner, V.P. Menon, a middle-aged Indian civil servant who looked like a benign bank manager in his dark European suit. Mountbatten, with his experience of assessing men, had very quickly come to appreciate

64

Menon's personal integrity, as well as his political useful-
ness as a close friend of Vallabhbhai Patel. But it was this
very friendship which discouraged the Viceroy from taking
Menon into his inner circle as quickly as he might have
done, a decision which Mountbatten regretted, insofar as
he dwelt on anything: he was a man of decision and of
action. If milk were ever spilt, he would not cry over it, he
would immediately seek ways of mopping it up, or of
rescuing what he could.

'This is a very significant occasion, Your Excellency,'
Menon was saying. 'The first ever party at Viceroy's House
to which ordinary Indians have been invited.'

Standing a little to one side, and noting the pleasure on
Menon's face, Ismay muttered to Abell, 'You know, I get
the distinct feeling that if we'd only done this sort of thing
years ago, we wouldn't be in the mess we're in now.'

'If you're right,' said Abell, 'let's pray that it hasn't
come too late.'

Edwina was approaching Menon and the Viceroy in the
company of an elegant Indian Princess, an observant and
gravely gentle woman in her late thirties.

'Darling, I don't think you've met Rajkumari Amrit
Kaur. She's Mr Gandhi's English language secretary.'

'How do you do?' said the Viceroy.

'I am so sorry to meet you just as I am leaving,' said
Amrit. 'But Her Excellency and I have been so engrossed
in discussing the problem of the nursing profession here in
India. It seems that our views on how to solve them
coincide exactly.'

'Then it is my sincere wish that you will do so together.'

Amrit smiled at the implied compliment. 'It has been a
delightful party, Your Excellency. I shall look forward to
meeting you again.'

As the Rajkumari left, escorted by an ADC, Edwina
turned glowingly to the two men. 'At last I feel as if I've
made a friendly contact! How could the memsahibs bear to
be so stand-offish, V.P.?'

Menon was a little embarrassed by the frankness of the

question. 'Not all were totally isolated, Your Excellency. Though it is true to say that most seemed to prefer it that way.'

'Then all I can say is, they don't know what they were missing!'

Pamela joined them. 'Everyone's gone,' she said, sadly. 'I was enjoying it so much. It's a shame.'

'I agree. I'm still in rather a party mood,' said Edwina. 'Darling, couldn't we go out somewhere? I can't bear the thought of just sitting and reading.'

To Menon's consternation, Mountbatten turned to him and suggested that the family drop in to a small party which Nehru had mentioned he was giving that evening at his home at 17, York Road. The suggestion staggered Menon. He knew that it was out of the question for a Viceroy to visit an Indian, however elevated, at home, informally. He expressed his regret, and Ismay and Abell backed him up. Apart from anything else, there would be no time to make security checks.

'It's just not done, sir,' said Abell.

Mountbatten looked at them. 'Well, it's damned well going to be done,' he decided.

Nehru had his back to the garden entrance when he turned to find out why the conversation, which a moment earlier had been buzzing happily around him, had suddenly faltered and died. But his concern turned to astonishment, and then, as the implications dawned on him, to delight, as he saw what had caused it.

'We heard you were giving a party,' said the Viceroy, approaching him with outstretched hand and a disarming smile. 'Hope you don't mind a few of us dropping in?'

For a few moments Nehru was confused. He simply didn't know how to react. The English half of him was already rejoicing at the compliment, and the Indian half considering the political advantage.

'This is a most pleasant surprise,' he said, introducing the Mountbattens to his sister and his daughter, who had

66

come up smilingly with drinks. 'And may I also present Maulana Kalam Azad.' Mountbatten shook hands with the aged, grey-bearded Azad, whose slight reserve he correctly attributed to his affection for Lord Wavell. But his loyalty to the departed Viceroy was not shared by his fellow members of the Congress Party, and Mountbatten knew that Azad, as an influential Muslim opposed to Partition and the Muslim League, and indeed until recently President of the Congress Party, was a man to cultivate.

As they moved on together, Nehru was unable to suppress a chuckle.

'What is it?' asked the Viceroy.

'Oh – nothing. It's just that I'd like to see Jinnah's face when he finds out who was my guest tonight.'

'Well, if he cares to send me an invitation, I'll be delighted to visit him.'

Nehru's smile didn't fade. He was impressed by the Englishman's fair-mindedness, and besides, he knew precisely what the likelihood was of Mohammed Ali Jinnah issuing social invitations.

'I'm sorry, Mrs Pandit,' said Edwina, 'but I just haven't got used to Indian names yet. 'What was your first name again?'

'I don't blame you for forgetting,' laughed Nehru's sister. 'It must seem so complicated.' They were walking, with Pamela and Indira, towards the pillared verandah where dancers were to perform. 'In the family they call me Nan. But my first name is Sarup.'

'I thought there was another – the one I'm trying to remember!'

'Oh yes. It is a Kashmiri custom to give a woman a new first name when she is married. And as the Nehrus come originally from Kashmir, I got one. So I am now Vijayalakshmi Pandit.'

Edwina repeated the name carefully, to Mrs Pandit's delight.

'Do you have a married name, too?' Pamela asked Indira.

'Yes. It is Priyadarshini.'

'Oh,' said Pamela, unable to begin to pronounce it. She blushed.

'Don't worry, my dear,' said Mrs Pandit. 'To us, it is compliment enough that you are interested.'

Mountbatten and Nehru were watching them laughing together. They smiled to each other.

'I shall look forward to our having another talk quite soon – on the future, Mr Nehru.'

Nehru immediately became serious. 'Yes, of course. But there is one thing I must make plain from the outset. I will only enter into discussions on the Independence of India in terms of a united country under one government.'

'The division of India has formed no part of my talks with His Majesty's Government,' replied Mountbatten, evenly.

'I am relieved to hear it, but I must emphasize my point. It is criminal of the Muslim League to stir up the violence we see around us to further their case for Partition. And may I tell you, Your Excellency, that the Muslim League is not a democratic organization. It is not only led by Jinnah, it *is* Jinnah. Remove him, and you remove the problem.' Nehru paused for a moment, warming to his theme. 'He refused, of course, to join the Interim Government himself. Instead, he manipulates the League puppets he has placed there. I think you have already had a meeting with Liaqat Ali Khan?'

'Yes.'

'Jinnah is the ventriloquist; Liaqat is the dummy. He is out to sabotage the Interim Government.'

'I have to see things from his point of view too, Mr Nehru. It may seem to him that that is the only way he's going to achieve anything, since he's outvoted in your Cabinet by two to one.'

There was a long pause.

'We had better go over, if we don't want to miss the beginning of the dancing,' said Nehru. They crossed the lawn in silence for a moment, which Mountbatten broke

68

by saying, 'Would it be out of order for me to ask your personal opinion of Gandhi?'

Nehru paused briefly. 'Bapu? I'm sorry. For years I have thought of him as Bapu – Father,' he explained, then hesitated and said simply, 'I revere him as another father, love him as a friend, and admire him as a guide. He is the conscience of us all. There can be no solution to any of the problems we face, without reference to the Mahatma.'

They met Edwina and the others coming towards them and Nehru led her to a chair placed under the great tree facing the pillared verandah. Lights had been strung across to illuminate the verandah like a small stage. Letting the rest of the ladies take the few seats, Mountbatten and he stood on either side of Edwina, applauding as the musicians came out, then the dancers in their delicate silk and brocade costumes and jewelled head-dresses.

To the music of flutes, drums and sitars, their gestures precise and stylized, their movements fluid and graceful, the dancers wove an immediate spell which held the guests rapt. Edwina glanced up at Nehru, her eyes wide with delight. In the half dark, she looked suddenly younger and very beautiful. 'But they're exquisite,' she breathed.

He leaned towards her. 'I'm very pleased you can see this,' he whispered. 'It's something special. They're a troupe of Masque Dancers from Seraikella. That is a small state dedicated for hundreds of years to the art of the dance.' Edwina smiled to him and turned back to watch.

Nehru straightened slowly, still surprised by his own reaction to her smile. It had been so warm and open, with no hint of reserve, that he had responded as to an old friend. He remembered her laughing as he and Lord Louis had pulled her from under the feet of that excited mob in Singapore, and in the drawing-room of Viceroy's House, cool and charming, making tea with the silver kettle brought to her by a turbaned servant and pouring it as though at home in London. Being part of that simple ceremony had swept him back to his years at Harrow and Cambridge and later at the Inns of Court, an ordered and

69

civilized world into which he had been completely absorbed. Part of him still missed that gracious world and, he told himself, that explained his response to this middle-aged English lady who personified it. He was watching her profile, caught by the light as she gazed at the graceful patterns of the dancers. Beyond her, Mountbatten looked round and smiled to him. Nehru answered the smile and turned back to the performance.

He found himself as disconcerted by that second smile as by Edwina's. He had earlier decided not to be distant, himself, but to remain guarded with both of them. It had been his political mentor, Krishna Menon, who had warned him against the charm of the Mountbattens, which concealed a steely determination, while his closest colleague, the strong man of the Congress Party, Sardar Patel, had laughed and assured them that Lady Louis was only a social butterfly who enjoyed being associated with 'good works' and that Lord Louis was lightweight and would prove easy to manipulate. Nehru was beginning to suspect that Patel's assessment was wildly inaccurate and that Krishna's warning had not been sufficiently forceful. The charm was beginning to work on him, so much so that he felt mean-spirited for holding back from it. He had many colleagues, his sister Nan, and Indira, who, although married, kept house for him. But there had been an emptiness in his life since Kamala had died and he had few intimate friends. He was watching Edwina's profile again, her eyes alight, her lips slightly parted.

The applause for the end of the first sequence of dances took him by surprise and he was a moment late joining in.

Six hundred miles away, Gandhi left the little village behind him and walked slowly off into the dusk, his staff in his left hand, his right resting on Manu's shoulder. He had told his divided children in the village that he did not expect them to agree on everything, only to agree to settle their differences without violence. The Muslim leader had wept.

'We hear you, Mahatmaji. It seems so simple, when you are with us.'

'I only speak what each of you has in his heart,' Gandhi had told him. 'I believe in Hindu-Muslim friendship because it is natural and necessary for both, and also because I believe in human nature.' The headman had begged him to stay with them, to teach them and pray with them, but he had many more miles to cover before nightfall to reach another, larger village, where already there had been several deaths and the communities lived in a state of armed siege. He had sat with them and taken a meal with them, since they had agreed to do the almost unthinkable and eat together. Before he left, he had taught them a prayer, which all of them might say together when there was need.

> 'Rama, King of the Universe,
> Who makes the sinner pure,
> Who is both Ishvara and Allah,
> Who gives his blessing to all.'

He had left his children sitting together at peace. But for how long would that peace last?

# FOUR

They had slowed the horses to a trot. On their left, the villages were waking up in the haze of morning. Few of the villagers paid much attention to them, but here and there a knot of children would cry out and wave. A man leading his oxen to the fields paused and stared at them in astonishment, his features breaking into a broad grin as he recognized them, and returned their friendly greeting. On their right, the River Jumna wound its sluggish course south towards Delhi.

This morning ride into the countryside to the north of town was a precious half-hour's relaxation with his wife and daughter snatched before the rigours of the day began. He was always pleased when the villagers recognized them. He remembered, smiling, how the Muslim newspaper *Dawn* had run a photograph of their arrival. The photograph had been captioned 'Lord and Lady Louis Mountbatten arriving at Palam Airport', but had shown Ronnie Brockman and Elizabeth Ward descending from the aeroplane. He looked across at his wife – she looked radiant, happier than he had seen her for some time and, although he knew that the headaches she suffered from so badly had not abated in the cruel heat of India, her love for the country and the stimulation of new company and new activity were doing her much good.

Her eyes drank in the yellow plains lying in the early sunshine. She loved the sense of space India gave her, and the quality of the light, so much richer than it ever is in England. The timelessness of the villages and of the villagers clad in their simple white cotton *kurtas* and *dhotis*, going about the eternal tasks of the peasant farmer,

72

unchanged for centuries, gave her a sense of inner peace which she had not felt for a long time.

'Isn't it glorious?' she said.

Pamela was watching the river. On its bank some women had just started their washing, beating the cotton on flat stones. 'I just want to ride on and on,' she said. 'Couldn't we follow the Jumna to its source?'

'I only wish we could, Pammy,' said Mountbatten, but he was glancing at his watch. 'Unfortunately, I'll have to be getting back soon.'

'Do we have to?' asked Edwina, knowing what the answer would be.

'It's a busy day.' Mountbatten knew that he faced a heavy session with Sir Conrad Corfield, who, as Secretary to the Political Department, was responsible for the interests of the Indian princes. Mountbatten's office of Viceroy covered not only the overall administration of the eleven provinces of British India, but as Crown Representative he also bore responsibility for the five hundred and sixty-five princely states which made up the rest of the subcontinent. The princes recognized the paramountcy of the British King-Emperor, but with the transfer of power that paramountcy would lapse. Mountbatten hoped that the states would throw in their lot with the new Indian republic, but he knew that Corfield believed that such a course would be injurious to the interests of the princes he represented. It was a further complication in an already intricate situation.

And then there was his first meeting with Mr Patel.

He reined his horse in. 'At least we gave our bodyguard the slip,' he grinned. 'I know they have their job to do, but I really can't be riding around in a convoy like that!'

Pamela had already turned her horse. 'Don't speak too soon, Daddy,' she laughed, ruefully. In a cloud of dust over a slight rise behind them a troop of mounted soldiers was riding fast towards them, the sunlight glinting on the polished buttons of their uniforms, and the harness of their horses.

'Oh well,' said Mountbatten. 'Let's race them back!'

Sardar Vallabhbhai Patel drummed his fingers on the desk. So far the meeting had not gone badly, though he might have wished for a more positive response from the Viceroy to his views on the Muslim League. In his view, no way forward could be made until the League was stripped of its power, at whatever cost. Well, he would have to be patient: there was still the question of compensation to departing members of the Indian Civil Service to be settled. This, Patel felt, was an open and shut problem. It also provided him with a convenient method of measuring the strength of the man sitting opposite him.

Patience did not come easily to Sardar Patel, for all that he looked like an elderly Buddha. Bald, leathery, with a pugnacious set to his mouth, and an alertness in his face which belied his seventy-two years, he prided himself on his reputation as the strong man of the Congress Party leadership. Nehru was too enamoured of Western diplomatic methods, he sometimes felt. If you wanted something, sometimes you had to grab it before the opportunity slipped by, and that meant confrontation, not pussyfooting.

'You British talk about giving Independence to India as if it were some great and noble gesture,' he said. 'You won't admit that the real reason is economic.'

'That is one of the reasons,' replied Mountbatten, mildly. Far from being tired, the discussion stimulated him. Patel was putting him on his mettle.

'You say that you're going to quit, but all we've heard so far is talk.'

'My one wish is to transfer power as soon as possible. And to discuss the ways and means.'

'Good. But there are others to be satisfied as well as Jawaharlal.'

'Naturally. Yourself for one.' Mountbatten paused. 'And, presumably, Mr Gandhi.'

He had touched a raw nerve. Like the other leaders of Congress, Sardar Patel had early allied himself to the ideals

74

and aspirations of the Mahatma. But recently there had been times when he had wondered whether Gandhi's belief that the soul of India lay in her villages was in fact still true, in a world increasingly concerned with industrialization and technological development. Patel decided to change course, to go straight into the attack. He drew a few sheets of typed paper from his briefcase and laid them on the desk.

'Something which I want settled immediately is this question of pensions to be paid to the British members of the ICS after Independence. The amounts proposed are too much. If they're not adjusted the British Government can pay for the lot themselves.' He pushed the typed sheets across the desk to Mountbatten. 'I've put the Home Ministry's terms into this Minute. I might add that if any Indian ICS member opts for compensation rather than continue service, he'll never work in this country again. As Home Minister, that is my last word.' He leant back, his face set and unyielding.

Mountbatten barely glanced at the paper in front of him, then he looked at the *dhoti*-clad figure in the chair across the desk. 'I'm afraid I must ask you to reconsider this, Mr Patel.'

'I'm not prepared to discuss it. Take it or leave it.'

Mountbatten was motionless, his even tone of voice unchanged. 'Then you leave me no alternative but to order my aircraft.'

'Why?' Patel was taken aback.

'Because I'm going home. I never wanted this job, and you've just handed me the perfect excuse to give it up.' He pulled the telephone towards him.

'You don't mean it!'

'Mr Patel, I didn't take on the Viceroyalty just to let myself be bullied by anyone who thinks he can walk in here and throw his weight around.'

The Indian scoffed. Mountbatten's expression did not alter one iota. He leant back in his chair and tapped the Minute on the desk between them. 'You obviously don't know me very well yet. Either you withdraw that document immediately, or I will send in my resignation. His Majesty, Mr Attlee and Mr Nehru will, of course, be fully informed of my reasons.'

Patel was unable to read the expression in the new Viceroy's eyes. For once in his life he was thrown. Should he call this man's bluff or not? He looked from Mountbatten's face to the hand resting lightly on the telephone. Resentment gave way to a new respect and he shrugged inwardly. At least he'd got the measure of the man. And if he was going to be this firm, he wouldn't let Jinnah order him around either. Perhaps, after all, they could work together.

He looked evenly at the Viceroy, picked up the Minute, and tore it in two.

Mizzen was behaving like a puppy again, thought Edwina, laughing as Mrs Pandit threw a stick for the old Sealyham to scamper after. During the course of this first private conversation together, she had greatly taken to the Indian woman, and she dared to hope that the feeling was mutual. One barrier, however, remained to be broken down. She knew how Indians tended to retreat into formality when dealing with the British – indeed, the British had done nothing to encourage them otherwise. Now she felt that the moment was right to unlock that particular door.

'May I ask you a favour?'

'Of course, Your Excellency.'

Edwina laughed again. 'That's just it! I hope very much that we are going to be friends, and my friends call me Edwina.' Mrs Pandit smiled, stooping to take the stick from Mizzen and throw it again. Here under the trees in the beautiful garden of 17, York Road, Nehru's white-painted, two-storey villa, it was still cool. Later, she knew, the dog would want to lie down in the shade and sleep through the heat of the day. There wasn't much difference between English dogs and Indian dogs, she thought.

'Thank you, Edwina,' she said. 'And I hope that you

76

will call me Nan.' They smiled to each other, and she continued, thoughtfully, 'You have the gift of friendliness. Forgive me, but that is a little unexpected from someone in your . . . position.'

'Oh, I am only Vicereine because Dickie is Viceroy! The war taught me how to be a nurse. Before then, I'd barely cared about anything beyond my own pleasure.'

'But you have had a most successful career. And when I consider what you are achieving here: the whole idea of an Indian Nursing Council had been well and truly shelved before you arrived.'

'Nevertheless, when I compare my career with yours . . .'

'Oh, being the daughter of Motilal and the sister of Jawaharlal Nehru was no handicap.'

Edwina laughed. 'Don't be modest. You are an inspiration to women everywhere – and we in the West should certainly look to our laurels, I think, when I consider what Indian women are achieving. Can you imagine an Englishwoman leading her country's delegation to the UN, as you do?'

Nan took the compliment smilingly, aware in all humility of its truth. Perhaps this was one of the advantages of being in at the birth of a new, free nation, unfettered by the prejudice of ages. But there was still much to be done. She was aware that she was one of a very small, very privileged minority, which had been able to learn from both the triumphs and the mistakes of the British.

'How do you find working with your brother?'

'Jawaharlalji? He's very good. Of course we do have our differences. And he has a fiendish temper.'

Edwina was surprised. 'He seems so charming.'

'Oh, he is. But he's not very patient. Especially when something strikes him as dishonest or unfair. Then it's best to take cover!'

They had been walking towards the villa, and at that moment Nehru himself came out onto the verandah, blinking in the sunlight and stretching his arms. Edwina was

77

pleased to see surprise give way to delight as he noticed her.

'I had no idea you were coming. Forgive me,' he said, advancing towards them.

'What are you doing away from your office?' teased Nan.

'I've been at it since six. And there's a Council meeting in an hour. I thought I'd choose my buttonhole and have a glass of fruit juice.' He smiled, looking at Edwina. 'And what have you two been chatting about? Me?'

'Oh, the vanity of men, Edwina.'

'As a matter of fact, Nan was telling me how bad-tempered you are!'

Nehru looked from the Viceroy's wife to his sister. So, they were on first-name terms. He remembered Lord Louis' behaviour towards him in Singapore. He had treated him like an Indian politician, not like dangerous revolutionary jailbait. The fact that the British had sent such a couple to preside over India's secession from the Empire was indeed encouraging. Behind him, a servant, bearing jugs of orange and mango juice on a tray, appeared on the verandah.

'Ah,' he said, smiling. 'Perhaps you would care to join us . . . Edwina?' It had been a calculated risk, using her first name unbidden and for a moment he was nervous. After all, she was Vicereine. But the beautiful English-woman smiled back.

'I should be delighted.'

The daily staff meeting was held first thing in the morning at Viceroy's House. Ever since he had read Maeterlinck's *The Life of the Bee*, Mountbatten had developed a working philosophy which he referred to as 'the spirit of the hive'. It had characterized his control both of Combined Operations and South-East Asia Command during the war, and he had found it so successful that he applied it now to the greatest task of his career. The meeting was an open forum, a chance for each and every key member of his team to air their views, to criticize and help one another for

78

the good of the job in hand. To help them all, Mountbatten, whose memory was acute, had established a system of devoting fifteen minutes after each personal interview he had with an Indian leader to dictating a résumé of it. He felt that a stenographer's presence at an interview would inhibit discussions, an instinct that had been proved correct by his session with Vallabhbhai Patel. It was Patel whom the men, crowded together at the small round table in the Viceroy's study, were discussing now.

'I'm glad you showed him who's boss,' said Ismay with characteristic frankness, 'but he does control the party machine, so we must do everything we can to get him on our side.'

'How much of a rival is he to Nehru?' Erskine Crum wanted to know. 'Could he nudge him out of the leadership?'

'We can't rule out that possibility,' Mountbatten said, looking for a comment to his Principal Secretary, Sir Eric Miéville.

'To me, it's strange that Nehru and Patel can work together at all. Patel's a practical capitalist, while Nehru's a romantic socialist. What seems to bind them together is Gandhi. He's still the presiding spirit, for all that he's withdrawn from direct involvement in politics nowadays.'

Mountbatten turned to his Press aide, Alan Campbell-Johnson, who had the job of taking down his verbatim reports immediately after each meeting. 'The question is, just how much clout has Gandhi got? What was it Patel said about him exactly, Alan?'

Campbell-Johnson consulted the file in front of him. '"I love and respect him, but in practical terms he is becoming out of date."' The men round the table assessed what he had read out. It was the old India hands, Ismay and Miéville, to whom it came as the greatest shock. The British had always considered Gandhi to be the decision-maker of the Congress Party. But if that were no longer the case?

'That,' Ismay said, 'as our American cousins put it, would make it a whole new ball game.'

Neither Abell nor Miéville were ready to accept that power might be slipping away from Gandhi. 'Oh, he bewilders his disciples by changing his mind,' Miéville said, 'but he is still the major force to be reckoned with. When are you meeting him?'

'I wish I knew,' Mountbatten answered. 'The sooner, the better. I even offered to send my own plane for him. He replied that he was in no hurry and that, if he did come, it would be by train.'

They laughed and the discussion turned to another tricky area. Mohammed Ali Jinnah had at last agreed to accept the Viceroy's invitation to a meeting.

'You're going to enjoy that,' Ismay said drily. 'He's the colonel of the Stonewall Brigade.'

As George Abell began to go over the reports of violent clashes which were attributable to Jinnah's policy of Direct Action, clashes which had now spread to include the Sikhs, there was a knock at the door and V.P. Menon, most uncharacteristically flustered, hurried into the study. 'I am so sorry to interrupt, Your Excellency,' the Indian civil servant said, 'but we've just had news and I thought you'd better know at once. Gandhi has arrived in Delhi. He is on his way here.'

Edwina had ordered tea, although she was by no means certain that he would take it with them. She was delighted that Dickie had asked her to be with him for this first meeting and could see that he was tense. Nan Pandit's assurance that Gandhi was the most charming man she had ever known did little to ease Mountbatten's nerves. 'How do you talk to someone who's been in and out of British prisons for the last forty years?' he asked.

'You'll just have to be completely natural with him,' Edwina said. 'And it's not only Nan. Indira says he's gentle and lovable.'

Mountbatten nodded. 'He may be lovable, but he has a

razor-sharp mind and as many tricks up his sleeve as a barrel-load of monkeys.'

The doors of the drawing-room were opening and Erskine Crumm announced, 'Mr Gandhi, Your Excellencies,' The Mahatma, as always, entered with his hand on Manu's shoulder and Mountbatten advanced to meet him.

'My apologies that I could not accept your invitation before now, Your Excellency,' Gandhi said.

'Not at all. I know what detained you,' Mountbatten replied. 'This is a rare pleasure, Mr Gandhi.' They shook hands. 'My wife has been very keen to meet you.'

Gandhi turned to Edwina and bowed. 'At last I see the famous Lady Louis.' She must have looked questioning, for he went on, 'My friends from Malaya and Burma have told me how you were the first into the jungle after the war with food and medical supplies. What better claim to fame than to have saved thousands of lives?' Edwina thanked him quietly. 'May I present my grandniece, Manu? I couldn't function without her. She is my walking-stick.'

Mountbatten and Edwina greeted Manu, who smiled, placing the palms of her hands together in the Hindu greeting of *namaste* before silently retreating to sit on the floor by the wall in a corner of the room.

Edwina still felt touched and grateful for Gandhi's compliment. It meant so much more coming from him. Seated opposite him, she was aware of a strange sense of humility. The force of his personality was different from anything she had ever experienced before. She saw him looking at them expectantly, clearly waiting for them to begin the conversation. There was something she wanted to ask, about his name. She had heard him referred to as 'Gandhiji'. Was this a more correct form than plain 'Gandhi'?

He smiled. 'My name is Mohandas Karamchand Gandhi. The 'ji' is added – by some people. It is a way we have to express . . . respect or affection. As one might say, "Lord Louisji".' He admonished himself. 'Oh, no, that sounds too Italian.' They laughed, surprised by his twinkling sense of humour. 'Do forgive me,' he continued. 'I am being frivolous, when we have important things to talk about.'

'Not at all,' Mountbatten assured him. 'I'd really prefer in this first meeting for us just to chat and get to know each other.'

'What a delightful idea!' Gandhi exclaimed. 'I confess I am very curious to know more about Your Excellencies.'

Edwina nearly laughed again, to see how neatly Dickie's ball had been returned. It was not quite what he had had in mind. 'I had hoped to learn something about your own background and experiences, Mr Gandhi,' Mountbatten said.

Gandhi glanced up at the chandelier, suspended from the ornate plasterwork of the ceiling's central rose. 'A great British principle which I learned in my early days in London,' he said, 'was the principle of "Fair Play". I believe it is known as Give and Take.' When he looked at them, his eyes were mischievous and this time Edwina did laugh quietly.

They were both delighted by his puckish humour and by his cultured, measured English, which briefly had seemed incongruous, coming from one whose appearance and dress were those of a simple villager. It did not, by any means, induce Mountbatten to underestimate him and he realized that any game of political chess played with this remarkable old man would be highly stimulating, as well as dangerous. He smiled, giving in. 'That does seem only fair.'

'People speak of a new atmosphere, of a Viceroy who is not remote, but approachable and understanding, human. Now I see what they mean,' Gandhi said. 'They say you have a genuine feeling for India. I know you were here during the war. Did you have any connection with us before?'

'The happiest,' Mountbatten told him. 'It was here that we became engaged. In New Delhi.'

'Did you meet here?' Gandhi asked, eagerly.

'No, we had already met in England,' Edwina said.

They found themselves telling him how Mountbatten

had come out on an official visit as aide to his cousin, the Prince of Wales, now Duke of Windsor. He had missed Edwina and wrote to her, asking her to join him. She had not yet come into her inheritance, so had to borrow the money from a great-aunt for a second-class ticket on the steamer. Once in Delhi, she had been taken under the wing of Lady Reading, the then Vicereine, who was fairly strict and did not entirely approve of Dickie. Yet it was an exciting time, with parties and balls and receptions and visits to maharajahs' palaces.

'Edwina was surrounded by all the young officers, all dancing attendance on her. Finally, I realized I'd better do something about it – so I proposed.'

'It all happened at the old Viceregal Lodge,' Edwina said, 'which is now the University.'

'Have you been back there since?' Gandhi asked with obvious fascination.

'We took our daughter the other day,' Edwina told him, 'just to show her where it all began.'

'What a romantic story!' Gandhi exclaimed. 'I do enjoy a romantic story.'

'So you see, Mr Gandhi,' Mountbatten said, 'here I discovered the three loves of my life. For my wife; for polo, which has become my favourite sport; and for India, herself.'

Gandhi considered him for a long moment, and sighed. 'What a pity . . . Lovers are the only people I can never reason with.' He was teasing again, and they laughed.

'You mentioned when you were in London,' Mountbatten said. 'You were studying law, I believe.'

'Like Mr Nehru,' Edwina added.

Gandhi nodded. 'Many years before him. But yes, like Jawaharlalji.' The slight, deliberate stress on 'ji' made them smile. 'And like Sardar Patel,' he went on. 'And for that matter, Mohammed Ali Jinnah.' He chuckled at Mountbatten's reaction. 'Yes, you see what you are up against, Lord Louis. A battery of London-trained Indian lawyers.'

In his turn, he told them of his early struggles in England

and South Africa, and of his return to India to begin the long fight for *Swaraj*. What impressed them both was his obvious lack of bitterness at his generally insensitive treatment by the authorities over so many years.

'May I say, I am one of those who have always admired you,' Edwina said, 'what you have fought for, and your love for your people.'

'Ah, but I also love Englishmen,' Gandhi smiled. 'I have tried to let nothing into my heart but love. In a heart filled with love, there is no room for resentment or the desire for revenge. With love comes understanding, and together they are the answer to everything.'

News of Gandhi's arrival had spread rapidly and a photo session had quickly been arranged. Alan Campbell-Johnson had to shepherd and placate a throng of Indian and international journalists and cameramen, as they waited on the terrace of the Mogul Gardens behind the House. He had informed them that no questions would be permitted on the nature or progress of the talks and that a press communiqué would be issued later. As the time dragged on and still no one appeared, he could hear them all speculating on what was going on inside. That was what they were all waiting for, to try to judge from the expressions how the talks were going.

As more time passed, he had to keep fending off queries about the delay, assuring the eager and impatient reporters that there would be a photo session and that there was no disagreement between the Mahatma and the Viceroy. He fervently hoped that was true, and was relieved when servants came out onto the terrace at last, then the duty ADCs and, finally, the Mahatma and the Mountbattens. They obligingly did as the photographers asked, as they all jockeyed for positions to get the best shots, but smilingly refused to answer any questions. 'Please, gentlemen,' Campbell-Johnson protested. 'We agreed – no questions.' They, however, had their job to do.

'Have you agreed a date for Independence?' one asked.

'How about you, Mr Gandhi?' an American correspondent called. 'Would you care to say how your talks are going?'

Gandhi merely smiled, not replying. He shook hands with Mountbatten, then moved to let Edwina be photographed between them.

'How about a comment, Lord Louis?' the American correspondent asked.

'Sorry, no statements,' Mountbatten said. 'Thank you, gentlemen.' He nodded to Gandhi and Edwina and turned, heading for the door. The session was ended.

There was a murmur of disappointment and speculation and the clicking of cameras stopped. As the others moved away, one photographer, Max Desfor of the Associated Press of America, came to Campbell-Johnson. He had been hanging on for the perfect shot, the picture that would capture the feeling of the meeting for the world, but it had not presented itself. 'Well, that was short and sweet,' he said. 'What do you think – ?' He had glanced towards the door and broke off, raising his camera quickly. Alan Campbell-Johnson looked round, and saw at once what had caught Desfor's eye.

Edwina and Gandhi were following Mountbatten. As they neared the door and were about to step up inside, Gandhi had laid his left hand on Edwina's right shoulder for support. Desfor's shutter clicked, capturing the simple yet eloquent gesture of affection and trust.

Edwina came into the Viceroy's study with Gandhi and helped to settle him in an armchair by the window. It was time for her to leave the two men alone together and here they would be more comfortable, and certainly quieter. 'Perhaps I'll see you again later, Mr Gandhi,' she said.

'I would like that,' Gandhi smiled. 'You have been most kind.'

Mountbatten took the seat opposite him and she headed for the door. As she was going out, she looked back and paused, seeing that Gandhi was shivering, drawing his

85

shoulder wrap round himself. Mountbatten had also noticed and was concerned.

'Are you all right, Mr Gandhi?' he asked.

Edwina had realized. 'No, he's not! It's the air conditioning. The poor man's freezing!'

'It is the cold air, I am afraid,' Gandhi told them. 'I am not used to it.'

There was a sweater of Mountbatten's lying folded over the back of a chair by the door. Edwina shook it out and draped it over Gandhi's shoulders. 'There, is that better?' But he was still shivering uncontrollably. 'It's no good, Dickie,' she said. 'You'll have to get the machine turned off.'

Mountbatten had a better idea. 'The Press should have cleared from the terrace by now. Mr Gandhi, why don't we talk there, while we have tea?'

Gandhi was grateful. The cold was really affecting him badly. 'Tea on the terrace sounds . . . very good,' he panted. 'But please don't provide anything for me. My greatniece has everything I need. She always . . . carries it with her.'

In the heat of the terrace, Gandhi recovered rapidly. Sitting opposite him again, now at a wicker table, Mountbatten poured and sugared his own tea, watching Manu as she poured a whitish liquid into a small wooden bowl and spooned a yellowish, curdled substance into another. Having served them to Gandhi, she retired again to a distance and sat on her haunches, waiting.

Mountbatten watched curiously as Gandhi picked up the bowl of liquid and sipped it. 'May I ask what you're having, Mr Gandhi?' he enquired.

'It is my daily diet. Lemon soup.'

Mountbatten was eyeing the yellow substance. 'And the other one?'

'Goat's curds. Would you care to try some?' Gandhi asked. He saw Mountbatten hesitate. 'Come along. Please. It's very good, very nourishing.'

Reluctantly, Mountbatten took a little of the yellow

86

curds with his teaspoon and put it in his mouth. He
found the taste unspeakable and had the greatest difficulty
swallowing, but finally forced himself.

Gandhi had watched him with great interest and asked
blandly, 'Would you like some more? Finish the bowl.'

'No, thank you,' Mountbatten answered with a grimace.
'Frankly, I don't know how you can bear to eat it.'

Gandhi laughed, seeing him drink his tea quickly to
wash it down. 'Perhaps one has to be born with a taste for
it,' he suggested.

They sat for a few minutes in companionable silence,
each aware that the time for serious discussion had come.
Gandhi sighed. 'I am grateful for your welcome – but it
feels unreal to be sitting here, after the horror I have
witnessed in these past months, whole villages slaughtered
in the name of God. . . . Can there be any greater
obscenity?' Mountbatten was silent, and Gandhi went on,
'Yet even more painful is the thought that it might lead to
India being divided. You must have heard this from others,
but hear it from me: there must be no Partition. It would
make a mockery of my life, of everything I have stood for.'

There was no mistaking his sincerity and Mountbatten
decided he could only try to be equally sincere. 'I shall be
completely honest. I came here with the firm determination
that India would never be split into two separate states. I
knew the option existed – but only as a very last resort.'

Gandhi was taut. 'Are you saying that you have changed
your mind?'

Mountbatten shrugged. 'I'm not sure what I *am* saying.
However, I admit that I am beginning to see no alternative,
if Mr Jinnah and the Muslim League go on refusing to
cooperate.'

'But if a solution were offered to you, you would not
reject it?'

Mountbatten heard the eagerness in Gandhi's voice and
answered cautiously. 'I'm willing to consider any suggestion
– especially if it comes from you.'

Gandhi sat back, smiling. 'Then perhaps we may still do

a good day's work.' He had foreseen the line of discussion and had been turning it over in his mind all day, from his arrival in Delhi and visit to the shanty town where the Untouchables lived in poverty and squalor and which he would make his headquarters as always when he was here, and on the journey to Viceroy's House. He had the solution worked out, a plan which should not only satisfy Jinnah, but would ensure the future of a unified India. It was not without its drawbacks, yet if he could persuade the Viceroy to support it, he was certain he could persuade the Congress leaders to accept it. There was always an element of risk, but it was one worth taking.

The house on Aurangzeb Road managed to combine austerity with luxury. Visitors said it reminded them of nothing so much as a mosque. It was the Delhi home of Mohammed Ali Jinnah. The study, panelled in dark wood and lined with law books, was meticulously neat and tidy; papers, books, even the pens on the desk were in perfect alignment. The room was dominated by a large map of India, which hung above the marble fireplace. The map was made of silver and the northern Muslim provinces to the east and west, Jinnah's dream state of Pakistan, were enamelled green, the colour of the Prophet.

Jinnah was standing by the desk, looking at a photograph in a newspaper. It was the one taken of Edwina with Gandhi's hand resting on her shoulder. He threw the paper down on the desk in anger. 'So! Apparently we have another Viceroy who backs the Congress Party!'

Liaqat Ali Khan, a short, stout man with glasses, watched his leader nervously as he fitted a cigarette into his jade holder, screwing it in with an angry twist. Even as Jinnah did so, his body was racked by a deep, hollow cough. Despite his attempts to control it, the cough had been growing worse. His doctor, a close friend, had told him bluntly it was a miracle he managed to survive on his regimen of whisky and cigarettes. It was only his willpower which kept him going. His frail body could not withstand for much longer the treatment to which he subjected it.

'I shouldn't read too much into that photograph,' Liaqat said, placatingly. He was nervous at disagreeing with his chief, but had a valid point. 'You know how unaffected, almost childlike Gandhi is. He behaves the same everywhere, as if he were in a hut in some village.'

'As simple as a fox, as childlike as a hyena,' Jinnah snapped. 'I shall never forget him squatting in that corner, with his granddaughter or whoever she is mixing his nasty little bowls of goat's curds. . . . It's a wonder they didn't bring the damned goat in here and milk it!'

Liaqat began to smile, but stopped when Jinnah glanced at him.

'The whole trouble with Gandhi,' Jinnah went on, 'is that you can never trust him. Just when you think you've reached a firm agreement with him, he goes back on it.' To break one's given word was inexcusable to Jinnah, yet Gandhi had demonstrated several times his ability to take part in exhaustive discussions and sign his name to a solemn undertaking, and then go home and reject it.

'Whenever he changes his mind, he says he's been prompted by his Inner Light,' Liaqat pointed out.

'To hell with his Inner Light!' Jinnah coughed again as he lit his cigarette. He had noticed over the years that Gandhi's famous Inner Light was inconsistent, except that it always worked to his own advantage. 'It is typical of him that when he returns to Delhi, he settles himself in the worst slum he can find, among the Untouchables.'

'His followers say that shows his humility.'

'A public humility that masks the ultimate pride,' Jinnah snorted. 'He wants to be thought of as a saint.'

'The point is,' Liaqat said, 'that he is just the sort to respond to the Mountbattens.'

'Oh? Why?' He had turned to the drinks cabinet behind him and paused, as he selected a bottle of vintage brandy.

'They have a way of making strangers feel like old friends

within a few minutes. I felt it myself,' Liaqat said. 'It is part of Lord Louis' technique.'

Jinnah poured himself a measure of brandy. Knowing Liaqat to be a practising Muslim, he did not offer him one. 'His technique for what?'

'He knows that the large conferences involving the leaders of all parties have always ended in bitterness and disagreement,' Liaqat explained. 'So he has started his own meetings on a one-to-one basis, to make friendly contact before the conference stage is reached.'

'Friendly contact,' Jinnah repeated. He added soda to his glass and, out of long habit, raised his glass to the silver and green map above the fireplace. As he drank, he saw only the green spaces. He coughed. 'I am always wary of a man who is too eager to offer me his friendship. Because I know that inevitably he will demand a high price in return.'

In the small, bare hut which the Mahatma had made his home in the slum of the Banghi sweepers' colony, he sat cross-legged on a reed mat on the floor in the centre of the room, his dark bald head shining in the yellow light of the single oil lamp. Sitting near him, with Vallabhai Patel on his other side, Nehru felt both eager and receptive, seeing him so alight with enthusiasm. He had summoned them both urgently to come to him, as soon as he had left Viceroy's House.

'It is the way, the perfect way, the only way,' he told them. 'I outlined my proposal to the Viceroy and, provided I can assure him that Congress accepts it, he is prepared to consider it.'

Nehru smiled. He could see that Patel was just as intrigued. 'What is the solution, Bapu?'

'One so simple no one has thought of it!'

Patel chuckled. 'Are we to be enlightened? If, as you say, it will secure the unity of India, I can't wait to hear it.'

'If Jinnah will not accept a government controlled by the Congress Party and insists on Partition,' Gandhi told them, 'you and the government simply resign.'

'. . . And call new elections?' Nehru asked.

Gandhi shook his head. 'No, no. Don't you see? You ask Jinnah to form a government – just hand it over to him.'

Nehru and Patel gazed at him in astonishment, while he smiled to them, willing them to understand and accept the concept.

Patel hoped he had misunderstood. 'Wrap up everything we have achieved – and make a present of it to Jinnah?'

'To prevent the greater evil of Partition.'

Nehru and Patel were both disturbed now. Reluctant to believe that he was really serious, Patel tried to laugh. 'What sort of future do you think our people would have under Jinnah?'

Gandhi beat one hand against the other. 'The essential thing is to preserve India, to stop her from being maimed.' That truth was self-evident. Why could they not see it?

'That's too high a price,' Patel said, dismissively.

'You don't understand, Vallabhai.'

'I don't even want to understand! Nothing on earth would make me hand over power to the Muslim League.'

Nehru was hurt by the shock he could see on Gandhi's face. At the same time, he could sympathize with Patel's rising anger. He tried to be conciliatory. 'I believe Jinnah is bluffing, Bapu, and the League is not so powerful as he is trying to make out. After all, many Muslims support us and Congress. They have not joined the League.'

'Will you do nothing to halt the shameful vivisection of our country?' Gandhi asked quietly.

Nehru found he had to phrase his answer carefully. 'I would do anything practical.'

The shock which Gandhi had felt at having his proposal rejected almost without consideration by his two chief disciples and friends was giving way to a profound sadness. He was convinced that an idealistic gesture such as he had proposed was the only move that could counter Jinnah's disruptive tactics. He pulled himself together. Obviously, they saw him as impractical, out of touch with reality. Very well. He would make them face the hideous realities that were left, if his way was not followed. 'I have offered you the least extreme of the only remaining alternatives.'

'Which are?' Patel grunted.

'You tell the British to get out now and leave India to chaos.'

Nehru was too appalled to be tactful. 'But don't you realize what that would mean?'

'Yes. It would lead to a bloodbath,' Gandhi said, his tone deliberately impersonal. 'But it would prevent Partition, and power would be yours to deal with unrest wherever it breaks out.' Nehru and Patel looked at each other. Moving slowly apart in ideology and increasingly wary allies, they were bound together by their distress at what Gandhiji was proposing, and by what he seemed prepared to sacrifice for his ideal of a united India. They each knew that what he was proposing would lead to more than unrest. There would be civil war in at least three major provinces, and chaos in the princely states, over which they had to gain control if India were ever to become a viable modern republic. Gandhi was speaking again. 'If you reject that, you are left with only one more option. Let the government resign without agreeing to the creation of Pakistan. The British will be forced to remain, to keep India united.'

'If we did that, we'd have them on our backs for another hundred years!' Patel muttered. What the old man was putting to them were not alternatives, they were nightmares. He rose abruptly, unwilling to remain any longer in case he lost his temper. He had come here praying that the Mahatma had found a solution – and now this. 'You have obviously been under a strain, Gandhiji,' he said, tightly. 'We would lose all credibility in the Party, and in the country, if we suggested such schemes. We would have declared ourselves unfit to deal with Independence.'

Gandhi did not answer. He had expected argument and opposition from Vallabhai. But surely Jawaharlal . . .?

To his dismay, Nehru was also rising, slowly. When he spoke, it was with difficulty, for he realized that his words symbolized a parting of ways which might never be brought together again. 'I am sorry, Bapu. I have followed your instincts before, but in this I cannot.'

Gandhi turned his head away from him, his eyes lowered. Nehru was stricken and made to speak, but Patel shook his head. There was no more to be said. They bowed slightly, their palms together, and left.

Gandhi sat motionless, after they had gone, brooding, wondering why he had not seen until now how far apart from him they had moved. After a time, he became aware that Manu and Abha had come in from where they had been guarding the door and were squatting in their usual corner, watching him.

'They call me Mahatma, Great Soul,' he whispered. 'But I tell you they treat me like one of those they call Untouchable.'

The main light shone on the marble-based billiards table. Mountbatten was playing with Ismay, Miéville and John Christie, his brilliant Joint Private Secretary, kept on from the previous Viceroy's staff. They talked quietly, conscious of the two turbaned servants standing by the butler's tray of drinks near the rack of cues on the far wall.

Miéville was still incredulous, which made him miss his shot. 'He really meant it?'

Mountbatten took over the game. 'No question. He wanted me to propose the scheme. But I said I'd only consider it, *if* it were given Congress approval.' He brought off a difficult cannon, leaving the red ball perfectly placed.

Ismay gave him another two points. 'But they'll never agree. Do you think so, John?'

Christie had been silent, considering Mountbatten. 'I don't think His Excellency expects them to,' he said slowly. 'I don't think he even wants them to.'

Ismay paused by the score board. 'Yes . . . Yes, I think we are being remarkably dull, not to see what is under our noses.'

93

Mountbatten was rechalking the tip of his cue. He glanced up and smiled briefly.

Miéville was no wiser. 'What? I don't follow.'

'The Mahatma's proposal to hand over the government to Jinnah is imaginative as His Excellency has said,' Christie told him quietly. 'So imaginative that there's little doubt the Congress Party will throw it out. And so the distance between them and Gandhi will widen.'

Miéville understood at last and was troubled. 'If so, was it fair to encourage him to suggest it?'

Mountbatten was lining up his shot and glanced up again. 'Oh, come on! I admire him tremendously, but I have enough problems without him confusing the issue still further.' Miéville was still troubled, but Ismay and Christie watched Mountbatten with a new respect. He grunted in satisfaction as his next cannon potted the red.

On Saturday, 5 April 1947, Mountbatten sat facing the Qaid-i-Azam across his desk in Viceroy's House. Outside, it was already fiercely hot and even the air conditioning did not fully protect Mountbatten from the heat. Jinnah, however, in his pale three-piece suit, his monocle fixed in his eye and his cigarette holder clamped between his teeth, showed not the slightest sign of discomfort. Impassive, gaunt and withdrawn, he sat stiffly, determined to yield nothing. 'I will enter into discussions on one condition only,' he stated.

Mountbatten smiled as he interrupted. 'Mr Jinnah, I am not prepared to go into conditions or anything else, until we are better acquainted, until I know more about you.'

'If your staff have not already given you all the relevant information, Your Excellency, then they have entirely failed in their duty,' Jinnah said, drily.

This one's going to be just as tricky as Pug predicted, Mountbatten thought. The open approach which had worked so well with Nehru and Gandhi, and had even gone some way to melt Patel, seemed to wash over Mr Jinnah like soft waves over an immovable rock. It was odd,

94

he thought. He spoke of Nehru already as 'Jawaharlal' and Gandhi as 'His Nibs'. But he could think of the Qaid-i-Azam in no other terms than as 'Mr Jinnah'. He did not let himself be thrown. He smiled. 'I know part of what the world knows. But I would like to hear the rest from you, yourself. I understand you were once a leading member of the Congress Party.'

With no change in his expression, Jinnah removed his monocle and examined it, before deciding it might be in his interest to reply. He coughed deeply and gained a little more time as he brought it under control. 'The policy of England has always been "Divide and Rule",' he said. 'I was convinced that with Muslims and Hindus united, Independence would come much sooner.'

'What led you to change your mind?'

'In a word?' Jinnah paused. 'Gandhi. And his call for civil disobedience. I warned that it would lead to violence and outrage on both sides.'

'Admirable,' Mountbatten smiled. 'And yet, recently, your party appears to have altered its opinion on violence.'

Jinnah's eyes said that he would not rise to any bait. 'My people had to prove they are capable of defending themselves,' he answered evenly. 'The division is not of my making. It was you British who introduced separate electorates for Hindus and Muslims, don't forget, and Congress has never been prepared to cooperate with Muslims on local government levels. I became convinced, finally, that the only true protection Muslims will ever have is within their own separate, sovereign state.'

'Pakistan.'

'Pakistan. The Muslims are a nation. If you grant that and if you are an honest man, you must grant the principle of Pakistan.'

'Have you considered, Mr Jinnah,' Mountbatten asked, 'that if it comes to Partition, I will have to divide the provinces of Bengal and the Punjab?'

'A man is not a Hindu or a Muslim, he is a Punjabi or Bengali,' Jinnah said. He coughed slightly and took the silk handkerchief from his cuff to dab his lips. 'The Punjab is a nation. Bengal is a nation. Each area shares a common language, not to mention internal economics. To divide these nations will lead to greater bloodshed.'

'Exactly,' Mountbatten agreed. 'Then, since Partition on Hindu-Muslim lines would inevitably mean the division of the Punjab and Bengal, you have given me the perfect answer against the idea of Partition.' He waited for a full two minutes, until it became clear that Jinnah was not going to reply. 'I would like you to consider again the plan put forward by the British Cabinet Mission,' he went on. 'Your provinces would become self-governing, but still part of India, which would become a federated state like America.'

Jinnah waved the question away with his handkerchief. 'The Congress Party would solemnly agree to self-government for the provinces to get Independence, then go back on it afterwards.'

'In this case, the British Government would guarantee that the promises were kept,' Mountbatten assured him.

Jinnah's lips pursed in denial. 'You will forgive me, Your Excellency. After Independence, your troops will leave this country and you will be in no position to guarantee anything.' He paused, and shrugged, holding up his handkerchief. 'That is why I tell you, I do not care if the Pakistan you give me is only the size of this handkerchief, providing you give it to me completely. It is the only solution acceptable to me.'

The newsmen waiting on the terrace were becoming impatient. The meeting had run long over schedule, more than three hours. Jinnah had arrived determined not to talk, and had evidently changed his mind. Alan Campbell-Johnson was relieved to see him come out into the Mogul Gardens at last, followed by the Viceroy and Vicereine.

'Oh-oh,' Campbell-Johnson thought, seeing the Muslim leader's set and severe expression, but the moment Jinnah spotted the photographers, he straightened and smiled as he walked forward.

'My God, he was cold,' Mountbatten whispered to Edwina. 'It took me half the meeting to unfreeze him.'

She was watching Jinnah wave to the photographers. 'He looks happy enough now.'

'He's making an effort. He's decided he wants me on his side.'

Jinnah turned, smiling and beckoning, and they joined him, shaking hands, posing for the newsmen. He felt like a monkey, grimacing and posturing, but he wanted to be seen to be on at least as easy terms with them as Gandhi. It was not what he was best at. Talking business or politics, he was in his element, and he knew the elation of addressing a vast, adulating crowd. He had known passion for a woman, too, but those embers were cold and dead. His only remaining passion was the elusive dream of Pakistan and he would do anything to achieve it. He would even try to match this couple's easy charm. Mountbatten was on his right, Edwina on his left. He turned to her and attempted a compliment. 'Fatima will be jealous of me being photographed next to such an attractive lady.'

Edwina was faintly surprised. 'Your sister? Why?'

He smiled gallantly. 'She tries very hard to keep me from contact with the fair sex. I think she is afraid I might be distracted.' Edwina smiled politely. Encouraged, he elaborated. 'But here we are. A rose between two thorns.'

No sooner had he spoken, than he saw the Viceroy and Vicereine glance at each other from either side of him. Edwina just managed to prevent himself laughing. Mountbatten was poker faced.

'That is to say – I actually meant – ' he began.

'It's quite all right, Mr Jinnah,' Edwina told him.

He stepped round behind her abruptly, drawing her over to stand between him and Mountbatten. He was erect and severe, in his embarrassment retreating once more into the grey fortress of his mind.

Some evenings later, Mountbatten walked with his 'Inner Cabinet' in the circular, sunken garden, chosen as the one place they were certain not to be overheard. Two guards were on watch at the gates and the group was silent, passing them.

Out of earshot, Mountbatten continued. 'What more can I say? After a whole series of talks with Jinnah, I'm no further forward. He won't budge an inch.'

'What about the other Muslim leaders?' Ismay asked.

'They dance to his tune, and it's called Pakistan,' Mountbatten said, sombrely. They walked on in silence, waiting for him to continue, almost afraid of what they knew was on his mind. He stopped, deep in thought. 'I am aware that none of you is going to like it, but I am very reluctantly coming to the conclusion that any plan for Independence will have to include some form of Partition – and it should be settled sooner rather than later.' He looked at them, waiting for an explosion of protest. It did not come.

Miéville was very serious. 'Sadly, I agree – if there is really no alternative. And I can't see one.'

Mountbatten looked at the others.

Ismay shook his head, his normally humorous, pug-like face drawn with concern. 'Neither can I. Unless something positive is done, we face the threat of a civil war in the very near future. So – it's against everything I believe in, everything I came out here determined to prevent, but . . . I agree.'

'So do I, sir,' Abell said. 'We talk glibly of "the Muslim Minority", forgetting that that minority is nearly twice the population of the United Kingdom.'

Mountbatten was genuinely surprised by their agreement, had secretly hoped that they would still hold out against him. 'Apparently we have all accepted the inevitable,' he summed up. 'But what chance, if any, is there of Congress going along with it?'

'On present form, none,' Ismay said, flatly. They might reluctantly have come to terms with the inevitability of

Partition, but the Congress Party never would. Any hope of a peaceful solution was fast receding.

Throughout, the brilliant Indian civil servant, V.P. Menon, had been listening and speaking little. He cleared his throat gently to gain their attention. 'Except . . . there is something which we may have overlooked,' he began. The others turned to him. As an Indian, he was better qualified than any of them to gauge the mood of the country. 'Some time ago,' he continued, 'I seem to remember a resolution being forced through Congress by Sardar Patel, a resolution recognizing the possibility of a future subdivision both of Bengal and the Punjab.'

For a moment the only sound to be heard in the garden was the dry staccato of the crickets. From the distance came the laughter of girls playing in the park.

'But that would mean the Congress Party has already accepted the idea of Partition – to an extent,' Ismay said. Menon gave the faintest nod.

Mountbatten had felt the surge of a new excitement. 'Right, then,' he decided. 'I'm not going to beat around the bush any more. This will have to be done in the strictest secrecy. I have to go on this tour of Peshawar and the North-West Frontier with Edwina. It can't be put off. While we're away, I want you, George, to work with Lord Ismay on a draft plan for a federated state of India, to include the Partition of the disputed territories. V.P., you'll hold yourself available for consultation.' He paused. 'Don't look so disheartened, gentlemen. Central government over a federation of states has worked very well in North America for nearly two centuries. In any case, any way forward is better than none!'

Later that night, a small black limousine drew up outside the house next to Nehru's in York Road. It was the home of Sardar Patel.

Grave and heavy-shouldered, Patel sat in the front next to his old friend V.P. Menon, who was driving. 'They saw how useful that resolution could be?' Patel asked.

'Straight away,' Menon told him. 'Ismay's working on a draft plan now.'

Patel's massive head moved approvingly. 'Good.'

Menon hesitated. He trusted his friend's instincts completely and felt sure that his interests and India's were identical, yet a doubt still nagged at him. 'You're sure we've done the right thing? That Partition's the answer?'

Patel's face was craggy in the faint light of the dashboard. 'It's the only answer left, if the whole apparatus of state is not to come crashing down. We must force this thing through before we lose control completely. Nehru would take another year to accept it. Gandhiji . . .' He shrugged. 'We had to get the ball rolling – whether we like it or not.' He opened the car door and climbed out, but before closing it again he bent down and said, 'Listen, V.P., there's a useful English phrase. Sometimes you just have to bite on the bullet.' He closed the door. 'Good night.'

'Good night, Vallabhai,' Menon said. He watched Patel start down the path to his house and slid the car back into gear. As he drove off, he thought, well, the die is cast. They would just have to see if the British Draft Plan matched in any way the plan they themselves had been considering privately for a divided India. For a while, he himself would have to tread carefully. He was utterly loyal to the Viceroy and the administration he served. He also had the greatest admiration for Patel, and for the moment their concerns ran together. Yet it would not do for anyone to guess the part the Sardar had played in this. His orderly mind regretted the need for the oblique approach, the hint of deviousness. But at least the deadlock was broken.

## FIVE

The York aircraft circled the runway at Peshawar, giving its passengers a magnificent view of Nanga Parbat, the 26,500 foot giant of the Karakorums, whose tall regular peak rose sheer to the sky in the north-east. Then the plane turned steeply for the final descent.

Partly for comfort, and partly because of the heat, the Mountbattens were simply dressed in working olive-green undress uniform. They knew there was unrest in the Province, but were surprised to see a detachment of troops ringing the small airfield. It was a worried Provincial Governor who came forward to meet them from the knot of officials and photographers, as the guard of honour came smartly to attention. He greeted the Mountbattens, Campbell-Johnson, and Major Martin Gilliat, the Viceroy's Deputy Military Secretary, who had also accompanied them.

'I'm very sorry to meet you with bad news, sir,' began Sir Olaf Caroe, 'but I'm afraid we have rather a difficult situation on our hands. Somehow or other news of your visit has got out, and Muslim agitators have been going round the hill tribes, whipping them up to make some sort of demonstration. The result is that we've had an invasion. Pathans mainly – perhaps seventy thousand of them. They say they have a list of complaints to deliver to you, and they insist on doing so.'

Mountbatten considered. The Pathans were fierce warriors, owing only token allegiance to other authority, British or Indian, while their adherence to Islam was absolute.

'We've got them penned up in Cunningham Park, behind the railway embankment,' continued Sir Olaf hastily. 'But they won't be put off seeing you, and frankly we don't have the men to hold them for much longer.'

Pamela Mountbatten had insisted on travelling up with her parents. Now, still unsteady from the bumpy flight to the extreme north-west corner of India, she drew closer to her mother.

'Well,' said the Viceroy, 'if they want to see me, I'd better go and show myself. We don't want any upsets, do we?' He smiled reassurance to Edwina and Pamela, but Sir Olaf caught the seriousness underlying his tone. The Pathans were working themselves up to fever pitch in the hot sun, and if they should decide to go on the rampage. . . .

'That would be best, Your Excellency,' said the Governor. Then he glanced at the two women. 'Unless, of course, you were to return immediately to Delhi.'

Mountbatten gave him a brief look and, signalling Gilliat to accompany him, headed for the waiting staff cars. As he reached the first, he heard footsteps behind him, and turned to see Edwina following.

'What are you doing?'

'I'm coming with you,' she said. He recognized the determined set of her mouth.

'Didn't you hear what he said? This could be damned dangerous.'

'I heard. And if you think I'll let you go alone, you have another think coming!' If there was danger, Edwina refused to let him face it alone.

It was barely a mile's drive. Some way behind them on the dusty road, other cars bearing the rest of their party followed. As they approached the park, they became aware of the roar of thousands of voices raised in a defiant chant.

'*Pakistan Zindabad!*

'*Pakistan Zindabad!*'

Along the outer base of the high embankment, a thin line of soldiers and police was strung out. The roar of the crowd beyond was deafening, like some monster throwing itself against the bars of its cage. The Viceroy glanced along the line of men, then over to where the other cars were drawing up. Pamela was climbing out of one with Edwina's assistant, Muriel Watson. Sir Olaf Caroe was already hurrying to him.

'Let's keep the men out of sight,' said Mountbatten. 'No troops or police to show themselves. It'd be like a red rag to a bull.' The Governor and the Viceroy looked at each other. Each knew what was at stake, but Sir Olaf, with his years of experience and his love of his wild province, was perhaps the better judge of the degree of risk involved. He felt nothing but admiration for the courageous younger man. Mountbatten reached out for Edwina's hand. It was taking all his self-control to prevent his tension from communicating itself.

'Well, old girl,' he said. 'Up we go.'

Together they began to climb the slope. As they reached its summit and the crowd below recognized them, the shouting reached a new crescendo. The concourse of people stretched as far as the eye could see, its outer limits obscured in the heat haze over the distant fields. Edwina noticed a large number of women and children among the wild-faced, bearded tribesmen, who waved their rifles violently in the air, occasionally loosing off a shot into the sky. As well as the rifles, innumerable flags swayed in the air above the Pathans' heads, the illegal green flags with the white crescent of Pakistan.

'*Pakistan Zindabad!*

'*Pakistan Zindabad!*'

Edwina let out her breath in a long, slow, expressive gasp, instinctively tightening her grip on her husband's hand. The dust swirled about their feet, rising to their nostrils, and with it the smell of that sea of humanity. Mountbatten knew that a speech was out of the question. In any case he couldn't speak to them in Pushtu and it was unlikely that more than a few of them would understand English, but the tension he sensed was a solid thing, and he was keenly aware of the tens of thousands of eyes fixed

103

upon him. The smallest wrong move and the Pathans' rifles would cut Edwina and him to ribbons.

'Wave,' he muttered to Edwina. 'Wave to them – and smile!'

With an effort, she made herself follow his example, as the whole ocean of people suddenly began to surge towards them. For a split second she visualized that ocean breaking its banks, and carrying them all away in a furious, uncheckable torrent. But now, just as suddenly, the forward movement wavered, faltered, and ceased. At the same time the pounding chant gave way to silence. The dust hung over them all for a long moment, when not a sound was heard. Not a horse jangled its harness and not a child cried. Then, out of the silence a lone voice, lost somewhere in the midst of the people, raised a new shout.

'Mountbatten! Mountbatten *Zindabad!*'

Within seconds, a thousand other voices had taken up the tribute. Sullen faces now returned smiles, broad glittering grins of welcome. Edwina could not believe what was happening. A minute earlier she had been preparing herself for death. Now she was flushed with a pleasure, a warmth, a triumph which she knew Dickie was sensing also. She looked at him.

'Come on,' she said.

Together they walked down the embankment's inner slope towards the crowd, which parted to welcome them. Soon they were surrounded by smiling, cheering tribesmen, vying with each other to shake their hands and pat their backs. The crowd seemed in danger of swallowing them up, but always the Pathans kept a protective area free around them, all their violence now turned to gentleness, and admiration for the couple's courage.

The rest of the party had climbed the slope behind them, and stood looking down at the scene below. None of them spoke. None of them could believe the impact those two friendly, confident personalities had just made.

'There's a lot to be said for undress uniform,' commented

Sir Olaf Caroe to Martin Gilliat, as they drove back to Government House for an extremely well-earned luncheon.

'How's that?'

'They're green. The same colour as the flags. The colour of the Prophet Mohammed. The Pathans must have taken that as a direct compliment.'

'But the Mountbattens behaved magnificently. Surely you're not suggesting that it was simply the colour of their shirts that saved the day?'

'Not at all. But it certainly helped.'

She lay in her darkened bedroom at Viceroy's House and gritted her teeth against the migraine. Someone was boring a needle of infinite length into each of her eyes. The pills hadn't helped, and nor could she escape into sleep. The memory of the past week's experience drove her back into consciousness. How could she have been so arrogant as to suppose that she could cope with it? How could she have said so blandly to Sir Evan Jenkins that she was sure she would have seen far worse things during the war, before she even knew what she was talking about?

Two days after their arrival in Peshawar they had flown south-east to Rawalpindi in the northern Punjab, where they had been met by the Governor. Like Olaf Caroe, Sir Evan Jenkins was an old India hand with a profound love and knowledge of the customs, language and history of his troubled province. The Mountbattens found him grey-faced and exhausted, as he attempted to describe to them the horrors which Muslim-Hindu tension had led to.

'I wonder what the leaders of the League, and all those comfortable middle-class Muslims in Lahore and Karachi, would say if they knew what whipping up the peasantry in the name of Pakistan would lead to?' he said. 'Everywhere, people are shedding blood. Even neighbours who have lived side by side in perfect amity all their lives are turning knives on each other.'

'Perhaps we had better see what you mean,' said

Mountbatten. 'I can't pretend to deal with a problem that only exists on paper for me.'

Sir Evan had driven with them to the village of Kahuta, twenty-five miles due east of Rawalpindi. It had been a village typical of the half-million villages spread across the face of India, with a population of some two thousand Hindus and Sikhs, and a slightly smaller number of Muslims. The villagers had lived together in harmony, until now. As they drove through the blackened and burnt main street, where only the dome of the mosque rose unblemished, Edwina and the Viceroy looked about them in dumb horror.

'Muslims did this,' explained Sir Evan, 'but the reprisals against them are just as bad, particularly those carried out by the Sikhs. The whole province is going mad. Everybody loses by this – and nobody gains.' He looked out of the window to where a small Red Cross team were carrying stretchers out of a still smoking house. From their twisted shape, it did not seem possible that the charred bundles on the stretchers were human beings. 'It's always the same – thugs – *goondas* – attacking the weak. It's the weak who suffer, who are raped, tortured and burned.' He bit his lip, glancing at Edwina.

'How did this happen?'

'A gang of Muslim *goondas* attacked at night – the houses you can see which are untouched are Muslim houses, though even they have fled off into the fields – and what kind of village have the poor devils been left to come back to? Their favourite weapon is fire. They use gasoline.'

'How?' asked Edwina, evenly.

Sir Evan hesitated. 'In terrible ways,' he said, finally.

After the experience of Kahuta, Mountbatten had made haste back to Delhi. The man who had fought the worst of the war in Burma against the Japanese was visibly shaken, and more convinced than ever that the only means to end the bloodshed and a fast deteriorating situation was by bringing Independence and an amicably settled Partition as fast as possible. June 1948 suddenly seemed a very long way off, in the light of what was happening in the Punjab.

Edwina had not accompanied him. She had insisted that she stay behind to work. 'At least I can help get things organized a bit up here – and I should think a full report on the situation ought to be made.' Reluctantly, Mountbatten had agreed. Besides, there was no moving Edwina once she had decided that there was work to be done. Before leaving, he had quietly enjoined Muriel Watson, who was staying on with her, to make sure that she did not overdo it.

She turned on her bed in an attempt to relieve the terrible headache by finding a more comfortable position, but it was useless. Another picture rose before her, of another devastated village. She remembered the insupportable humidity: you had barely dressed before you were wet through. And she remembered everywhere the stench of death. She had never known the name of the village, but she could remember the corpses lined up in the street – corpses without names, without histories, and with no one to attend to them but the buzzards and vultures which hovered patiently overhead, awaiting their opportunity.

The nursing staff to attend the survivors was minimal. She remembered the harassed Medical Officer, who had made the most dreadful discovery.

'Please, Your Excellency. It is best we leave here.'

'Why?'

'This village has been struck by cholera.'

'Well, what can we do about it?'

'Nothing,' said the man, helplessly. 'We have no staff, no spare beds. There is not even any serum.'

Edwina's eye caught a woman sitting hunched by the door of her hut.

'Is she infected?'

'Not yet, Your Excellency. But she cannot leave. Her father is in there, and he is dying.'

The Vicereine stepped past him and pushed open the door of the hut. The smell and the heat practically took her breath away, but in the light from the door she could see an old man lying on his *charpoy*. His face was sunken and blue, and his almost naked body covered in sores, over which the flies teemed to feed. She bent to pick up the tin bowl of water by his bed, and, placing his head on her lap, poured a little of the liquid onto his parched lips.

In the bedroom at Viceroy's House, Edwina turned over again, to cool her head on the other side of the pillow. Her eyes opened wide in the darkness as another picture flashed into her brain. They had been driving along a road, when their way was blocked by a village bus slewed across the track. It had seemed empty, but as they drove round it, they saw that all its passengers were dead. A little child lay on the road near its mother, like a broken doll. The mother's severed head had been placed obscenely between her spread and naked thighs.

There was no sound but the buzzing of flies.

Finally Edwina gave up trying to sleep and sat instead at her dressing-table. She had thought to put on some make-up but sat motionless, too tired to do anything, watching the patterns made by the light slanting through the slats of the closed shutters. A gentle knocking at the door interrupted her reverie, and she looked up to see Dickie softly entering the room.

'Ah, you're up. Sorry I couldn't get away sooner.'

He had been unable to interrupt his work even for a moment since her arrival back that morning. Even in the dim light of the room he could see how haggard she was looking. His heart ached for her. If only she would take less on. . . . 'How was it? Pretty rough?'

She gave a dry sob as he took her in his arms, soothing her. Fighting for self-control, she started to tell him at least the gist of what she had seen. The image of that broken child drummed most constantly on her mind. As she spoke, Mountbatten wondered how Nehru would react if he could hear her. Perhaps if she could tell him, too, what she had seen, it would help channel his mind more quickly in favour of Partition. The sooner everything was sorted out, the Viceroy reasoned, the sooner the killing would stop. He felt he knew Jinnah well enough now to know that the Muslim leader could watch hundreds of thousands die impassively, before he would concede one inch of his stand on Pakistan. With Nehru, things might just be different.

'Is there no way to stop them? My God, there was one village where Sikhs had roasted Muslim babies on a spit!' Edwina sobbed. 'Babies!. . .'

Mountbatten caressed her cheek with his and decided. 'It is not me you should tell,' he said.

Since the Mountbattens' arrival in India their hard work had set an example for everyone to follow, but Nehru and many more of the Indian leaders had been working just as hard for years, some of them with the handicap of health being broken by frequent terms of imprisonment. Jawaharlal Nehru could not remember when he had last had more than five hours' sleep in a night, and today he had worked through a particularly heavy pile of paperwork. He was concerned, too, about the Independence Plan which Mountbatten was working on with Ismay and Abell. Menon and Patel were reassuring, but he would have liked to be kept more closely informed. He felt confident that on a personal level at least Mountbatten would be unlikely to favour Jinnah at his expense, but he was both weary and preoccupied when he received Edwina in his study at York Road. He knew that she had just returned from the Punjab, and he knew what her reactions must be. But as he listened to her catalogue of horror he himself grew more and more affected. Astute politician though he was, he was also a man of deep and volatile emotion. He knew about the Punjab, but perhaps he had not allowed himself to think that the situation was as bad as it was.

'I'm supposed to write a report on it,' she was saying. 'But how am I to put down things that no one in England would believe? Wells choked with the bodies of children – men blinded and mutilated – girls forced to watch their mothers being raped and murdered. . . .'

He turned away from her, leaning on the desk. The circles under his eyes were heavier and darker. 'Please, Edwina. . . .'

'How can you let it go on? In the name of humanity, how can politicians expect people who hate one another to live side by side?'

'The hatred you speak of is new. It is the work of a few extremists. Do you think Jinnah and the Muslim League would have any foundation for Pakistan if they didn't whip the peasantry up into a nationalistic fervour? And the only thing he has to base it on is Islam – certainly not race or language!'

'The hatred is there, nevertheless. Does no one in Congress realize that? How many more must die, how many families must be wiped out before something is done to stop it?'

Nehru tried to soothe her. 'There are many places where Hindus and Muslims still live peacefully side by side. In any case the problem is confined to Northern India, where the majority of Muslims live. And the police have orders to – '

'The police are powerless! Even the army can only control a few areas. And how long do you imagine it will be before *they* split into their Hindu and Muslim factions?' She rounded on him. 'Have you *seen* what is happening to your children, living in terror? They are your future – yours as much as Jinnah's! For God's sake, let there be a Pakistan if that is what it will take for the children to grow up free of fear!'

On the evening of 2 May 1947 Lord Ismay and George Abell boarded the York MW 102 at Palam Airport to start their flight to London. They had with them the new Draft Plan for the transfer of power. Mountbatten was so confident of its success that he had already arranged with Alan Campbell-Johnson to issue a communiqué, saying that the plan would be announced to the Indian leadership on 17 May. The Viceroy had even roughed out the speech he would make on All-India Radio for the occasion. London, he felt sure, would only wish to make minor emendations. He was on the best of terms with Lord Listowel, who had replaced Lord Pethick-Lawrence as Secretary of State for India, and he knew that he had Attlee's backing. Churchill's Conservative Opposition was a force to be recognized, but they stood in such a minority that any objections they had would be shouting against the wind, barring the unlikely event of their being able to block any legislation following acceptance of the Draft Plan until the end of the Parliamentary Session, which was still a long way off.

Sir Eric Miéville had warned him that V.P. Menon had raised some objections to the Plan, but the Viceroy told himself that despite the fact that it was the brainchild principally only of British members of the ICS and his staff, it offered the fairest and most sensible solution. The Plan provided for each of the eleven British Indian provinces to show by a plebiscite whether they wished to join India or Pakistan; Bengal and the Punjab, exceptionally, could opt for being split between India and Pakistan, for acceding to one or other country in their entirety, or for going it alone. The independent states could also opt to join one or other of the newly Independent countries, or continue to enjoy independence of their own. Mountbatten felt that political reality might ultimately impose responsibility for foreign policy, defence and communications on a central government, and foresaw the need for the smaller independent states to group themselves together for administrative purposes, but all that lay in the future. As far as possible, Muslim majority areas forming the new land of Pakistan would be geographical neighbours.

The Viceroy was aware that the Plan left a lot of questions unanswered, and posed a great many more questions of detail. He was also aware that the Plan was by no means regarded favourably by all his own staff. He was, however, driven by the conviction that movement towards Independence had to be made at the fastest possible pace. Patel,

Nehru and Jinnah, though not yet *au courant* with the details, had accepted the Plan in principle. Patel had accepted it at once, and Jinnah had commented laconically, on accepting the inevitability of a divided Punjab and Bengal, 'Better a moth-eaten Pakistan than none at all.'

Mountbatten was not at the airport to see Ismay and Abell off. He was taking his family to Simla to snatch a few days' rest before the next round began.

Simla lies barely two hundred miles north of Delhi, but it is set seven thousand three hundred feet up in the foothills of the Himalayas. The little town is built on a steep slope and looks out over a stunning tumble of fir-clad green hills and lush valleys. Beyond it, the distant peaks of the Tibetan Himalayas, another two hundred miles north, rear up against the sky.

The British had discovered it a century earlier. They had gratefully accepted the relief it offered from the remorseless summer heat of Delhi, and they had made it their own. It was dominated by Christ Church Cathedral, the epitome in yellow stone of a Victorian Gothic English country church, and the baronial Viceregal Lodge, completed in 1888 and reminiscent of Balmoral. The main street was called the Mall, and Indians in native dress were not allowed to walk there. Apart from the Indians, and its location, and the hordes of brownish-yellow monkeys which patrolled its streets, Simla might have been an English market town.

On the morning of their first day there, Mountbatten stood with his wife and daughter on the rich garden lawn of Viceregal Lodge, drinking in the refreshing sight of green vegetation again, the clear coolness of the air, and the magnificent mountains on the horizon. Mizzen was busying about the kaleidoscopic herbaceous borders, nose to the ground and tail wagging.

'Headaches gone?' Mountbatten asked his wife.

'Nearly,' she smiled. She still looked tired, he thought. Never mind, she could have a good rest here. He himself had only brought a copy of the Draft Plan with him, and did not aim to have to do much work. Menon had come up, and they were expecting Nehru for the weekend. But that was a social visit as much as anything. Mountbatten was delighted that Edwina and Jawaharlal had taken to each other so much. It could only help his work, and it seemed to do them both so much good. For himself, he aimed to spend at least some of the time in Simla working on his neglected hobby, the genealogical tables of his own family. Who knows? Perhaps one day he would be able to map the family tree back to his distant ancestor, the Emperor Charlemagne.

'Mizzen's dying to go exploring. Look at him,' said Edwina.

'I'll take him,' said Pamela. 'I'm dying to go exploring myself!' Laughing, she set off down the path which led back round the side of the house, the old dog trotting at her heels. Edwina watched them go, biting her lip. Her headaches were by no means better, but she was not going to bother Dickie with them, and perhaps the air up here might help.

'Well, what do you think of our country cottage?' said Mountbatten.

'It'll be fine, once we've built the extension!' she joked, and he chuckled with her.

'Have you seen my study here? It's painted the most wonderful shade of pale green. First thing I'm going to do when we get back to Delhi is have the study in Viceroy's House painted the same colour. Much cooler, and much more restful. In fact, I can't imagine how all my predecessors stood that dark panelling for so long.'

Later, Mountbatten was closeted in his light green study with V.P. Menon. He was feeling more than pleased with himself after a cable from London. No problem is insuperable, he told himself, if only you attack it resolutely. In the act of locking his copy of the Draft Plan into his safe, he remembered Miéville's telling him that Menon had a low opinion of it. But Miéville always tended to be over-cautious, looking on the gloomy side of things. He would ask Menon himself.

'No, I don't like it very much,' Menon answered straight-forwardly. 'And I doubt if Congress will.'

Mountbatten was thrown. It was the first criticism he had heard of the Plan, which the British Cabinet thought workable and fair.

'I had a cable from Ismay to say that Mr Attlee has accepted it wholeheartedly,' he said. 'Tell me, is your opinion that of a civil servant, or an Indian national?'

'Both. I think the Plan creates more problems than it solves. And it offers too many options. It could lead to India being fragmented.'

'Well, I can't agree with you, V.P.,' Mountbatten said, recovering.

'May I ask about the princely states, sir?' Menon said. 'Suppose they choose total Independence?'

'I think it unlikely, but that would be their right,' Mountbatten said. 'We cannot dictate to them. I promised His Majesty to find some way of maintaining links between them and Britain. Many of the maharajahs are his personal friends, and their services to us during the war created a debt we will find it difficult ever to repay.'

'An Indian constitution drawn up for only half the country's land area will never work, Your Excellency.'

Menon had raised a doubt in the Viceroy's mind, but he brushed it aside. 'These are matters to be ironed out. Personally, my only disappointment is that India will not remain within the Commonwealth when she achieves Independence.'

He had touched the very point that Menon had hoped he would. The question of India's joining the Commonwealth had been much discussed by the leaders of Congress, and he knew that the League had been engaged in similar consultations. For some, the idea of joining the Common-wealth appeared to run counter to Independence. It gave the impression that the member countries still acknowl-edged the paramountcy of the British Crown. Menon and Patel, however, had seen that by accepting a place in the Commonwealth, several advantages would accrue to them.

If they were granted Dominion status, as Australia and Canada, and acknowledged the British king as constitutional head of State, they would not need to draw up their own constitution immediately, a task which would hamper the speedy transfer of power, and one which would in any case be next to impossible while India's future physical shape and size remained uncertain. They would also enjoy the support of Britain, and British goodwill, for as long as they needed it. As a brand new nation, unsure of its economic future, this would give them a bedrock on which to build. Furthermore, the British would be delighted and, if Pakistan also became a Dominion, then a degree of Indian unity centred on shared Commonwealth membership was assured. Once the Indian leadership realized that Dominion status did not mean the sacrifice of one iota of Independence, the advantages were clear. And as Patel had pointed out, 'We can always walk out of the Commonwealth any time we are ready.'

'Why should India not join the Commonwealth?' asked Menon, carefully.

Mountbatten was astonished. For a moment, hope leapt high in his heart. 'What do you mean?'

'I've heard it suggested that we might be prepared to stay in.'

'By whom?'

'Sardar Vallabhbhai Patel.'

'But he's been agitating for fifty years for complete separation!'

'He has revised his opinion, in view of the fact that Independence could thereby be achieved so much sooner.'

Mountbatten knew that V.P. would not have spoken, unless authorized to by Patel. He looked down at the quiet, bespectacled civil servant sitting in front of him, barely the glimmer of an expression on his face. Here was the most splendid solution, acceptable, surely, even to Nehru. And Nehru would be with them at the weekend. The Viceroy laughed out loud. 'V.P., did I ever tell you you're a genius?

The Dominion of India. . . . That makes the whole thing perfect.'

So far the weekend had gone well. Shortly before Nehru's arrival, a long cable had arrived from Ismay in London incorporating the British Government's emendations to the Draft plan. Nehru himself had been in fine form, playing with Alan Campbell-Johnson's children and demonstrating to the others a technique for hill-walking designed to save oxygen and spare the calf muscles, by walking uphill backwards. Miéville and George Nicholls had shown some dismay at the Viceroy's openness with the Indian leader, but Mountbatten chose to ignore them.

He was in fact nursing a hunch that had been nagging at him ever since his conversation with Menon. Despite his continuing optimism for the Plan, Menon's contention that it would not be well received by Congress had given him more than usual pause for thought. Mountbatten set great store by his instincts: often wayward, they had served to get him out of a hole more than once in his career, and now he was building himself up to give them free rein once more, whatever the risk involved. After dinner on the Saturday night, when Edwina had gone to bed, he invited Nehru into the study of Viceregal Lodge for a nightcap.

As he provided whiskies and soda for them both, Nehru noticed the genealogical charts spread over a table against the wall.

'Your family tree?'

'It's a hobby of mine. Trying to fit in all the twigs and branches.' The Viceroy handed Nehru his drink, and then quite suddenly crossed the room to the safe and unlocked it, taking out the amended Draft Plan Ismay had cabled to him earlier. Only in some minor details did it differ from the original. Nehru felt a tense excitement rise in him as Mountbatten handed him the papers.

'Is this what I think it is?'

'Yes,' said Mountbatten, trying to control his own height-ened feelings. He had gone too far to back out now. 'I'd like you to have a quick look at it.' He sipped his whisky. If Jinnah should find out about this . . .

'I don't know how to thank you, Your Excellency.' Nehru took the Draft Plan eagerly and sat down with it, immersing himself in it immediately. Mountbatten watched him for a moment and then turned his attention to his genealogical charts. But he was unable to concentrate for long, and looked across at Nehru again. The Indian had stopped reading the Plan, and was riffling angrily through the final pages. His face was drawn and pale. Mountbatten's heart sank.

'Take your time,' he said, placatingly.

'There's no need. I can see that this is completely unacceptable!' Nehru stood up and threw the Plan onto the desk. Mountbatten was shaken. He had never seen Nehru so furious.

'What's wrong with it?'

Nehru laughed incredulously. 'Everything! If this goes ahead it will split India into another Balkans! Is that what you British want?'

'Well, can we go through it?'

'There would be no point!' Nehru made an effort to control himself. 'I am sorry. It is unfortunate that I have to leave first thing in the morning. But I will try to summarize my thoughts tonight and leave you a note of my objections. This much I can tell you now: Congress will never agree to a Plan which admits the very real possibility of India's fragmentation into – ' he fought to find the right words, ' – a host of little states, dotted about piecemeal! Don't you see what that would do to a central government? It would be a mockery!'

'I see.'

'One other thing. It should be made clear that it is Pakistan that is breaking away from the mother country. The Plan makes no such provision.'

Mountbatten was breathing hard. 'Very well. That is something we must consider. Please do as you suggest and put your suggestions in writing. I will cable London immediately to let them know the Plan's been scrapped. I'll get a roasting, but I dare say we can still save the day if we can come up with a revised plan quickly.' Never a man to brood over setbacks, Mountbatten was getting into his stride again. And thanking God that he had played his hunch. This was a disaster, but at least it wasn't an irredeemable one.

'I must leave for Delhi tomorrow morning,' Nehru said coldly.

'There can't be anything more important than this! Please – there's a train in the evening. Will you at least stay until then?'

Nehru considered. The Viceroy had done him a great courtesy by showing him the Plan. By giving way to anger now he could place in jeopardy all that he had spent his life fighting for.

'Very well,' he said.

The following day, the Viceroy sat on the secluded rear terrace of Viceregal Lodge while V.P. Menon read over Nehru's promised memorandum of objections. Menon was privately gratified to note that there was nothing here which he had not foreseen.

'It is not as bad as all that,' he said. 'Mr Nehru only questions certain sections of the Plan.'

'Yes – the key ones!' snapped Mountbatten. 'I'm sorry, V.P., it's been one hell of a night. Look, we'll have to redraft and resubmit immediately, in the light of his comments. Can you do it?'

Menon paused before replying. He had talked to Nehru already that morning and although there had been a very awkward moment when the Indian leader had learnt that Menon and Patel had discussed the possibility of Dominion status without consulting him, the civil servant had managed to convince him of the desirability of accepting it. The British king would have to drop the title of 'emperor', of course, but the likelihood of his refusing to was small. It seemed that Jinnah, in charge of a small new nation which would also be relatively poor, would not only desire

Pakistan to be in the Commonwealth, but insist upon it. The redrafted Plan would provide for two governments, of Pakistan and India, each with its own Governor General. Nehru had been quick to see the advantages: the independent princely states, too, could be persuaded to accede to a powerful central government in return for some degree of internal autonomy, a kind of regional government which could actually be to the advantage of the new régime, which would in any case have a host of more pressing problems to deal with first. An additional advantage was that, once the disposition of the eleven British Indian provinces had been resolved into the new countries of India and Pakistan, Independence could come very quickly – could come, indeed, easily by the fixed time limit of June 1948.

'Very well, Your Excellency,' said Menon. 'On the understanding that the provinces will choose between Pakistan and India on the basis of geographical affinity and religious majority.' It was more a statement than a question.

'As far as possible.'

'And that Bengal and the Punjab have separate referenda to determine whether or not they are to be split.'

'Yes. Though I think we both know that it is inevitable.

Menon looked at his watch. It was a little before two. 'Well, if you want this immediately, I'd better be getting back to Delhi now.'

Mountbatten looked up. 'I don't think you understand, V.P. By immediately, I mean right away – now. How soon can I have it?'

'It'll take a week. I should think.'

The Viceroy stood up. 'That's no use.' He shook his head. 'I need it by six o'clock this evening.'

For once in his life Menon was at a loss for words. Even with the gist of what he had to do already sketched out in his mind, no one could expect him to draw up a plan which would seal the fate of four hundred million people forever – in four hours!

'Six o'clock, V.P.,' Mountbatten was saying. 'If we don't

get Nehru's agreement to a new plan before he leaves here today, we might as well pack our bags.'

The events of the following days transfigured Edwina's week's rest in Simla into a whirlwind of activity. In a sense, she reflected wryly, it should have come as a relief, for it was triggered off by Nehru's acceptance of Menon's rewritten proposals for the transfer of power. The Indian civil servant had performed the demanded miracle in the allotted time, with no more help than solitude and a very stiff whisky. The next step had been a hasty return to Delhi, where Campbell-Johnson had faced the unenviable task of announcing the deferment of the 17 May leaders' meeting which the Viceroy had so over-optimistically caused to be announced before his departure for Simla. Close on the heels of that had followed the expected summons to London. It was polite but terse, but Mountbatten had no intention of behaving like a naughty schoolboy summoned to the headmaster's study. Besides, he held a new trump card: out of the ruins of his original Draft Plan he had not only scooped guaranteed agreement to his new one, but all-round agreement on joining the Commonwealth.

By flying non-stop, Mountbatten and V.P. Menon reached London in twenty-four hours, a near-record time for the flight. They were met by Ismay and George Abell, who were both terse and distant.

In the taxi taking them to 10, Downing Street, Ismay could no longer control his irritation. 'Believe me, you're in for a grilling,' he warned. 'Sending George and me over to talk them into one Plan and then sending them a cable to forget it! They're hopping mad and asking themselves if you really know what you're doing.'

Mountbatten accepted that Pug had a right to be annoyed, but he had not flown all this way to give in. 'It's up to me to show them,' he said. 'I'm going to ask for five minutes, and if I haven't convinced them by then – well, it's back to the navy.'

'Start packing your hammock,' Ismay advised.

After an initially cool and hostile reception by Attlee and his Cabinet in the Cabinet Room, Mountbatten swiftly had them all sitting forward, following him with great attention. He was at his most incisive and convincing. 'And let me assure you, gentlemen, this time I guarantee not a qualified, but a positive acceptance of the revised Plan by all Indian parties. Without it, without the certainty of full Independence in the near future, the prospects are for the loss of any hope of our retaining Commonwealth ties and the inevitable escalation of violence into a nationwide civil war.'

It was obvious from the Cabinet's reaction that they were profoundly impressed. So was Ismay. It was the most assured and persuasive *tour de force* of sustained reasoning he had ever witnessed. Events had pulled something extraordinary out of Dickie, he realized. He had touched greatness before, but had never reached this level.

'Lord Ismay,' Cripps was saying, 'do you agree with Lord Louis' estimate of the likelihood of civil war?'

'Emphatically, Sir Stafford,' Ismay Confirmed. 'I'd go so far as to say that our original suggestion of June next year is far too late.'

There was little more that could be said. Attlee sucked for a moment on his unlit pipe. 'Well, it seems that Lord Louis may well be right.'

Mountbatten heard the murmur of agreement from the Cabinet and allowed himself to relax slightly. He glanced at Pug, who shrugged, acknowledging that he had won. Beside Ismay, V.P. was smiling broadly.

'However,' Attlee observed, 'there is a serious problem with passing the Indian Independence Bill.'

'Surely with your majority, Mr Attlee, you could get it through Parliament before the end of this session?' Mountbatten said.

'Yes, it can be passed by the Commons with no difficulty,' Attlee agreed. 'The problem is the Conservative majority in the House of Lords. Mr Churchill's opposition to Indian Independence is unwavering and he can block the Bill in the Lords for two years.'

Mountbatten was shaken. 'By that time, it would be too late! Tragically late. It would mean complete disaster. Can't you explain that to him?'

'Unfortunately, for some time Mr Churchill and I have been unable to communicate,' Attlee said. He was examining the bowl of his pipe, and glanced up. 'This needs a personal approach.'

'Oh, no.' Mountbatten shook his head. 'Don't look at me. He hasn't spoken to me since I took on the job.'

'Nevertheless, Lord Louis,' Attlee said, 'I'm afraid it is up to you. There's no one else who can do it. You will have to see him and – somehow – get his approval.'

Winston Churchill, wearing silk pyjamas and dressing gown, black-rimmed half-moon spectacles on his nose and a large Double Corona in his mouth, sat up in bed at Chartwell, surrounded by papers on which he was working. He enjoyed working in bed increasingly, as he grew older, but today he was in a vile mood. Well, he'd agreed to see Dickie. He could hardly do otherwise. But that was all he would do.

Mountbatten could hardly remember ever feeling so nervous, as when the secretary announced him and ushered him into the bedroom. He had taken a deep breath and hoped his nervousness did not show. But Churchill did not look up. He went on reading the paper he had in his hand. His wispy hair was ruffled and his mouth set in that pouting scowl which always signalled his extreme disapproval. At last, when Mountbatten repeated his respectful greeting, his eyes shifted and he stared at his former protégé for a long moment, before nodding grudged acceptance of the visit. The secretary went out, closing the door.

Churchill cleared his throat. 'Dickie. I hear you've been having a high old time.'

'Fairly hectic, sir.' Aware of the gulf that had opened up

between them, Mountbatten knew he had to proceed with caution. 'I'd like to talk to you about it.'

'About India? No, I don't want to talk about India. Not to you, anyway.' He flicked his cigar and turned pointedly back to his papers.

'I came to appeal to you,' Mountbatten said. There was no response. Damn it, he thought, there's no use beating about the bush with him. 'We have to get the Independence Bill passed as soon as possible.'

Churchill flicked his cigar again angrily, not looking up. 'And you expect me to help you? To help you destroy two hundred years of British history? To abandon our duty to those millions whom we have protected and administered for so long?' Churchill's stance on India had not moved since his earliest days as a subaltern stationed in the North-West Frontier Province. He loved the country, his attitude both sentimental and paternal in the old Victorian manner.

'We have to accept that the coming transfer of power is a fact, sir.'

'I do not blame the Indian people,' Churchill growled. 'For them I have only respect and affection.'

'It is they who will suffer,' Mountbatten said. 'If we do not get the legislation through quickly, India will face anarchy on an unimaginable scale.'

'That is what will happen, anyway,' Churchill snapped, 'once British administration is withdrawn. It is all the fault of the leaders, those fanatics, with their obsession to destroy the Empire. . . . With the loss of India comes Britain's decline as a great power. Our position in the world will be diminished.' He looked at Mountbatten. 'What could possibly induce me to assist in bringing that about?'

'I imagine . . . your sense of history, perhaps. And it would allow me to honour a promise I made to His Majesty.'

'What promise?' Churchill was interested despite himself. He had to admit that Dickie knew how to cast a line. He had taught him well.

'To keep a link, somehow, between England and India.'

Mountbatten paused. 'To be granted Independence immediately, the leaders of both the Congress Party and the Muslim League are prepared to accept Dominion status.'

The ex-Premier's attention was fully engaged at last. He puffed on his cigar. 'Do you have that in writing?'

'I left a letter from Pandit Nehru at 10, Downing Street.'

'H'mph . . . And what about that sophisticated old fakir? Does he still run around dressed in one of his old bedsheets?'

Mountbatten smiled briefly. 'Mr Gandhi is well. I regret you two have never met.'

'Perish the thought,' Churchill grunted.

'But the fact is, although he is both the most powerful figure and the unknown quantity, he will not influence Congress on this, not if it means freedom by the end of the year.' Mountbatten had fired his best shot. If Winston failed to respond now . . .

Churchill smoked in silence, thinking, his eyes shrewd. 'At least . . . if India remains as part of the Commonwealth, all might not be lost. The British public will back you.'

'And you and the Conservative Party?' Mountbatten asked, tensely.

Churchill appeared to be considering. Privately, he had already decided, but he intended to make Dickie sweat for it. Cocky son-of-a-prince . . . But by God, he appeared to have brought off the impossible.

'I will help to get the necessary legislation through Parliament without delay,' he said evenly. 'And in that case, India can have her damned Independence sooner than she ever expected.'

Mountbatten and his party arrived back in Delhi to find that Mohammed Ali Jinnah had tried to drop another bombshell. Now he was insisting that the agreed areas of East and West Pakistan should be linked by an eight hundred mile-long 'corridor'. This demand was only one of a series of events which had led to a slow but steady breakdown in goodwill which had been continuing throughout the Viceroy's absence in London. However, Mountbatten had arrived back with a viable Plan which enjoyed London's backing, as well as Indian approval, and his mandate now was to proceed to Independence as quickly as possible. At least Jinnah's demand had come too late to be included in the Plan by which Independence would be granted.

Nehru met them at Palam. Mountbatten, dressed once more in his white admiral's uniform, noticed that the crowd at the airport was much larger and more excited than it had been on his first arrival just over two months earlier. Together with Edwina, he walked with Nehru to the shining Viceregal Rolls Royce.

'It's good to have you back, Your Excellency. How was London?'

'Cold and wet.'

'You know I wasn't talking about the weather,' smiled Nehru.

'I can tell you very little more than you must have heard already. HM Government has accepted, almost without alteration, our revised Plan for Independence.'

'And Mr Jinnah should give you no more trouble,' put in Edwina. 'He's got his Pakistan.'

Nehru felt a slow surge of quiet excitement. So, it was confirmed at last. His tiredness gave way to elation. The task confronting him now was so great that he hardly dared think about it, but it would be *his* task. He was prepared now completely to accept the creation of Pakistan as the lesser of two evils. 'At least by cutting off the head, we get rid of the headache,' he murmured to Edwina.

They had reached the huge open car. Nehru stood aside to let Edwina and the Viceroy get in first. The Viceroy stood and waved to the crowd, as they cheered. Then Nehru waved. The cheering redoubled.

'*Jai Hind!*' they shouted. 'Nehru *ki jai!*'

A meeting had been arranged for the following morning. That night after dinner the Mountbattens discussed it. Edwina had gone straight to bed, the hectic pace of the past few weeks having brought her headaches back in their wake. She would barely admit it to herself, but she was profoundly tired. Mountbatten undid his bow tie and poured her a glass of water. Gratefully, she swallowed her pill with it.

'It's the flying,' she said. 'You know how I hate it. It always leaves me feeling wrung out. You should get some rest too.'

'I will, darling. But there's a lot to be done now, and none of it will wait.' He sat on the edge of the bed, and ran a hand over his face. He was quiet, thinking.

After a moment she said, 'Is it the meeting tomorrow?'

He nodded. 'So much hangs on it.'

'Will Gandhi be there?'

'We invited him, but he turned it down. He said that since he was neither a member of the Government, nor an official of the Congress Party, he wouldn't attend.' Mountbatten paused. He knew that the real reason was that Gandhi felt freer to act if he remained on the outside. His power might be waning, but it was still his voice alone that the masses of India listened to. Mountbatten knew that the Mahatma might still upset the apple cart, which

126

was why it was vital for him to get the round table meeting of the other leaders to accept the new Plan unanimously and immediately. He could not afford to give them time to start making new conditions, like Jinnah with his damned 'corridor', and above all he could not afford to give Gandhi time to work on Nehru again.

'Where are you going to have the meeting? In the Council Chamber?'

'Too portentous. We've got to get this through with the minimum of fuss. Make them think it's already a *fait accompli*. No, I'll meet them in the study. Which, I'm delighted to see, has been transformed in our absence.'

'Yes. A lovely shade of pale green.' They smiled to each other, but then she became more serious. 'Can you do it?'

'Who knows? But I'm damned well going to try!'

The *jamadhar chaprassis* were busy early in the morning on Monday, 2 June. They had rearranged the study for a small conference, and placed a circular mahogany table by the large map of India which almost covered one wall.

Mountbatten was dressed informally in a lightweight grey double-breasted suit. He sat with his back to the map, while behind him to his right were Ismay, Miéville, and George Abell. The Conference Secretary, Vernon Erskine Crum, waited at the side of the room, and not far off stood Campbell-Johnson with the official Indian photographer. To Max Desfor's disgust, he and the other press cameramen had been banned from this meeting. The Viceroy wanted to concentrate on the job in hand with as little fuss as possible.

There had been a last-minute crisis of form concerning which of the Hindu and Muslim leaders should be invited, but it had been ironed out and now all of them, save one, sat round Mountbatten at the cramped table, fiddling with the pencils and writing paper which had been set before them. To his right were Nehru, then Patel, then the thin-faced, dapper new President of the Congress Party, Acharya Kripalani. Next to him sat the bearded, turbaned Baldev

127

Singh, who represented the interests of the Sikhs. To the Viceroy's left were Liaqat Ali Khan, plump and looking deceptively benign in a grey business suit. Lastly, Sardar Abdur Rab Nishtar, with his fierce Mogul moustache, and his white *sherwani* coat and tight *churidar* trousers, the Muslim member for Communications in the Interim Government. As they waited, Mountbatten attempted a few words of light conversation, but the response was desultory. Was he deliberately late, in order to make an entrance? Nehru could not help wondering.

Finally the double doors were opened by a uniformed ADC to admit Mohammed Ali Jinnah. The sticklike man, immaculate as ever, was coughing into a cream silk handkerchief which he had bought, with several others, in an exclusive little shop in the Burlington Arcade off Piccadilly.

'Ah, Mr Jinnah, good morning,' said Mountbatten, rising. Inwardly he breathed a sigh of relief. He had begun to wonder whether the Muslim had decided not to come.

'My apologies for being late, Your Excellency.' Jinnah glanced at Liaqat and Abdur Rab, who each hastened to move along one chair to leave the one immediately to Mountbatten's left free. Even a round table was not without its order of precedence for Jinnah. Campbell-Johnson nodded to the photographer. He arranged his camera on its tripod and quickly took one flash photograph.

Nothing escaped Mountbatten's eye for detail: as it was, the photo would only have caught the back of Baldev Singh's head. 'One more for safety, I think,' he said. 'Perhaps you could move round a little, Mr Singh.'

The Sikh turned to his right, presenting his profile to the camera. The shutter clicked once more. As Campbell-Johnson and the photographer left, Erskine Crum distributed neatly typed copies of the Plan, placing one in front of each of the men at the table. Mountbatten opened the meeting with crisp confidence.

'I wish first to thank you all, gentlemen, for accepting my invitation. We are here for no less a reason than to settle the future of India.' He looked around the table. Jinnah sat alert and watchful. Nehru seemed almost sad, gazing at the blank notepad before him. 'In my view,' he continued, 'and that of the British Government, the sooner power is transferred, the better for all.'

'I think we all agree on that, Your Excellency,' said Nehru, quietly. Like a duellist's, his eyes met Jinnah's, and flicked away again as quickly.

The Viceroy turned to Jinnah. 'My first duty is to ask you once again, formally, Mr Jinnah, if you will accept the Cabinet Mission Plan for a united, federated State of India.'

Almost without hesitation Jinnah replied, 'It is totally unacceptable to myself and to the Muslim League.' He glanced challengingly at the Hindu representatives across the table.

'We must now discuss the details of the new initiative,' continued Mountbatten, his voice remaining calm, almost neutral. 'It provides for the Independence and Partition of the country.'

'A question,' broke in Baldev Singh. 'We need to know where the new boundaries will run. The Sikh community is very worried if it means that the Punjab, our homeland, is to be divided.'

Mountbatten sympathized with his concern. The rich farmland of the Punjab depended on the integrity of the province for its survival. What if a boundary line severed irrigation systems from the river sources which fed them? 'That will be settled at a later date, Mr Singh,' he answered, finally. 'But the division of India into two separate nations, sadly, appears to be the only option left open to us. You are already aware of the dilemma. Congress does not agree to the principle of Partition, but if it is unavoidable it insists on the Partition of the provinces involved – the Punjab and Bengal – to avoid large numbers of Hindus or Muslims from being forced to live in a country they would not choose. The Muslim League, on the other hand, resists this division of the provinces, but insists on the Partition of India.'

Jinnah, still coughing slightly, was fitting a cigarette into his holder. 'The Muslim League may find itself in a position less opposed to the division of the provinces in question if we were assured of a corridor linking East and West Pakistan.'

Sensing the tension in the Hindu leaders, Mountbatten turned to Jinnah. 'I can only discuss the Plan as it stands. That is what we are here to approve. It contains no mention of a corridor, nor is there provision for one.' To his relief Jinnah's eyes remained lowered as he lit his cigarette. He did not reply. At least he had the sense not to push his luck, thought the Viceroy, and turned again to Baldev Singh. 'I am acutely aware of the situation facing the Sikh community. The dignity and spirit with which your people are prepared to accept the division of the Punjab, with its unavoidable effect of separating many thousands of your people from their families and friends, is an example to us all.'

An hour ticked by as the meeting continued. Jinnah was smoking so heavily that Mountbatten and Nehru both thanked God for the air conditioner, which whirred away relentlessly under the window, the only thing which stood between them and a racking headache.

'Let us now turn to paragraph 20: "Immediate Transfer of Power".' There was a surge of increased interest, a rustle of paper as pages were turned. 'As you will see, HM Government suggests that it can best be achieved by the granting of Dominion status to both India and Pakistan.'

'But do we get total control if we are a Dominion?' asked the Congress President.

'Total, Mr Kripalani.'

'But we would simply be exchanging a Viceroy for a Governor General,' put in Liaqat Ali Khan.

'A Governor General's position is constitutional. He would act in a purely advisory capacity. He is responsible both to your governments and that of Great Britain.' The Viceroy looked round the table. Some of the faces still expressed doubt. 'This offer is made,' he explained, 'not

130

from any desire of Great Britain to retain a foothold here beyond her time, but as an answer to any charge that we are quitting our obligations to India. Our assistance will not be withdrawn as long as it is still required, but in no way will it be a further imposition of British power.'

'I for one welcome the opportunity for Pakistan of retaining a link with the Crown, and of remaining in the British Commonwealth,' said Jinnah, in his dry, measured voice.

'And of course there's no obligation to stay in for ever,' countered Patel. He wanted to make sure that this was clear to everyone.

They had virtually reached the end of the paper. Only a last formal note of 'Further Announcements by the Governor General', and an appendix relating to the Muslim majority districts in Bengal and the Punjab remained. The men around the table sat back, stretching.

'These, then, gentlemen, are the bare bones of the Plan,' said Mountbatten, winding up. 'I would like you now to go away and discuss it privately, and then let me know your decisions. I don't expect you to agree fully with every clause. I am seeking your acceptance of the broad lines of the Plan in principle.'

Jinnah shifted uncomfortably in his seat. This should have been his moment of triumph: at last Pakistan was an acknowledged reality. But years of gaining ground by saying 'no' had made the practice a habit with him. His elderly lawyer's mind baulked at any hint of rush. 'I . . . enter into the spirit of the proposals,' he said. 'But we cannot make any final decision without consulting the people we represent.'

'Mr Jinnah,' said the Viceroy, patiently, 'there are times when leaders must make decisions by themselves, and trust to carrying their followers with them afterwards.' Again he paused, and stood up. 'I should like your reactions in writing, gentlemen – by midnight tonight.'

The men around the table were startled.

131

'Tonight?' Patel queried, momentarily caught off his guard.

'This needs no more lengthy discussion,' said Mountbatten positively. 'You either know it is right, or wrong.'

Baldev Singh rose. 'You shall have the reaction of the Sikhs by this evening, Your Excellency.'

Kripalani stood up with Nehru and Patel: 'And ours, too.'

Jinnah sat where he was, saying nothing.

The meeting had ended at 11.00 am and Mountbatten had arranged to see Gandhi at 12.30 pm. To counterbalance this, he had diplomatically also arranged an interview with Jinnah alone immediately following the momentous morning's work which came to be known as the '2 June Meeting'. Before the other leaders departed, Mountbatten secured one more agreement from them, that they would join him in broadcasting to the Nation on All-India Radio the following evening. At the same time, Attlee in London would be breaking the news via the BBC. It was only by driving relentlessly forward, not allowing time for doubt or second thoughts, that Mountbatten felt he could succeed.

Before Jinnah left him, the Viceroy had at least made some progress. The Muslim leader would not commit himself to paper, but said he would return in the late evening and give a verbal report of his reactions to the Plan. Mountbatten knew that he could only press so far. Jinnah had withdrawn from the game once before and the result had been disastrous. Now, it would be catastrophic. What the Viceroy simply could not understand was why the Muslim was holding back now – with all that he wanted about to fall into his grasp.

'All right, Mr Jinnah, you come and just tell me what you think. But Lord Ismay must be present as a witness to what is said.'

The Muslim had inclined his head, stared at the Englishmen for a moment with those impenetrable eyes of his, and left. By now Mountbatten's usually strong nerves were on edge. He was elated by the success of the morning's meeting, but at the same time he was keenly aware of how thin the ice on which he was skating still was. He hardly had time to splash his face with cold water and snatch a cup of coffee and a cigarette before it was time to meet Gandhi, possibly a more crucial interview than the one he had just survived. Would the ice hold his weight? he wondered ruefully, as he hurried along the corridor to the small drawing-room where he was to receive the Mahatma.

Gandhi was dressed as always in his plain white *dhoti*, always so spotlessly clean, and shoulder wrap. His feet in their leather sandals looked huge at the end of his spindly legs. Mountbatten, a consummate actor when he had to be, gave the impression of absolute composure and calm.

'Good afternoon, Mr Gandhi.' The old Indian looked at him with an expression which was very difficult to read, and answered him not a word.

'I hope you haven't come to bully me,' said Mountbatten, but Gandhi merely smiled and placed a finger to his lips. 'Forgive me – won't you sit down?'

They sat opposite one another in silence, a silence which began to be increasingly disconcerting to the Viceroy. Gandhi fished in the folds of his clothing, finally producing a stub of pencil and some old, used envelopes stapled together for use as a notebook. He considered it a sin to throw anything away until it was well and truly used up. As Mountbatten proceeded with a one-sided conversation, the old man wrote quickly and with concentration.

'I want to explain the situation to you as I see it,' the Viceroy explained. 'I've already outlined my ideas to Jawaharlal and Mr Patel. Nobody knows better than you the dangerous increase in violence that threatens India. I am seeking the best way to stop it, or at least contain it . . .' He trailed off, as Gandhi raised his hand, and gave him the note he had written. Mountbatten glanced at it in astonishment, and then looked at Gandhi again. He still could not read the expression on the old man's normally open face.

'I am sorry I can't speak,' Gandhi had written. 'When I took the decision about the Monday silence, I did make two exceptions . . . that is, speaking to high functionaries on urgent matters or attending upon sick people. But I know you won't want me to break my silence. Have I said one word against you in my speeches? . . . There are one or two things I must talk about, but not today. But if we meet each other again, I shall speak.'

Mountbatten did not know what to think. Had Ghandi given in, or was he biding his time? And if so, what for? Certainly the implication was that if he was adhering to his usual rule of keeping Monday as a day of silence – even *this* Monday – he would not only not speak to Mountbatten, but Nehru and Patel as well. The Viceroy could only welcome the unexpected reprieve. By tomorrow, it would be almost too late even for Gandhi to turn the tide.

Pug Ismay sat next to Mountbatten in the study at Viceroy's House. In front of them on the round table lay formal letters from the Sikhs and the Congress Party accepting the Partition Plan. Opposite them sat Mohammed Ali Jinnah. He had accepted a whisky, and was now meticulously fitting a Craven 'A' into his holder. Each breath he took seemed to cause him pain, and frequently he wet his lips, pursing them. His careful movements were those of an invalid. His mental stamina was that of a giant.

It was a little after midnight. The conversation had been general for the first few minutes but now Mountbatten had had enough of polite fencing and went on to the attack. It was the only way to deal with this devious old politician.

'Well, Mr Jinnah, you have seen the depositions of the Sikhs and the Congress. Pakistan is assured. All we need now is your own formal acceptance.'

Jinnah regarded him with curiously dead eyes. 'I regret that I cannot give it, Your Excellency.'

Mountbatten was astounded. Had things gone so far

with Jinnah that he was incapable of saying 'yes' even when it was to his own advantage? He glanced at Ismay, who looked similarly shaken.

'May I ask why?'

'It is as I have explained. I must put the proposition first to the membership of the Muslim League. I shall do my best to persuade them, but the final decision must be theirs.' He drew evenly on his cigarette. Mountbatten, after his earlier experience that day with Gandhi, was beginning to wonder if he would ever wholly come to terms with the Indian mentality. But he would gain nothing by being impatient. Privately he thanked God that his duty lay in bringing the Raj to an end, rather than continuing it.

'You do realize that after all your years of struggling and dreaming, you risk ruining everything?' he pointed out. 'Congress has insisted that adoption of the Plan by all parties must be simultaneous. If you don't accept now, Nehru and Patel will immediately suspect a political motive, and they will withdraw their own acceptance. The Plan will be wrecked.'

'What must be, must be,' said Jinnah, with no change in his expression. 'I cannot consult the Council of the League for at least three days, possibly longer.'

Considering that this man practically *is* the Muslim League, thought Mountbatten, he is taking a bloody high line with me. The truth is, he's incapable of taking the final step unless I bully him into it.

'Mr Jinnah,' he said. 'I am not going to allow you, for whatever reason, to throw away the dream for which you have worked for so many years. I'll tell you what I'm going to do; and if later your Council refuses to ratify the Plan you can put the blame on me. At tomorrow's meeting, I am going to say that we have discussed everything and that I have accepted your assurances. Then I shall look at you. You don't have to say *anything*. You merely have to nod your head.' The Viceroy paused. 'If you do not do that, Mr Jinnah, everything will collapse – everything. You will have lost your Pakistan, and as far as I am concerned you can go to hell!'

Light poured into the Viceroy's pale-green study on the morning of 3 June as the Indian leaders once again took their places round the table. Mountbatten did his best not to allow the tension he felt to communicate itself to the Congress Party members on his right as he formally asked them to confirm the sense of their letter of the night before, accepting the Plan. He went through the same formality with Baldev Singh.

Now for it, he thought. Jinnah had refused to catch his eye at any point during the meeting so far. True, the evening before he had finally agreed with Mountbatten's proposal, after protecting himself with various stipulations and qualifications. He had even agreed that the broadcast message publicizing acceptance of the Plan should go ahead from Delhi and London that evening. But, faced with triumph, Jinnah was proving himself as unpredictable as Gandhi, and his mind was so convoluted that it seemed unable to recognize simple advantage even when it stared him in the face. In the eight hours since he had last seen him, Mountbatten had no idea whether Mr Jinnah might once again have changed his mind.

'Last night,' he said, 'I had a long and informative discussion with Mr Jinnah, in the course of which he gave me assurances *vis à vis* the Plan on behalf of the Muslim League, which satisfy me and which I have accepted.' He paused, and looked at Jinnah. For an eternity which lasted no more than five seconds, the Muslim leader did not move. Then, with an angular movement, he looked bleakly at Mountbatten and jerked his head in a curt nod.

Watching them both, Pug Ismay shut his eyes in relief. It was just as well that so few people knew how delicately balanced this great moment of history had been. If Jinnah had *not* nodded. . . . The consequences did not bear thinking about.

'This must be a unique moment,' Mountbatten was

saying. 'We all seem to be in agreement.' Ismay looked at him in admiration as the others round the table smiled in the release of tension. How does he do it? he wondered. But no sooner had general agreement to the Plan been formally ratified, than Erskine Crum placed before the Viceroy an awesome pile of identical buff folders. Each contained a document of some thirty closely typed pages, prepared by John Christie, Joint Private Secretary to the Viceroy, and his staff. Mountbatten was sticking to his policy of making the Indian leadership run so fast that they wouldn't have time to stop and think. He called the meeting to order again.

'Good. Now, this is what we have to consider next, gentlemen. It's a paper we've prepared on a subject to which very little thought seems as yet to have been given.' With perfect stage timing he raised the top copy above his head and brought it down with a crack upon the table which made everybody sit up.

'"The Administrative Consequences of Partition."'

Early that evening, the leaders gave their speeches on All-India Radio. The Viceroy spoke first, his voice measured and subdued in accordance with the solemnity of his announcement.

'. . . To my great regret, it has been impossible to obtain agreement either on the Cabinet Mission Plan, or on any plan that would preserve the unity of India. But there can be no question of coercing any large areas in which one community has a majority to live against their will under a government in which another community has a majority. And the only alternative to coercion is Partition.'

Nehru spoke next, and his simple, eloquent words revealed him as the scholar and artist whom the politician sometimes overshadowed. Frustrated in victory, he nevertheless held his head high. Shortly before the broadcast, and speaking at the end of his regular evening prayer meeting, the Mahatma had rebuked his disciple. 'Jawaharlal is our King,' the old man had said, 'but we should not be impressed by everything the King does or does not do. If he has devised something good for us we should praise him. If he has not, then we should say so.' Whether Gandhi would act upon his veiled threat was a question Nehru had to consider.

The last to speak were Jinnah and Baldev Singh. Baldev, aware of the tensions Partition would create in the Punjab, appealed for calm. In his heart he knew that the legislatures of his home province would opt for division, and that the Sikhs' homeland would thus be torn in two. He knew that the consequence of that would be blood.

Jinnah could not speak Urdu, and so an interpreter had to deliver his English words in the language the majority of his newborn state would understand. In contrast to the others, his main concern was for greater broadcasting facilities to be made available to him, 'to enable me to voice my views and opinions, which will reach directly to you, live and warm, rather than in the cold print of newspapers.' The self-esteem which was to dominate his personality in the coming months was beginning to show itself. Jinnah finished with some of the few words he could speak in the language of his nation. He said, '*Pakistan Zindabad!*' but his tone was so clipped that many of his listeners had taken him still to be talking in English, and saying, with a frivolity no one could possibly associate with the Qaid-i-Azam, 'Pakistan's in the bag!'

On the morning of 4 June the Viceroy made his way to the Legislative Assembly, to face the Press. Copies of the twenty-one paragraph '3 June Plan', or the 'Mountbatten Plan' as some were calling it, had been published, and now the questions the public wanted to ask had to be dealt with. Dressed in his grey double-breasted suit, Mountbatten stood at the high rostrum of the Assembly, with Vallabhbhai Patel, who was chairing the Press Conference, on his right. Below him sat his aides. Mountbatten had neither a prepared speech, nor any notes. It was in situations like this, in total command of the facts, that he flourished. Now he was fluent, charming, incisive, and backed by a natural charisma which few could withstand. He had finished his brief introductory speech, and Patel invited questions from the floor. The Assembly chamber was packed with Indian and foreign newsmen.

'On what basis are negotiations between the independent princes and His Majesty's Government to be carried on?' asked an Indian journalist.

'There will be no direct negotiations. The British Government has individual treaties with the princely states. Those treaties will lapse automatically on Independence. It will then be up to the princes and their advisors to decide which of the two nations to join.'

A British correspondent stood up. 'How did you fix the position of the boundaries in the provinces to be divided, Your Excellency?'

'On the basis of the predominantly Hindu or Muslim areas. But let me remind you that they are only for voting purposes. The actual boundaries will be determined by an impartial Boundaries Commissioner – if they are required.'

'There may be unfairness caused by simple geography,' a Muslim newsman pointed out. 'For example, if Hyderabad in the south wants to join Pakistan, it cannot do so.'

'The states are absolutely free to choose,' came the reply. 'Although, normally, geographical situation and communal interests will have to be considered.'

Another Muslim correspondent stood up, and posed a loaded political question. Clearly asked on Jinnah's behalf, it was about the provision of 'corridors' from one part of Pakistan to another. There was a momentary hush as other journalists waited to see how the Viceroy would deal with it. Mountbatten picked up a copy of the Plan and made as if he were reading through it in puzzlement. 'I don't remember where that comes,' he said. 'Which paragraph are you referring to?' The Muslim correspondent sat down again amidst laughter. His cleverly planted question had misfired. There was no provision for 'corridors' in the Plan.

Reverting to the subject of the princely states, an Indian journalist asked, 'How will you keep control until June 1948, if the people in states like Hyderabad reject the rule of the princes?'

Mountbatten had been prepared for that question. Now his plans to transfer power at a much earlier date would have to be made public. 'The date of the transfer of power is going to be much earlier.'

Patel's head whipped round towards him. An excited buzz of conversation ran round the Assembly Room, fading to silence as the Viceroy continued, 'The date you mean is in this year – 1947. The British, including this chap here,' he pointed to himself, 'may have left by the end of it. We may have booked our berths and be gone.'

'May I ask whether you mean that British troops will also be withdrawn?' asked the British correspondent.

'So far as I am concerned, the answer is "yes".'

Excitement in the room was rising fast as an American reporter rose. 'How long will His Excellency stay as "His Excellency"? Might you not stay on as Governor General?'

Mountbatten paused. He suddenly saw that here was a golden opportunity to fix his time limit, once and for all, and in public. Once committed to it, they would all have to work like Trojans to meet it. Without it, there was still a strong possibility of the energy he had concentrated in the Indian leadership over the past three days being dissipated once again. But he had not discussed a date, even with his personal staff. He thought quickly.

'That is far from being decided,' he began. 'As for staying on, I think the transfer of power could take place on – oh – the 15th of August this year.'

He had spoken as casually as possible, hoping to under-play the effect of this announcement. In a moment, however, the room was in an uproar of excitement.

After the Press Conference was over, Mountbatten hurried back to Viceroy's House. He had placed a bombshell under his staff and the Indian leadership together, but just as great a bombshell was waiting for him. He had received word that Gandhi was intending to speak out against the Plan at his prayer meeting that evening.

Mountbatten was by no means sure what effect such a denunciation might have, but there was no underestimating Gandhi, and so the Viceroy sent word to the Mahatma suggesting a meeting that afternoon. Gandhi arrived at Viceroy's House at 6.00 pm, an hour before his prayer meeting was due to begin. Mountbatten was shocked to see the change that had come over the old man. He seemed to have shrunk into himself.

'I know how you must feel about all this,' said Mountbatten, gently.

'No one can know that.' Gandhi drew himself up. 'I have come one last time to ask you to reconsider.'

'If the only thing Hindus and Muslims can agree on is Partition, we are left with no choice,' Mountbatten explained.

'There must be another! Have you thought of the bitterness, the violence Partition will cause? What I have seen in Bihar and Calcutta will be as nothing compared to it!'

'I have thought of little else. Yet at least I know that Partition will not be forced on your people. The referendum will ensure that the people of India will be free to choose their own destiny.'

The old man looked away. Mountbatten realised that he had to convince him that the Plan *was* the only way forward, that his dream of a united India could never now become a practical reality. Things had gone too far for that.

'You told me yourself that I should leave the choice to the people of India and that is what the Plan is about. The newspapers are calling it the 'Mountbatten Plan'. Perhaps they would have done better to call it the 'Gandhi Plan', since so much of your thinking has gone into it. To cast doubt on it now in the people's minds would throw them into confusion and would certainly lead to bloodshed throughout the country.'

'But Partition . . .' Gandhi remained unconvinced, yet he was listening now.

'You must see that this is what is best for India. It is what India wants.'

Slowly, the old man turned to look at him. 'Yes . . . yes . . . I have always said, we must trust the people. I must trust them now. I see that it is too late for me to intervene without making things worse.' He looked at his battered Ingersoll. 'I must go soon. I will tell them that you are not to blame for this Partition. Many will be angry with me for this. . . .' The ghost of a smile appeared on his face. 'But I think I am still a match for the extremists who would prefer war to a divided India.' He fell silent again, and then, unexpectedly, he asked, 'How is Edwina?'

Mountbatten let out a sigh of relief which could not have escaped the old man, though he did not comment upon it. 'Working too hard, as usual,' he replied. 'She and Pamela have been touring the countryside around Delhi. She's trying to organize a regular steady supply of medicines to the villages.'

Gandhi smiled. If only his fellow countrymen would follow that frail woman's example of dedication and love. But if at least he could bind them together in brotherhood, then in the heart, if not on the map, the unity of India could be preserved.

At seven o'clock precisely he mounted the low, makeshift rostrum in the middle of the dusty square in the sweepers' colony. Surrounding him were Hindus of all classes, men and women, and he was pleased to see a handful of Muslims, too. He tried to gauge the underlying mood of the crowd, as they joyfully called out his name. He waited, smiling, until they fell silent. Then he raised his arms.

'My friends – at our prayer meeting tonight we have historic questions to resolve, our answers to which may affect the lives of generations to come.' He paused, looking slowly round the sea of expectant faces. 'But first, before we begin, would anyone object if I recited some verses from the Holy Book of Islam – from the Koran?'

The reaction cut him like a knife. Dismay and shock quickly gave way to anger. The few Muslims present looked worried, and then hastened away as the shouting began. 'The Koran has no place here! These are Hindu services! It would be a defilement!'

Gandhi was silent, looking at the gesticulating hands, the faces contorted with rage and fear. Again he waited for them to be still.

'So be it,' he said quietly into the silence. Turning his back on them, he leant on Manu for support as he made his way back to his hut. Never had he felt more isolated or more useless.

On the rear verandah of the house in York Road, Mountbatten sipped his drink and watched the dusk creep over the trim lawn. He stretched out his legs in front of him luxuriously.

'It's so peaceful here. I envy you, Jawaharlal. For weeks I never seem to have stopped talking.'

Nehru smiled briefly. 'You may be at peace, but you've ruined mine. Independence on 15 August? Do you realize that it's barely two months away? If HMG set such an early date, why on earth didn't you warn us?'

'They didn't choose the date. I did. We've got to keep things moving.'

'When did you choose it?'

'At the Press Conference.'

Nehru looked at the tall Englishman in amazement. 'I'm not at all sure we can get everything ready in the time.'

Mountbatten sipped his drink. 'Well, I'm afraid the die is cast, and somehow or other we'll have to.'

'So, it has begun,' said Gandhi sadly. His guests in his humble hut in the sweepers' colony today were the Vicereine and Rajkumari Amrit Kaur. They had just returned from a tour of inspection of the hospitals in the Punjab.

There, they had seen the first results of the impending threat of Partition. Already, thousands of people were on the move. People who had lived in the same place for generations had suddenly become refugees, fleeing from those areas where almost overnight they had become the victims of a witch-hunt by virtue of their religious beliefs. Now, a steady stream of Hindus headed east, and Muslims west, hoping to place themselves far from the danger zones when the carnage they feared started.

'For each who rejoices at Partition, another weeps,' sighed the old man.

'I have heard you have been having trouble at your own prayer meetings, Bapu,' said Amrit Kaur tentatively.

'It is no sin to speak the name of God in Arabic. If they had *all* objected, I would have read from the Koran and died at their hands, speaking the name of God. I broke off every meeting, though, until there were no more protests. In the end, *ahimsa*, non-violence, prevailed. As it always will.' Gandhi had quickly regained much of his moral strength since the black days at the beginning of June. He had found stability in applying the principles which he had lived by all his life, since his hard schooling as a young lawyer fighting for human rights in South Africa at the turn of the century, and his agile mind had adapted to the situation it now had to confront. He would preach religious tolerance and brotherhood to his people until they learnt the lesson of its goodness. This was the unity towards which he now strove.

'With all that I've seen in the last few days in the Punjab, I'd almost lost my faith in humanity,' said Edwina. 'But you give it back to me.'

'You must never lose your faith in humanity, my dear. Humanity is an ocean. If a few drops of that ocean are dirty, it does not mean that the whole ocean becomes dirty.' He smiled to her.

'Gandhiji, we must go,' Amrit Kaur said at length. 'There are so many people waiting to see you.'

'Ah, they come to me for answers that I no longer have.

144

But before you go, will you pray with me? I have been thinking of a very simple prayer which can be said by anyone, anywhere, at any time. And which is very suitable for us now.' Edwina and Amrit Kaur knelt with him and repeated the words as he spoke them.

'Oh Lord,
Lead us from darkness
Into light.'

But death was in the air. On the sunny afternoon of 9 June, none of the fashionable British and Indian couples strolling in the gardens of New Delhi's luxurious Imperial Hotel paid enough attention to the shabby gardeners working there to notice that each of them carried a sharp-edged spade known as a *belcha*, and that several of them seemed to be spending more time honing the blades of their implements than actually using them in the garden. This was nothing unusual. It would have been the height of bad form to notice servants of such a low order.

9 June was not a typical day in the life of the hotel. In the foyer, and especially at the foot of the staircase leading to the first-floor ballroom, a number of Muslim League National Guards stood at the ready, armed with long bamboo *lathis*. In the ballroom itself, the members of the All-India Muslim League Council were awaiting the arrival of their leader. They would not have to wait long. His dark American sedan had just pulled up at the garden entrance of the hotel.

The gardeners let Jinnah get as far as the foyer. Then as one man they rushed through the french windows which gave onto it on either side. Whirling their *belchas*, and yelling, 'Get Jinnah!' they scattered guests and furniture alike in their forward rush. An Englishwoman screamed as she was hurled to one side across a dainty table laid for tea. The scalding water from a silver jug splashed over her face and neck as she fell. Beyond her, the swing of a sharpened spade severed a gilded wooden pedestal, bringing the huge vase of lilies it bore crashing down.

Halfway up the stairs, Jinnah turned. The Muslim National Guards had managed to check the undisciplined onslaught of the assassins, but they still struggled to reach him. He was transfixed by the fanatic zeal in their eyes as they sliced the air with their horrific weapons and yelled without stop, '*Pakistan Zindabad*! Get Jinnah! *Pakistan Zindabad!*'

'So, who were they?' Field Marshal Sir Claude Auchinleck wanted to know.

'Some of his own people. They call themselves *khaksars*,' said Mountbatten. 'It took the police with tear gas to clear them out.'

'I know about *khaksars*,' said Auchinleck. 'The name means "the servants of the dust". They're Muslim fanatics, zealots. They sort of correspond to the Hindu *Rashtriya Swayam Sewak Sangh*. Bloody dangerous extremists. They had a crack at old Jinnah back in '43. What has he done wrong this time?'

'They want an undivided Pakistan right across northern India from Karachi to Calcutta. They think Jinnah's sold them out.'

'Just as dotty as the RSSS – though maybe not quite as dangerous. I'd watch the Hindu lot. Their motto's death rather than the division of India.'

'There are so many problems, Claude, that I think one more won't make much difference to the load. Drink?'

'No thanks.' At sixty-two, Auchinleck had reached the zenith of his career as Commander-in-Chief of his beloved Indian Army. A battered veteran, his bluff charm concealed an extremely stubborn nature. Now his attention had been caught by something new in the Viceroy's study: a large calendar with the day's date at the top of the displayed page. Under that was printed the huge figure '63', and below that in capitals, 'DAYS LEFT TO PREPARE FOR TRANSFER OF POWER'.

'Like it?' asked the Viceroy. 'Had them printed for my

146

staff. I think the reminder every day helps keep them on their toes.'

Auchinleck grunted. Privately, he thought the thing was a bit of a gimmick. He had tried to avoid this meeting for as long as possible, but it could no longer be put off. And he had a pretty shrewd idea of what Mountbatten had in mind. The Indian Army, his army, the finest standing force of fighting men in the world, was going to be split up. Split up, like everything else, because of this damned Partition. Damned Independence! They even had two lawyers, one Muslim and one Hindu, beavering away at it, sorting out the nuts and bolts: how many office chairs went to Karachi, how many stayed in Delhi. How many typewriters, bottles of ink, reams of foolscap. He'd even heard it said there'd been an argument about the bloody rubber bands! 'Administrative Consequences of Partition', indeed! Well, he admitted grudgingly to himself, it had to be done. Chaos otherwise. But, damn it all to hell, not the *army*!

'To split it up would be to ruin it, Dickie!'

Mountbatten was exasperated. The warrior in him saw the truth of what Auchinleck was saying, and he sympathized with him. But now he had to be an administrator and a realist. There was no time for what had to be seen as sentiment. 'Nehru and Jinnah insist on having their own national armies, under their own control, by 15 August. It is a natural wish, and we've agreed to it.'

'I bloody didn't.'

'Claude, I don't want to fall out with you over this.'

Auchinleck rubbed his chin. 'Not a question of that. But have you thought of the complications? Ever since the Indian Mutiny ninety years ago, every single regiment has been organized into communal battalions, Hindus, Muslims and Sikhs, to balance one another.'

'Well, that should make it easier, shouldn't it? Detach the Muslim battalions to Pakistan.'

Auchinleck nearly laughed. 'You're asking me to unscramble an omelette, Dickie. Don't you see the shambles that will cause in every single divisional command? Hundreds of disconnected units being shipped back and forth across the country, just when we might need them most! And that's without going into the whole question of who's to command them. Apart from a few Indian brigadiers, the entire general staff is British!'

'Then you'd better select some Hindu and Muslim officers and promote them, double-quick,' snapped the Viceroy. 'It's got to be done, Claude.'

'At least let us keep some British troops as a strong central force until after Partition.'

'Out of the question.'

'Listen, Your Excellency,' said Auchinleck, controlling himself. 'I was appointed C-in-C to defend and maintain security in the subcontinent. Circumstances prevent me from doing that, but I do still have a solemn duty to protect the lives of British citizens.'

'I appreciate your concern, Field Marshal. But they are in no danger.' Auchinleck started to protest, and Mountbatten's patience came to an abrupt end. Didn't this lumbering fool see that what he was proposing would not only fail to keep the Hindus and Muslims from each others' throats, but would turn them against the British too? 'Don't you understand what I'm saying?' he rapped out. 'I'm not discussing it! We just have to get on with it. You just have to get your staff busy organizing the armed forces. And no bloody nonsense about it, Claude!'

The divison of the spoils, thought Lieutenant Commander Peter Howes ruefully. Drawn up in front of him in the great stable-yard at Viceroy's House were the last of the stables' contents to be shared out, the two State carriages. They vied with each other in magnificence, though one was trimmed with silver and the other with gold. Soldiers wandered about the yard, carefully directed to carry all the accoutrements of the stables, from dress tack to cans of dubbin, and deposit them in piles. One pile for India; one pile for Pakistan.

The job of adjudicating all this was not an enviable one, he thought, though he had derived a certain vicarious pleasure from the obvious delight of his two companions. Major Yakoub Khan for Pakistan, and Major Gobind Singh for India were in charge of what went to each of their countries. Howes was simply there to ensure fair play. His military mind hated to see the appurtenances of British administration, which after all was efficient and still in good running order, being broken up like this, but at the same time he recognized its inevitability. Like the carriages themselves, the Raj had been overtaken by time. There was no place for it in the modern world and to think otherwise was foolish and sentimental. All the same, it was a great pity.

'Over there,' he said to a passing soldier, who was pushing a rack of horse-trumpeters' uniforms. Then he turned to the two majors. As the day had worn on, their enthusiasm had dulled. Now, like people who had eaten too much cake, they were becoming ill-tempered.

'Now then, gentlemen, there are two sets of ceremonial carriages, one of gold, and one of silver.'

'The agreement clearly states that eighty per cent of assets should go to India, twenty to Pakistan,' put in Gobind Singh quickly.

'It would be criminal to break up the sets,' said Yakoub Khan. 'In any case, why should the Governor General of India need more carriages than the Governor General of Pakistan?' The two majors, brothers-in-arms a week ago, glared at each other.

'Gentlemen, please,' said Howes, 'we've arranged everything so far without losing our tempers. There's a time-honoured way of settling this. We can toss a coin, heads for gold. Agreed?'

The majors muttered their consent. Howes pulled a rupee out of his pocket and spun it.

'Heads!' cried Gobind Singh as Howes caught the coin and flipped it onto the back of his hand.

'Heads it is, Major Singh.'

With a whoop of triumph, the Sikh turned to a group of grooms standing by one of the carriages. 'Gold for India! You *syces* see that the cushions, harnesses and bridles that go with them are divided correctly.'

Howes was relieved. That seemed to be the lot. But at that moment another *syce* appeared, carrying the long, ceremonial Viceroy's post-horn. Oh Lord, thought Howes, we can't divide *that*. Major Singh was insisting that the horn should go with the gold set, which Major Yakoub categorically denied.

'We'll toss for it,' suggested Gobind Singh.

'So you will win again!' retorted Major Yakoub. 'I refuse to gamble for it.'

Howes had had enough. He took the horn from the groom and put it under his arm. 'There's only one fair solution, then,' he said. 'I'll keep it for myself.' Smiling, he saluted and left.

The women were walking in the garden of Nehru's house. They had been talking of Gandhi, and how he had remarked that India was secretly run by the women of the country.

'Some of us would like to think that was true,' said Mrs Pandit, smiling.

'It's not, though,' put in Maniben, Patel's plain daughter.

'I don't think he was joking,' said Edwina. 'At least, not completely.'

Mrs Pandit agreed. 'We are the lucky ones. But we must try to do something for all the millions of Indian women who are the prisoners of our country's worst traditions – all those poor creatures who have never had a day's education, or any opportunity to become more than just their husband's property.'

'But where are the opportunities?' asked Indira Gandhi. 'To create capabilities and expectations before the jobs exist in which women might be used, would be to make matters worse.'

'There are opportunities in nursing,' said Edwina. 'The whole field is wide open in India. What you should be looking at is ways of improving recruitment and working conditions. That is an area where you and other women of influence could have an enormous effect.'

They had arrived at a terrace where white-robed servants were laying tea. As the three Indian women sat, Edwina noticed that Nehru had come out onto the verandah of the house. Making her excuses to the others, she walked across the lawn to join him.

'We've just stopped for a tea break. I've no idea how much progress we're making, but there's no lack of ideas. Won't you join us?'

'No – but if you are not too terribly thirsty, perhaps you would have a walk with me?' he said.

'Gladly. But can you bear to tear yourself away from your work?'

'Oh, I have a few minutes.'

'I'm so grateful,' Edwina murmured.

He glanced at her, wondering if he had offended her, but saw that she was only teasing him. Nevertheless he felt he should apologize. 'I'm sorry, Edwina. That sounded terrible.'

'I assure you I'm used to it.'

'Yes. Lord Louis, too, works hard.' They walked towards the rose garden, away from the tea party. 'We haven't had a chance to talk for weeks.'

'I had noticed,' she said quietly, her head lowered.

As always, his reaction to her disturbed him. 'I really have been very busy,' he explained, 'with the division of all our assets with Pakistan. From the money in the banks to elastic bands.' She smiled. 'Yes, it would be funny, if the reason were not so tragic.'

'I saw Gandhi today,' she told him, as they walked on. 'He spoke very fondly of you.'

'I am relieved to hear it,' said Nehru, tensely. 'Do you remember what he said?'

'That he loved you, and respected you.' She stopped, turning to face him. 'He asked me to tell you that you were always in his thoughts.'

Moved and relieved, Nehru took her hand in his. The gesture seemed so natural that he hardly noticed that he had made it.

'Thank you . . . thank you,' he said, moved. 'His words mean much to me. There has been a coolness between Bapu and myself lately. It has been hard to bear.'

Edwina returned the pressure of his touch. 'He knows you have been under a great strain. And the violence distresses him. It just goes on and on.'

Nehru paused before replying. He remembered the nights he had been unable to sleep, thinking of the bloody birth of his new nation. 'We can only hope the fires cool with Independence.'

He looked into her warm, intelligent eyes. He wished he could tell her more, that as the violence mounted, he was becoming afraid of India's freedom. But what greater carnage might have followed, if they had not dared to take this step?

They stood in silence for a moment, aware of the heavy scent of the roses.

'We seem to be holding hands,' said Edwina.

Nehru laughed.

# SEVEN

The ball spun high in the air. Mountbatten moved back quickly, sidestepping so as not to be under the direct downward arch of the lob. Then he stretched his racquet high over his head and brought it slashing down. The ball cannoned off it and shot back low over the net and into the opposite corner of the court.

'Game, set, and match, H.E.!' Peter Howes called from the side.

'Let's not hear the scores, thank you!' Campbell-Johnson called back and they laughed. As he shook hands with Mountbatten at the net, he pointed out that this was the first game they had which had not been interrupted, a good sign. 'Everything seems to be proceeding fairly smoothly.'

'Don't tempt providence, Alan,' Mountbatten smiled.

They walked off the court together. It was really too hot for tennis, but after three months of non-stop exertion, Mountbatten in particular had felt the need to relax and take a little hard exercise. Since the announcement of the transfer of power, unrest in the provinces had lessened somewhat, and yet the Viceroy knew that any breathing space he had would be severely limited. As predicted, Bengal and the Punjab had opted for division, and London had appointed an eminent lawyer, Sir Cyril Radcliffe, who had a wealth of administrative experience, to be Boundaries Commissioner responsible for drawing up the new frontiers which would split the provinces. So strict had been Indian insistence on impartiality in this job that what recommended Radcliffe to them was his complete ignorance of India. Mountbatten hoped the man was a fast worker. Then, too, there was the whole question of the princely states to be settled. He was not so naive, nor so optimistic, as so assume that their future was something which could be sorted out amicably by the new Dominion Governments after 15 August.

It took him barely ninety seconds to shower and change, and when he came out, he saw V.P. Menon waiting for him. I knew we shouldn't have tempted providence, he thought wryly, seeing the tension on the civil servant's face.

'Good morning, V.P. What's up?'

'Good morning, Your Excellency. I thought you'd like to know that Mr Patel has arrived. He's waiting in your study.'

'Well, we'd better not keep him.' Patel was responsible for Home Affairs. It did not take Mountbatten long, as they walked towards the house, to guess what he had come about. He was only surprised that it had come up so soon, but at least that meant that the furious pace he had set was infectious.

Patel was examining the wall map as Mountbatten and Menon entered the study. Forthright as ever, his manner was nevertheless formal and the Viceroy could see that he was worried.

"Forgive me for calling on you at such short notice, Your Excellency, but you did say that if anything important cropped up . . .'

'Yes, indeed.' Mountbatten indicated chairs for the two Indians, while he himself perched on the edge of the desk. His mind felt clear and bright after the game.

'There's an itch that's become a sore, and could turn into a cancer,' Patel said bluntly. 'Some of the most powerful rajahs think Partition means they can opt for total Independence for themselves. Well, we know that's their privilege under the Plan – in theory, in any case. The problem is that they're ready to enforce it.'

'How could they?'

Patel pointed to the map. The princely states indeed covered a dominating area of India. The larger ones,

Mysore, Hyderabad, Rajputana, and Kashmir were bigger than major European countries. 'All they have to do is close their borders. By cutting post, telephone and railway communications, they could bring India to a standstill.' Patel was becoming angry. 'Even some of the smaller states have caught the disease. I dare say the next thing is that we will have some of them playing Pakistan off against India for the best accession terms! Well, I'm not going to let them sit like undigested lumps in the belly of India. If they want a fight, they can have it!' He paused. 'Unless you do something.'

So now we get to the point, Mountbatten thought. Patel was a past master at the bullying technique, but he would avoid plunging India into internal wars at the moment of her birth. The cost alone would cripple a tender economy. 'I take it you would be pleased if I could find an alternative solution?'

Patel relaxed slightly. 'You know how to talk to these people, and what's more, they'll listen to you. You're the King-Emperor's cousin: they'll regard you as one of their peers, if not more.' Patel's own origins were in the Gujerat peasantry.

'They are absolute rulers within their own states. I cannot order them to do anything.'

'No, but you can persuade them.' Again, Patel's brusque manner overcame him. 'They can choose to join Pakistan or India – or we send in the army.'

Mountbatten knew that this was not the answer. He also felt fairly confident that Nehru and the rest of Congress would put a brake on Patel if he actually tried anything so drastic. He was aware that even Menon had shifted uncomfortably in his chair each time Patel had mentioned using force. Nevertheless, the states would constitute a major problem if it were not resolved at an early stage. It was true that he knew the Indian princes. Many of them were personal friends, made on his trip to India twenty-five years ago, and reinforced during his term as Supreme Commander of SEAC during the war. He also knew how their minds worked. They had ruled feudally, for better or worse, for centuries. Some ran their countries well. One state imposed no taxes, for example, as its ruler had invested his private income so that the interest from his investments was more than enough to cover the cost of running his country. But in Kashmir, Hari Singh spent four million rupees a year on his palace and court, five on his army, but only three on his people. Mountbatten had to admit, too, that the British had not set as good an example as they might have done. Edwina had come to him in a rage only the other night. She had been shocked to discover a set of statistics gathered in 1939 which showed that, out of India's four hundred million souls, there were only 1,306 students of agriculture, 2,413 of engineering, and 719 of veterinary science. Only 150 technologists were being trained, and a mere 63 foresters. In 1939, only 3,651 Indians were medical students.

'Mr Patel,' he began, 'I will certainly talk to them. But you can't expect them to give up their sovereignty, their heritage, without offering something in return.'

Patel made a gesture of impatience. The princes had had a good run for their money, and in his view their day was done. To him, they represented an effete element which India would be better off without. 'Well, what do you suggest we offer them?'

'They should be permitted to keep personal possessions and fortunes, together with their status and titles.'

'Their titles will have no value,' scowled Patel.

'They have value to them. Take the line of least resistance, Mr Patel. India will have enough problems to deal with without creating more.'

Patel thought hard before replying. 'Very well. I'll accept that. But I want all of them to accede, or there's no deal.'

Menon cleared his throat. 'I should perhaps point out that we are talking about 565 people – the members of the Chamber of Princes.'

Mountbatten immediately saw the impossibility of the task in hand, especially given the time limit involved. He looked at his wall calendar. '54 DAYS LEFT TO PREPARE FOR TRANSFER OF POWER' it admonished.

'You must allow me a number of refusals. Say, fifty.'

'Three,' rejoined Patel flatly and without hesitation.

'Then I can't do it,' replied Mountbatten just as quickly. The man was impossible.

Patel thought for a moment. 'All right, I'll double it. Six. Bring me no more than six refusals and I guarantee that Congress will meet your proposals.'

'Then I shall ask Mr Menon here to make contact with the Secretary of the Chamber of Princes, and I will have a word myself with Yadavindra Singh, the Chancellor of the Chamber.' He looked at the neat little civil servant. 'I'm afraid I'm going to need rather a lot of help from you on this, V.P.'

'It's what I am here for,' smiled V.P.

Later, Mountbatten discussed the question with Nehru, who was, he thought, looking deeply tired and strained. He would have to get him away from that office of his and bring him up to Viceroy's House for a swim every now and then. They had met in the Viceroy's study, but Mountbatten had had enough of the room for one day and suggested a walk in the gardens. Nehru, too, was grateful for the opportunity to breathe some fresh air.

He agreed that the princely states would have to be brought into line, either with India or Pakistan, and he supposed that what would happen would be that those states with Muslim majorites would accede to Pakistan, and those with a Hindu majority to India. But the practice would by no means be as easy as the theory: the Nizam of Hyderabad, a miser reputed to be the richest man in the world, was the Muslim ruler of a vast land-locked country in southern India whose population of twenty-five million was predominantly Hindu. The Maharajah of Kashmir, on the other hand, was a Hindu who ruled a mainly Muslim people. The Nawab of Junagadh was in a similar position, a Muslim ruling Hindus. Less powerful than Kashmir or

Hyderabad, Junagadh nevertheless had a western seaboard which could be useful to Pakistan.

'I daresay we can deal with Junagadh if he tries to play us off against Jinnah,' Nehru considered. 'In any case, he's only really interested in his pet dogs. Do you know each of them has its own suite, with its own servants and a telephone by the bed? He mated a couple of them a year or two ago, and spent £60,000 on the "wedding". Sometimes our country passes even *my* belief!' He grew serious again. 'But if Hyderabad opted for Pakistan, that would indeed be a lump in the belly of India, and I do not think we would tolerate it. However, this is the difficulty. If we allow Junagadh to accede to Jinnah, we can hardly stand in the way of Hyderabad's accession to Pakistan. The principle for both countries is the same. On the other hand, by that same principle, Jinnah could hardly object if we gained Kashmir.'

'And what of Kashmir?'

'I cannot speak with detachment of my family's home-land. It will be difficult. Hari Singh will want to maintain his independence for as long as possible. I have no doubt in my mind that Jinnah has ambitions for it – after all, the "K" in "Pakistan" stands for Kashmir.'

They talked further, but without reaching any conclusion beyond establishing that the great majority of the leading princes, and all of the smaller ones, would accept the inevitable, and accede without raising an objection. Indeed, some of the younger rajahs were already active in central government. The old guard could not hold out for ever. 'I would be more worried about Hyderabad if it had a coastline,' was one of Nehru's parting comments.

'Won't you stay to tea?'

'No. I have another meeting, with Mr Birla and Mr Tata. You see, I am not so much of a socialist as not to realize how much the encouragement of private enterprise will mean to my country in the next few years.'

'Well, you mustn't keep India's two biggest industrialists waiting. Though Edwina will be disappointed.'

'I, too, am disappointed.' Nehru paused, aware that Mountbatten was watching him closely. 'Oh,' he continued seriously, 'there is one formal request I must make before I go.'

Mountbatten waited. Throughout their meeting, he had been aware that Nehru had something on his mind, something he was debating whether or not to raise.

'We have been discussing whom we should like to see as the first Governor General of the Dominion of India after 15 August,' Nehru told him. 'What would your reaction be, if I told you we would like to invite you?'

Edwina sat at her dressing-table and brushed her hair. She was furious. 'You always said you wanted to do your job here, and then get out as soon as it was done! I still think that's what we should do, before we get . . . too involved here.'

'Darling, it's a tremendous honour Nehru's offering me. And to be honest, it's a tremendous challenge. Added to which I could see the states safely integrated into the new Dominion by staying on. I think I owe that to old friends like Bikaner and Bhopal.'

The hairbrush continued to flick angrily through the rich auburn hair. 'You've already decided.'

'By no means. For one thing, it would be unfair to Pakistan.'

'How do you mean?' She stopped brushing, her anger deflected by interest, and turned on her stool to look at him.

'Attlee and the Cabinet feel, as I do, that both countries should have a joint Governor General, at any rate for their first years as Dominions, to handle mutual problems and to arbitrate when there's friction. It'll take a long time for these new countries to settle down amicably as neighbours, and as we're handing them both ready-made armies . . .'

'What does Jinnah think?'

'I'll give you one guess.'

'He won't commit himself?'

159

'Exactly! And I can hardly just walk up to him and ask him.' He paused. 'I hate to ask this, but could you bear to have him to dinner again?'

Edwina sighed. She had expected the Muslim leader to be his usual reserved self when they had first invited him to dine with them, and had foreseen an evening of unallayed boredom. Instead, Jinnah had completely monopolized all conversation and, to make matters worse, had seemed driven to prove his sociability by telling interminably long and excessively unfunny jokes.

'Do we have to, Dickie?'

'It's not so bad for you. You don't have to sit next to his sister, Fatima.'

Edwina smiled. She had partly recovered. 'All right. But let's pull the stops out and have it in the State Dining-Room. That'll flatter him, and besides, there's safety in numbers.'

The State Dining-Room was one of the show-pieces of Lutyens' monument to the Raj. The beautifully patina'd and vast rectangular dining-table stood in the centre of a huge blue-and-white Mogul carpet. Between the windows, and along the opposite wall, hung full-length portraits of former Viceroys, and of King George and Queen Elizabeth. Above them, below the domed ceiling from which five heavy chandeliers were suspended between the electric fans, bayonets and swords were fixed to the walls in displays. The concourse of people was resplendent, glittering dress uniforms mingling with silk evening dress and saris. At the centre of the table, Edwina and Mountbatten sat facing each other. Fatima Jinnah sat next to the Viceroy, and next to her came Rajendra Prasad, President of the Constituent Assembly.

Jinnah's eyes glittered with pleasure. His thin figure looked magnificent in the severe formal full evening dress which suited him so well. He was just coming to the end of one of his stories.

'. . . and so the other person said, why don't you try

pulling the stopper out?!' Fatima roared with laughter as her brother looked round the table for appreciation, but the others could only muster polite chuckles. Edwina had to nudge Pug Ismay, who had stopped listening some time ago.

'We must not let people think the Congress Party has a monopoly on humour,' smiled Jinnah. 'Although to listen to most of their speeches, one would think that they had.'

'Oh, Jinn,' laughed Fatima, 'that's very naughty!' She turned to the Viceroy. 'He is so funny, isn't he?'

'Most amusing.'

Jinnah had turned to Edwina. 'Did I ever tell you the one about the two men?'

Seeing her expression, Mountbatten came to the rescue. 'Before we hear it, there is something I'd like to ask you, Mr Jinnah. You were saying earlier that you doubted the impartiality of the All-Indian Editors' Conference, since it was entirely Hindu.'

'Yes.'

'But surely *Dawn* is a Muslim newspaper – and I believe that you are the proprietor.'

'That is so. But although you may not believe it, I have never exercised any direct influence over its policy. That is solely the responsibility of the editor. Fortunately, he has always been in total agreement with my views.'

Pug Ismay chuckled. It seemed that Jinnah could crack jokes after all, but he was silenced by the icy glare that met him from Fatima and her brother. Jinnah had not been joking in the least.

Later, in the drawing-room, Mountbatten drew Jinnah aside and gave him a large Armagnac. Stepping very softly, he confided to him Nehru's offer of the Governor-Generalship. The Muslim leader raised his eyebrows slightly, but did not otherwise express surprise, asking instead if congratulations were in order. Mountbatten explained that he had not accepted the post, and put forward his own argument for a joint Governor General. He was dismayed to see that Jinnah at once became aloof, his face masked by the unreadable expression that Mountbatten had come to recognize as the prelude to trouble ahead. However, Jinnah made a counter-proposal to the effect that, while he felt that both Pakistan and India should have their own Governors General, the Viceroy should stay on in the capacity of Supreme Arbiter. Mountbatten pointed out that there was no constitutional provision for such a post, and that in any case, if he stayed, he should prefer a more practical, less remote role to play. Jinnah received this frostily, remarked with glacial politeness that he had better not neglect his hostess any longer, and walked away in search of Edwina. Moments later Mountbatten could hear him remorselessly continuing his story about 'the two men'. 'Let us call the first one A, and the second one – eh – B.'

The dinner party had not been an overwhelming success. What was more, it was now clear to Mountbatten what lay behind Jinnah's obstructiveness. The Muslim leader intended to be Pakistan's first Governor General himself.

The Viceroy considered the difficulties. With himself as Governor General, and the pliable Liaqat Ali Khan as Prime Minister, Jinnah would be able to accord himself virtually dictatorial powers. On the other hand, if he overstepped the mark, he would oblige the British officers so vital to the establishment of the Pakistani Army to resign. Perhaps it would still be in Mountbatten's power to keep a brake on Jinnah, at any rate until the question of the states and the provincial boundaries had at last been settled. But the agreement was that India and Pakistan should not know precisely what the final boundaries, and those dividing the Punjab and Bengal, would be until immediately after Independence, when they would accept them unconditionally. Sir Cyril Radcliffe, the man responsible for drawing them up, would be working in total isolation from the moment he arrived in India, with only two Indian and two Pakistani magistrates to advise him. He would have no official contact even with the Viceroy. That was the agreement. What the reaction to the division would be he had no idea. And then there was the question of the princely states. It could be a very long time before that was settled. Kashmir's position in particular, with its strategic importance, and saddled as it was between the two new countries, might very easily prove to be a powder-keg.

Under these circumstances, Mountbatten considered, it would not be inconsistent with his duty to accept the Governor-Generalship of the new India. And there was something else. Partition was not welcomed by everyone. The Hindu extremist group, the RSSS, led by the sinister neo-fascist Veer Savarkar, looked bleakly upon events in New Delhi from its power base in Poona. And in Lahore, the sophisticated, elegant, Muslim-dominated town in the Punjab, Sikhs began to register their protest at the vivisection of their homeland, in blood. Lahore lay only thirty miles west of the Sikhs' holy city of Amritsar. Whirling their *kirpans*, their sacred swords, and hurling their blood-curdling new war cry of '*Sat Sri Akal*' – Death to Pakistan – into the air, the killer gangs of *Jathas* began to move on the Muslims of Lahore.

Mountbatten prayed that by 15 August it would not already be too late.

The middle-aged man in thick glasses and a formal three-piece suit climbed out of the aeroplane at Palam on 8 July. He felt as if he were walking into an oven. By the time he had descended the steps to the tarmac his shirt was sticking to his body, and rivulets of sweat ran down his back. The heat was his first and most enduring impression of India. 'It is so appalling that at noon it looks like the blackest night,' he recorded in his diary later, 'and it feels like the mouth of hell. After a few days of it, I seriously began to wonder if I would come out of it alive. I have thought ever since that the greatest achievement which I made as Chairman of the Boundary Commission was a physical one – in *surviving*.'

He was driven by fast car directly to Viceroy's House,

noticing on the way a confusing whirl of glimpses of the country he had come to divide. The shanty towns of the poor gave way to opulent suburbs, and these in turn to New Delhi and the last imprint of the Raj. Driving along the Raj Path, the magnificent avenue leading up to Viceroy's House, he noticed women washing themselves in the ornamental canals which flanked it.

He was driven straight to the Comptroller's bungalow on the Viceregal estate, where he was to be quartered for the duration of his stay. Now, having showered and put on fresh clothes, Sir Cyril Radcliffe was facing his first interview with the Viceroy. A lawyer of the most unimpeachable integrity, and by no means a man to fall victim to anybody's charm, Sir Cyril was quickly put at ease by the younger man's manner. He was reassured when the need for him to have an armed guard at all times was explained to him, and he understood the imperative need for secrecy until the work was completed and the boundaries drawn up. The best maps available had been put at his disposal and area offices had been organized for him in Delhi and Lahore. One question still bothered him, however.

'I should point out, Your Excellency, that in view of the immensity of the territory and populations involved, to pick out a credible frontier through the maze of small communities should take several years. I appreciate that this is a matter of some urgency, however, and I am ready to work with that in mind. But how long, exactly, do I have?'

Mountbatten smiled at him. 'We're all a bit pressed for time, I'm afraid.' He glanced at the calendar on the wall. 'It must be finished by 15 August.'

Radcliffe was stunned. 'I cannot hope to present anything remotely adequate in that time – ' he started.

'Nevertheless, I must ask you to try. You have exactly five weeks.'

Already, refugee camps were springing up on the outskirts of the capital. The trickle of Hindus travelling hopefully away from their threatened homelands had developed into a stream, and the stream flowed towards Delhi.

Edwina stood outside one of the tent dispensaries she had set up with Amrit Kaur to take some of the strain off the city's existing medical facilities, themselves hoplessly inadequate for the work they had to do. She paused for a moment longer, looking at the long, patient queue of India's poor, waiting. There was no time for rest. She turned and re-entered the tent.

Inside, Pamela was trying to explain to a woman how to give her baby medicine. 'Give him half a spoonful every four hours. Do you understand?' She bit back her frustration. With no common language, it was hopeless. 'Mummie, have you seen Rajkumari?'

Edwina was about to reply when Amrit Kaur entered the tent. To Edwina's surprise she saw that she had Nehru with her.

'This is a splendid place,' he said to her.

'So many people can't afford doctors. At least here we can give them some kind of basic treatment. But there are so many of them.'

'I know. I have just come back from Panipat. Gandhi wanted to visit the refugee camp there.' He paused, troubled. 'I cannot describe what I felt, seeing all those despairing, angry people. All looking to me to solve their problems. Some had their homes and crops burned. Others had lost their wives and husbands. It is terrible.'

'Why are they at Panipat? I didn't think the camp was ready.'

'It isn't. They scarcely have any food or water. But what could we do? The numbers took us by surprise. We had to put them somewhere.'

Edwina thought quickly. Panipat was only some thirty miles north of Delhi. 'They'll need water first of all, and proper sanitation. If there are no facilities, they'll have to be improvised.'

Nehru was silent. How tired he looks, she thought. In a different way, he needs help as much as all these people.

'Will you help, Edwina?' he said finally. 'I know how overworked you are, but you have dealt with these problems before – you have expert knowledge.'

Edwina smiled. 'Dickie isn't the only one who can work round the clock, you know.' She looked round the dispensary. 'I think things are pretty well organized here, and Pammy can hold the fort, can't you, darling?'

Pamela finished administering a spoonful of blue medicine to a tired infant. 'Of course, Mummie.'

'In that case, I think we'd better leave at once. You'd better come too, Amrit.'

In deference to the princes he was about to address, and also to identify himself as one of them, Mountbatten was wearing his full-dress white admiral's uniform together with all his orders and decorations, which outshone the most decorated maharajah there. From the rostrum he glanced around the small, semi-circular wood-panelled chamber at the gathering of maharajahs, rajahs, and nawabs, as the photographers took their final shots and filed out of the hall. Among those present were many *diwans*, prime ministers representing their own absent rulers. A few had boycotted the meeting altogether. Others, either uncaring, or unaware of its import, had simply not bothered to attend. The Viceroy sensed an atmosphere of tense uncertainty as he looked at the intent, proud faces around him. It was an atmosphere he relished. Confused, these men would follow any strong lead, provided that the demands made upon them were not too great. The room was stiflingly hot, yet Mountbatten remained cool and alert. He had no notes, and no prepared speech. He knew that direct, man-to-man contact, with no hint of plotting behind the scenes or the suggestion of any other authority at work than his, was the way to win the confidence of this disparate assembly, and to make them go in the direction he wanted them to. At the same time, he was aware that he was overstepping his brief in what he was about to do. He had no mandate from London to press the states into accession by 15 August, and he knew that Sir Conrad Corfield, the Political Secretary with responsibility for the states, would make things as difficult as possible for him. Against that, he had to balance the fact that Vallabhbhai Patel was now in charge of the States Department, with Menon as his secretary. Once again, the Viceroy was juggling eggs, and he needed to call up all his most eloquent powers of persuasion if he was to carry the day.

The princes settled into silence as he began. On a low key, he reviewed first of all the events and decisions of the past few months, before coming to the core of his argument. From the back of the hall, Alan Campbell-Johnson watched him with pride. The Viceroy was in his element.

'To be fair to you, the Rulers and Princes, I have submitted a draft agreement through which the two new Dominions will take overall responsibility for defence, external affairs, and communications. *But* – the central governments will have no authority to interfere with internal affairs or your sovereignty. I must make it clear that I have still to persuade the Government of India to accept such a tremendous concession, but if all of you are prepared to cooperate with me and are ready to accede, I am confident of my success. Remember that the day of the transfer of power is very close at hand, and if you are prepared to come, you must come before 15 August. I have no doubt that this is in the best interests of the states, and every wise ruler and wise government would desire to link up with the Dominion of India on a basis which leaves you great internal autonomy and which at the same time gets rid of your worries and cares over external affairs, defence and communications. I urge you to sign the Act of Accession.'

He paused for questions, still unsure of the effect he was having. Please God don't let it all come crashing down now, he thought. A tough, bearded maharajah in uniform stood up. 'Many of us have our own armies. Why can't we look after our own defence?'

'I'm not talking about internal security, but of defence against attack from outside.'

'Independence means being able to deal with both.'

Mountbatten nodded, his expression reasonable and reassuring. 'I know that your state is land-locked, Maharajah, but even if it were not my answer would be the same. If you imagine you can keep your independence by defying the Dominion that surrounds you, you'd better remember you would be in a permanent state of siege. You would be cut off from supplies, and sooner or later you'd run out of ammunition.'

The maharajah gave a brief nod, conceding the point, and resumed his seat. After a moment's hesitation, a small man in a black coat rose.

'Your Excellency, as *diwan* to my Ruler I am authorized to sign on his behalf. But,' he continued in embarrassment, 'he has given me no instructions.'

'Then why don't you ask him?'

The little man's embarrassment increased. 'He is on a ship sailing to Europe, and I am unable to contact him. I don't know what to do.' His words hung in the air. There was an atmosphere of expectancy in the chamber. All eyes were on Mountbatten. How would he react?

The Viceroy looked down at the flat top of the lectern in front of him. On it lay a round glass paperweight. He picked it up. 'Let me look into my crystal ball,' he said. What he was doing was a huge risk, but it was too late to worry about that now. He gazed intently at the paperweight for several seconds. Finally he set it down, and spoke confidently.

'Your Ruler says you are to sign.'

There was a moment's shocked silence. Then as one man the assembled rajahs and *diwans* of the Council of Princes burst into loud applause and laughter.

Not all the rulers signed the Instrument of Accession at once. Afraid that the socialist Congress Party would strip him of his chief amusements, flying, dancing girls and conjuring, delights which he had only just begun to indulge since he had only recently succeeded his father to the throne, the young Maharajah of Jodhpur arranged a meeting with Jinnah. Jinnah was aware that both Hindu majorities and geographical location meant that most of the princely states would go to India, but he was gratified by the thought that he might be able to snatch one or two from under Patel's nose. He gave Jodhpur a blank sheet of paper.

'Write your conditions on that,' he said, 'and I'll sign it.'

Elated, the maharajah returned to his hotel to consider. It was an unfortunate move on his part, for V.P. Menon was there waiting for him. Menon's agents had alerted him to what Jodhpur was up to. He told the young ruler that his presence was requested urgently at Viceroy's House, and reluctantly the young man accompanied him there. The urgent summons had been an excuse, and once they had arrived, Menon had to go on a frantic search for the Viceroy, and tell him what had happened. Mountbatten responded immediately. He solemnly reminded Jodhpur that Jinnah could not guarantee any conditions he might make, and that accession to Pakistan would spell disaster for his state. At the same time, he reassured him that accession to India would not automatically mean the end of his pleasures.

The maharajah appeared mollified, though he remained sullen, and Mountbatten left him alone with Menon to sign a provisional agreement.

'Here we are,' said the Indian civil servant politely, placing the document on the desk at which the maharajah sat. Jodhpur pulled a slightly cumbersome fountain pen out of his pocket and signed. Relieved, Menon was gathering up the paper when to his horror he saw that the young prince had unscrewed the barrel of the pen to reveal that it was also a miniature pistol. He was pointing it at the civil servant's head.

'You won't get me to give in to your threats as easily as that!' shouted the maharajah excitedly, waving his gun.

169

Fortunately, Mountbatten overheard the noise and hurried back into the room, quickly disarming Jodhpur.

'This is a jolly little thing,' he said. 'Where did you get it?'

'I had it made in my own workshops,' said the young man, then added, with rather more pride, 'It's a good trick. I am a member of the Magic Circle, you know.'

'Are you now? Well, as it happens, so am I. And I am sure you would want to donate this to their museum in England.'

Three days later, Menon was dispatched to Jodhpur to get the young man's signature on a full Instrument of Accession. This time the maharajah signed without demur, but afterwards, in desperate celebration, insisted that Menon get drunk with him. Whisky and champagne succeeded each other in inordinate quantities, and were followed by a banquet. By this time, the Indian civil servant simply wanted to crawl into a hole and die, but his ordeal was not over yet.

'Tell you what,' said the drunken maharajah, 'I'll fly you back to Delhi in my private plane.'

'That would be too great an honour.'

'Nonsense. We'll go now!' the maharajah insisted.

'Now . . . ?'

To his horror, V.P. found himself bundled into a tiny two-seater aircraft which rocketed off the runway and, once airborne, looped the loop twice before setting an erratic course for Delhi, where it landed at dawn.

'Tally-ho,' chirped the young prince, as Menon crawled towards the airport buildings and freedom.

In his shirtsleeves, sweating and uncomfortable, Sir Cyril Radcliffe sat at his desk by the window, checking a list of figures from the 1941 census. The numbers danced before his eyes, but he forced himself to concentrate. He made a note, and then turned to the maps spread out on a great table behind him. He had already discovered anomalies on them: river courses and the location of villages in some cases could vary by as much as ten miles. He sighed. Well, there were no other maps and he would have to do his best with what he had. An armed sentry passed the window as Radcliffe took out a handkerchief and wiped the sweat from his hand. He picked up a pen and added a quarter of an inch to the snaking line which on the map in front of him was gradually splitting the Punjab into two. A bead of sweat fell from his brow onto the map, and he dabbed at it with his handkerchief.

The soup kitchen at Panipat was nothing but a line of trestle-tables set up in what little shade there was. Wearily, Edwina doled her hundredth ladleful of rice and *dahl* from the massive tin cauldron into the wooden bowl held in front of her. For what seemed like hours, she had seen nothing but the food and the skinny brown arms holding out every imaginable receptacle to receive it. To rest her eyes, she looked along the queue of people still waiting to be fed. It did not seem to have diminished at all. An immaculate young British lieutenant stood at the end of the tables. She thought what a contrast he was to the ragged man standing in line near him. She looked again at the man. He was swaying, and she could only see the whites of his eyes as his pupils rolled up. Hastily handing her ladle to one of the volunteers working with her, she ran across to the man, just in time to catch him as he fell.

'I think it's dysentery,' she said to the lieutenant. 'We'll have to get him to a bed.' She looked up, blinking in the sunlight. The lieutenant had not moved. 'Are you going to help me or not?' she snapped, as she slung one of the ragged man's arms round her shoulder.

The lieutenant came to attention, blushing, then swiftly took the man's other arm. The man's odour made his stomach heave. How can she stand it? he thought.

The calendar on the wall by the map announced in bold letters: '7 DAYS LEFT TO PREPARE FOR TRANSFER OF POWER'. Around the table below it sat Mountbatten, with Nehru,

171

Patel, Baldev Singh, Jinnah and Liaqat Ali Khan. Pug Ismay and Sir Eric Miéville were in attendance.

'How near is Radcliffe to finishing?' Jinnah wanted to know. Like all the men in the room, he knew that they were now on the home straight, and like all of them, his mood was quiet and businesslike. The reality of power was not yet there, but they could feel its closeness.

'It's difficult to say,' answered Mountbatten. 'We deliberately have no contact with him, to avoid influencing him in any way.' He paused. 'At least the absorption of the princely states should now take place automatically.'

Vallabhbhai Patel grunted his approval. 'I must say you are to be congratulated, Your Excellency. To persuade all but three to sign is a remarkable achievement.'

'Yes, but Kashmir and Hyderabad are of the utmost importance. And I do not think we should underestimate Junagadh, either.' Privately, Mountbatten was worried that these key states should not yet have committed themselves.

'For the moment I think our best plan is to sign Standstill Agreements with them – we just leave everything as it was under the British, until they have had time to make up their minds,' suggested Patel.

'As long as that leaves them perfectly free to make their own decision when they do,' put in Jinnah, as ever overly quick in sensing intrigue.

Mountbatten rapped the table briefly. 'If we might move on . . . I have gone ahead with setting up a special Boundary Force, under the command of Major General Rees. With these continuing reports of unrest in the Punjab, we can't risk not having it ready to deal with any larger outbreaks of disorder after Partition.'

'You must be prepared, of course,' Jinnah conceded, 'but I assure you it is unnecessary, Your Excellency. Partition, I have always believed, is the answer to everything – the suspicion, the communal riots, everything.'

'I used to think so, too,' Nehru said, quietly. 'I pray you are right.' He was taking a cigarette from his case and was surprised when Jinnah leaned across and lit it for him.

'You will see,' Jinnah told him.

Patel shuffled the papers in front of him. 'There is another matter of some urgency on which we must make a decision,' he announced. 'The astrologers are very worried. They are very firmly against the date of 15 August for Independence.' He saw Mountbatten looking at him blankly and added gravely, 'To millions of Indians it is of profound importance.'

Mountbatten had begun to smile, but checked it. 'You mean, we should take it seriously?'

'With the utmost seriousness. The astrologers have predicted – unanimously predicted – 15 August as a disastrous day to begin Independence.'

'If that is true,' Baldev Singh said carefully, 'although I do not subscribe to such superstition myself, it could cause great alarm and agitation.'

Jinnah was lighting his own cigarette and clicked his lighter shut. 'It is all mumbo-jumbo. But since so many believe in it – ' He shrugged.

Mountbatten looked around the worried group at the table incredulously. 'So what are we to do? Are you telling me – actually telling me you want to postpone Independence to a later day?'

Liaqat Ali Khan shifted uncomfortably, placed his fingertips together and separated his hands, bringing them together again. 'Although, as Mr Jinnah has said, it is pure superstition . . . it might be wise to consider a postponement.'

Mountbatten dropped his pencil on the table and sat back. Now, he thought, I've heard everything. He simply could not believe it.

Nehru had been thinking and tapped the ash of his cigarette into the tray in front of him. Today it was nearly as full as Jinnah's. 'There may be a possible compromise that would satisfy the astrologers,' he suggested. 'We could proclaim Independence on 14 August – precisely at midnight.'

'Midnight?' Mountbatten queried. At least that would

not throw all the elaborate arrangements into total confusion, not to mention the innumerable administrative details which had all been geared for a transfer of power on the 15th.

'That would do it,' Patel confirmed. He was unable to conceal a certain relief. It was also noticeable in Liaqat Ali Khan and Baldev Singh.

They were all looking at Jinnah, who had crossed his arms, withdrawing from the discussion. 'It is of no consequence to me,' he told them. 'The creation of Pakistan will take place on the previous morning, in Karachi.'

Mountbatten was the most profoundly relieved of them all. He could just imagine the reaction of the British Government to his announcement of a postponement, and of the reason for it. He tapped the table. 'Very well, then, gentlemen, we are agreed. Independence for India will be proclaimed on 14 August, at midnight.'

The small private party in the state drawing-room of Viceroy's House was relaxed and informal, despite the setting. Edwina looked round the room, seeing Nehru chatting with Pamela and Alan Campbell-Johnson's pretty wife, Fay. Mrs Pandit was holding court to a group of the Viceroy's aides, and Dickie stood in conversation with Indira and Rajendra Prasad. The immaculate *khitmatgars* moved unobtrusively about the room, refilling glasses and proffering canapes. She wondered how these perfectly trained, inscrutable servants felt about the time that was coming.

Next to her, Amrit Kaur was drinking coffee. Edwina burrowed her spoon and tapped her glass with it. The room fell silent and all eyes turned to her. 'Relax, everyone – I'm not going to make a speech,' she smiled. 'All I want you to do is to raise your glasses with me to celebrate the formation of the Indian Nursing Council.'

'The Indian Nursing Council!' they toasted, calling out congratulations to her and to Amrit Kaur. They had reason to feel proud, as they smiled to each other. Together they had achieved in a few months what might otherwise have taken years of hotly disputed legislation.

'I have a toast, too,' Mountbatten said, raising his glass. 'Let us not forget the old Indian Civil Service, which is coming to an end. To the ICS for a job magnificently done. Without you, we couldn't have done it.'

George Abell responded to the toast, yet he felt oddly detached from the celebration. At least, India would be left with a highly efficient civil service of her own, he thought. The transfer of power had been an administrative miracle, but he had been acutely disturbed by the events and the pace of these past months. A brilliant and conscientious man, he had not enjoyed being part of a bulldozer team. The Viceroy, he conceded, deserved all praise, and yet he could not help wondering if Wavell's more cautious, steady approach might not have served better. Yet it was idle speculation, as Wavell's method would have taken much longer and the Indian leaders were not prepared to wait one day longer than necessary. He prayed that the harvest sown in haste would not be reaped in bitterness.

Abell's last months of intensive work had been crowned that morning by a knighthood at the Viceroy's hand. He had resisted the temptation to stay on, knowing that he represented the Raj too positively for the new Indian leaders ever really to accept him. A major phase of his life was coming to an end, and shortly he would be leaving the country he had loved so much and to which he had given so unstintingly. He was aware of a well of emptiness within him, and preferred not to think of the future.

Peter Howes was next to him. 'I must admit, these last few months have been an experience,' he said.

'Haven't they just,' Abell drawled, and they laughed.

Hearing the laughter, Edwina glanced around. Beyond George and Peter, she saw Nehru standing alone, detached and brooding. No one seemed to be paying him any attention. She wanted to go to him, but Indira was with her, and the poetess, Sarojini Naidu. They were congratulating Amrit Kaur on her appointment as Minister of Health in the new Government and Nan Pandit on being appointed Ambassador to Moscow. It was a great step forward for Indian women. She added her congratulations, excused herself and moved round to join Nehru, who was so lost in his thoughts that he did not notice her for a moment. Always unable to hide his feelings, it was his expression of sadness which had drawn her over to him. She could not understand it. 'You're being very quiet,' she said.

He did not reply at once. 'I find I have a lot on my mind.'

She hesitated, then, speaking softly, said, 'I'm glad now that Dickie accepted your offer. I'm glad we aren't leaving.'

He smiled briefly, at last. 'So am I.'

She felt almost ashamed at all the fuss she had caused. He was part of the reason she had wanted to leave, although she could never say so. Dickie had tried to persuade her, had commissioned Alan to write a paper with all the reasons for staying on laid out. He had even called in Gandhi to talk to her. Well, it was over now. 'When the excitement's died down,' she said, 'you mustn't be such a stranger.'

Nehru was very still. 'I have never been a stranger. I felt that from the moment we met. You and Dickie and I. I feel . . . I don't have to be with you to be near you.' He paused. 'Is that foolish?'

'No.' Her head was lowered. They were standing very close, and she wished suddenly that she could be alone with him. She looked up and smiled. 'It's all coming true, your new India. Aren't you happy?'

He could not return her smile. 'Yes . . . part of me is alight with happiness. But how can I rejoice when cities like Lahore are in flames?' The news had just been brought to him. 'Enchanted Lahore. I am afraid that when you fly to Karachi tomorrow, you will see fires burning throughout the Punjab.'

Sir Cyril Radcliffe was annoyed. He was in the middle of dressing for dinner, and now the Viceroy had sent these two minions to check up on him. Did the man never relax?

Alan Campbell-Johnson and John Christie saw that it was not going to be a cosy meeting.

'I'm so sorry to interrupt you,' Campbell-Johnson said, noticing his mood, 'but His Excellency is leaving for Karachi in the morning for the Pakistan Independence ceremony.'

'He's asked us to find out if you have finished, sir,' Christie added.

Radcliffe stared at the two young men. 'The Awards for the Punjab and Bengal are complete,' he told them. 'As are the main frontier lines. I have yet to finish the Sylhet district.'

'So they're not ready?' Christie asked, seeking confirmation. The point was that, with the weekend and the National Holiday of Independence Day, if they were not ready now, they could not be printed until the 16th.

'I have said so. If the Viceroy wishes to make an issue of it – '

'Not at all, sir,' Campbell-Johnson put in. 'All he said was, if he can't have all of them, he doesn't want any.'

As the Boundaries Commissioner saw them out of his bungalow with relief, Campbell-Johnson knew that the Viceroy would be even more relieved. He had been under pressure from both Pakistan and India to reveal the boundaries before Independence, but he had been reluctant to do so until after power had been transferred, when any dispute – and Mountbatten had no doubt that there would be dispute – would be a matter for the Pakistani and Indian governments to settle between them. The fact that the award to Sylhet was incomplete would give him the perfect excuse.

Dawn broke in Karachi over the now legal flag of Pakistan flying proudly from innumerable rooftops. Already, excited crowds were beginning to line the streets, and roads into the new capital were all but blocked as from all over the new country people streamed to see the inauguration of their leader. By the time the military band struck up 'God

Save The King' to welcome the Viceroy officially, for the last time, it was all but drowned out by the cries of *'Pakistan Zindabad'*.

As the last bars of the National Anthem faded, an English soldier hurried up to Mountbatten. Colonel William Birnie was Jinnah's Military Secretary. Whispering urgently, he drew the Viceroy aside.

'. . . eight Hindu fanatics, RSSS, we think, with hand grenades, stationed somewhere along the route . . .' Edwina overheard as she followed them. 'We've no idea who they are, so we can't pick them up. Be next to impossible in the crowds anyway. But we know for sure they plan to strike during the drive back from the Legislative Assembly to Government House.'

Mountbatten's face was set. 'What does Mr Jinnah have to say about this?'

'I'm afraid he's unwilling to cancel the procession, sir. But obviously he doesn't want to risk your life. We've made arrangements to get you to Government House by another route, and you can meet him there.'

'Nonsense, Bill. I'll go with him. Oh, don't look so shocked, I'm not being foolhardy. Those chaps won't be so keen to kill *me*. Anyway I can't let him go alone, can I?'

'Well, I'm coming with you,' Edwina broke in.

'Oh, no. Not this time,' Mountbatten told her firmly. 'We'll follow the arrangements to the letter, which means you go with Fatima in the car behind. And I'm going to make damned sure your driver stays *well* behind!'

The Legislative Assembly's small, shell-shaped chamber was packed. Throughout the ceremony Mountbatten had been aware of one thing above all others. It was the aura that now hung about Mohammed Ali Jinnah. Invested as Governor General, sitting on his gilded throne, he had reached his apotheosis. Mountbatten could think of nothing so much as a butterfly emerging from its chrysalis. Not that Jinnah had physically changed. The only difference in him was that that he wore the *sherwani* and *churidars* of his

178

nation, but the Baluchi jacket and trousers were no less immaculately cut than the former Savile Row suits, and the monocle still hung in its place. If a difference could be discerned it was one of inner light, detectable only through the eyes and the set of the mouth. Cold though his power was, Jinnah radiated it. He was like some bleak king come home after long exile.

Within an hour the Investiture was over. Amidst the applause the two principal actors in the drama looked at each other. The time for the drive back to Government House had arrived.

Outside, the light and the noise were enough to make them recoil. The shouting made up a cacophony of sound in which the only recognizable word was 'Zindabad', and as they climbed into the waiting open Rolls, the roar of the motorbikes of the outriders drowned even that. Slowly, inexorably slowly, the cavalcade moved off. To Mountbatten it seemed as if they were driving down a tunnel, a tunnel made up of half a million cheering people, their brown faces contrasting with the blinding white of their dress. And amongst that dense mass – eight men . . .

Mountbatten scanned the faces of the crowd, knowing as he did so the futility of it. Even if he identified the face of a would-be killer, it would already be too late. He grasped the hilt of his sword. Beside him, Jinnah sat impassively, but although there was no expression on his face, Mountbatten knew that in his mind he, too, was beseeching the driver to go faster. The Muslim's hands clenched the jade holder, but for once Jinnah was too preoccupied to light a cigarette. Despite the blazing sun, white in the sky above, Mountbatten was aware of terrible cold. He knew that there were plain-clothes policemen in the crowd, working desperately to locate the waiting assassins – but how could they find them in this press of people, so tightly packed that they could hardly move? Mountbatten looked away from them. He had faced death before, but on equal terms, and not passively like this.

Finally, finally, around the bend of a long slow curve,

179

Government House came into view. Mountbatten calculated the distance: five hundred yards . . . two hundred . . . one . . . .

The Rolls purred to a halt at the foot of the steps. Behind them, the sentries closed the high iron gates against the cheering crowd. They were safe.

He felt a hand on his arm. Jinnah was trembling, and in his eyes was something Mountbatten had never seen there before, relief and a deep and genuine affection.

'They must have lost their nerve. Thank God, I have brought you back alive,' said the new leader of Pakistan, his voice unsteady.

Mountbatten laughed in the release of tension. There was obviously no changing Mr Jinnah. 'My God,' thought the Viceroy, 'it was *I* who brought *him* back alive!'

He had ordered no ceremonial. All over India the Union Jacks were lowered at dusk, as they always had been, to the haunting call of the bugle. And at dusk on 15 August there was no special addition to the ritual. Only in their minds did the British acknowledge the red, white and blue flag of their motherland would fly no more over the magic continent it had dominated for two hundred years. But at Lucknow, where the flag had not been struck for ninety summers, a soldier cut down the flagpole, and others cemented over its base. No other flag should ever fly there.

In Viceroy's House, the bustle continued: one of his last orders as Viceroy was that all the insignia of the Raj, on ashtrays, on bookmatches, on writing paper, on seals, should be removed before dawn. Even the great coat-of-arms in the Durbar Hall was to be screened off. At the stroke of midnight the building itself would change its name to Government House.

In his study, Mountbatten and Campbell-Johnson had tied the last paper into the last dispatch box and locked it.

'Is there anything else, sir?'

'No, Alan. Off you go.'

He looked at the clock on the wall. He had not thought about what he would do as midnight struck. He toyed with the idea of joining Edwina, but decided that he would prefer to be alone, here in the study, where so much of it had happened. He thought of Gandhi, who had left for Calcutta a week earlier to attempt to quell the rioting which had already broken out there. Some would rejoice but many would weep that night, the old man had told him. He smiled ruefully. Gandhi would be asleep now. Not even the dawn of Independence would shake him from his inexorable routine.

The last Viceroy crossed the room to the calendar. '1 DAY LEFT TO PREPARE FOR TRANSFER OF POWER', it read. He tore the sheet off and dropped it neatly into a wastepaper basket. Below, the next sheet read simply, 'Friday 15 August 1947'. He moved over to the small drinks tray and poured himself a glass from the only bottle there, a vintage port. Then he turned and stood before the portrait of George VI that hung in the room. He raised his glass, and came to attention.

'The King-Emperor,' he said, for the last time.

Not half a mile away in the massive red-and-white sandstone pile of the Legislative Assembly, Jawaharlal Nehru was addressing a crowded Congress. His tone was quiet and even, but the excitement in his breast reminded him of his favourite dream, in which his weightless body would soar effortlessly through the air.

'. . . a moment comes, which comes but rarely in history, when we step out from the old to the new; when an age ends, and when the soul of a nation long suppressed finds utterance.' He paused and looked around the men he was addressing, men at whose side he had laboured for this moment for nearly thirty years. And he thought of Bapuji, peacefully asleep with Manu and Abha near him. He drew himself up, touching the rosebud in his buttonhole. Gone was all his tiredness. His voice became stronger, more vibrant.

'Long years ago, we made a tryst with destiny, and now the time comes when we shall redeem our pledge, not wholly or in full measure, but substantially. At the stroke of the midnight hour, while the world sleeps, India will awake to life and freedom.'

# Part Two
# Dawn of Freedom

# EIGHT

Except for the chiming of the clock, there was total silence in the Legislative Assembly. Eight . . . nine . . . ten . . . eleven . . . twelve . . . . As the sound of the last stroke died away, high in the gallery above, an Indian dressed in *khadi* slowly raised a great, rose-pink conch shell to his lips. As he blew upon the ancient, primitive trumpet, which the people of India had used since before the time of Buddha to salute the dawn, the silence gave way to a murmur, which in turn gave way to an exultant shout. 'Long live India! *Jai Hind*!' Outside, the waiting crowds took up the cry, which rose to a triumphant climax as Nehru appeared to them, waving from the wide balcony of the Legislative Assembly building.

In Viceroy's House, which she must remember from now on to call *Government* House, Edwina paused on her way to Mountbatten's study to listen. Around her there was a flurry of activity as Viceregal staff and Indian servants alike hastened to remove the last remaining vestiges of the Raj. Nearing the study, she nodded to Alan Campbell-Johnson, who was striving to contain the patience of a waiting gaggle of pressmen and photographers.

'Any time now, gentlemen. I can't tell you exactly when, but Mr Nehru and Mr Prasad will be making their way here as soon as the business at the Assembly is completed.'

She knocked softly on the door of the study and entered. In contrast to its appearance of the past five months, it now seemed empty and orderly, a room without a function. Her husband stood by the window, looking out into the night.

Edwina could not conceal her elation. 'It's like Piccadilly Circus out there,' she laughed. 'And it wouldn't have happened if it weren't for you. Well done, darling!' She paused, sensing the quietness of his mood. 'What are you doing here all alone?'

He did not move or turn. 'I'm sorry, I just wanted a minute or two by myself, after all the bustle. And I was thinking – it's not only the birth of India. It's the death of the British Empire . . . . Oh well, there was no getting away from it.'

She went to him, and said gently, 'I don't suppose your great-grandmother would have believed it possible.'

'I wouldn't myself, a few years ago. But the world has entered a new age. Two world wars have seen to that.' He had been looking out of the window still, but now he turned to her, smiling, breaking the mood.

'By the way, congratulations.'

'Oh? On what?'

'I've just had a call from London. I've been elevated to an Earldom. Which means that you are now Countess Mountbatten of Burma.'

Edwina was not the kind of woman who set great store by such honours, but she knew what it meant to Dickie, and in her heart she acknowledged the honour to which this great gesture of thanks from the British Monarchy and people testified. He took her hand, and kissed it.

'I've been meaning to tell you something else. If I haven't said it before, forgive me, but my silence didn't mean that I hadn't realized how tremendously hard you have worked since we've been here, and how effectively. Well done.'

She squeezed his hand and looked warmly up at him. Rare praise from him meant a thousand times more to her than becoming a countess.

There was a knock at the door, and Peter Howes, Mountbatten's personal ADC, looked in. 'Sorry, sir. The Press are piling up ten deep out there.'

'Good luck, darling,' said Edwina. 'I think I'd better leave you to receive India's first Prime Minister by yourself. But – congratulate him for me.'

She was gone. Mountbatten nodded to Howes. 'It looks

186

as if space is going to be at a premium in here. We'd better push some of the furniture back.'

The Press poured into the room, directed by Campbell-Johnson and Howes, and wedged themselves around the walls. Nevertheless the small room was soon so crowded that it was only with difficulty that they managed to keep a space clear round the desk. Mountbatten stood by it to welcome his two distinguished guests as, similarly dressed in *achkans* and Congress caps, they entered the room.

'Mr Nehru, Mr Prasad – welcome to Government House.'

In his elation, Nehru had totally forgotten that the Press had been invited to the ceremony. Now, as Prasad stood opposite Mountbatten, who was simply dressed in a white linen suit, India's first Prime Minister perched himself unselfconsciously on the corner of the desk, all formality forgotten. In fact, Nehru thought, it all seemed like a dream. He could scarcely bring himself to believe that everything, from this room he was sitting in to the jails in which he had languished for nine years of his life, no longer belonged to the British, but to his country. He looked across at Rajendra Prasad, who was obviously thinking the same. Grinning broadly, he was stumbling over every second word in his prepared speech.

'Your Excellency – er – Lord Mountbatten, that is, we come here for a unique occasion – er – for a unique reason . . .' The President of the Constituent Assembly was behaving like a shy sixth-former on Speech Day. He blinked in the glare of the photographers' flash bulbs. 'Let us – er – let us gratefully acknowledge the consummation of the historic tradition and democratic ideals of the British race.' He beamed. It was true, Nehru thought; this man, Mountbatten, had by his actions and personality brought an end to colonial power more honourably than anyone had before him in history. It would redound to his own, and his country's, credit for ever. Prasad was looking lost.

'Independence,' prompted Nehru, smiling gently.

'Ah, yes,' muttered Prasad, continuing more formally.

'Three-quarters of an hour ago, the Independence of India was proclaimed. At the same time, the Assembly unanimously endorsed the request of the Indian Government to invite you, sir, to be our country's first Governor General.'

Mountbatten bowed as the photographers unleashed a fresh battery of flash bulbs. 'I am proud of the honour, Mr Prasad, and will do my best to carry out your advice in a constitutional manner.' He shook hands with Prasad, and then with Nehru, warmly, smilingly. The Prime Minister bowed in his turn and produced a large vellum envelope, with a flourish.

'May I submit to you the portfolios of the new Cabinet?'

'Thank you, Mr Nehru.' He laid the envelope on his desk and unstoppered the decanter of port which stood there on its silver tray, filling three glasses. 'I'm sorry I don't have anything more suitable to offer you, but I feel that I would like to propose a toast.' He handed the two Indians their glasses. 'To India.'

The three men raised their glasses and drank. Then Nehru said, quietly, 'I, too, should like to offer a toast.' Turning to the portrait which hung on the wall and drawing himself erect, he raised his glass once more. 'His Majesty, King George VI.'

Deeply moved, the Governor General drank the toast.

'You'd better get some sleep, darling,' said Mountbatten. 'We'll have to be up in two hours, and tomorrow's probably going to be the biggest day of our lives.'

'Yes.' Edwina was sitting up in bed. She was really too excited to sleep, and did not dare take a pill. She knew that tomorrow – well, today now – would call on all her resources. 'I think it was amazing of him to toast the King.'

'After all the British have put him through. Few men have the greatness of spirit to be so generous in victory.'

'What's in the envelope he gave you? It looks terribly important.'

'It does, doesn't it? It's the list of the new Cabinet ministers.' He opened the envelope, and as he felt inside an expression of surprise, then of amusement, came over his face.

'What is it?'

Mountbatten laughed. 'It's empty! In all the excitement, "someone hath blundered"!'

Mahatma Gandhi had taken up residence in a run-down dwelling in the Muslim quarter of Calcutta called Hydari House. He awoke shortly before 3.00 am on the first day of India's freedom, as was his invariable habit, to say his morning prayers and take breakfast. But his routine was almost the only thing unchanged on that 15 August – his routine, and that of the lives of the millions of peasant farmers in whose hands he felt the future of India rested, and most of whom had never in their lives felt the presence of the British Raj directly. He awoke and drank from the tin bowl of water Abha proffered him, as Manu massaged his legs and feet, the one sensuous luxury he permitted himself, and even that not without a practical purpose. The Mahatma's customary mode of transport was walking. He listened, far and near, to the sounds of the great, dirty, cruel, vibrant city celebrating. Even Pyarelal, his faithful secretary, was smiling.

'Today they laugh,' said the Mahatma. 'Tomorrow they will weep.' He pushed away the bowl of curds which Manu was offering him. 'No food. Today I will observe as a day of sorrow. Now India is divided, and it is not a time to rejoice. It is a time to pray.' He looked around at his companions, and composed himself, closing his eyes, and pressing the tips of his fingers together.

'Listen to us, Thy children, in their need. A great evil is about to fall on our land. Turn the hearts of Thy people, my brothers and sisters, aside from it.

> Hé Rama, King of the universe,
> Who makes the sinner pure,
> Who is both Ishvara and Allah,
> Who gives his blessing to all.'

The liveried heralds in their scarlet and gold raised their silver trumpets to their lips and sounded, as they had done for twenty Viceroys before him, the State entrance of Earl Mountbatten of Burma to the Durbar Hall. No point of the pomp and circumstance of the former Raj was missing as the new Indian Chief Justice, Dr Kania, solemnly swore the Dominion's first Governor General into his Office. There was a moment of tension as a photographer's flash bulb exploded, but if they had suspected a bomb, the Mountbattens gave no sign of it. In solemn state, they moved outside, across the magnificent blue-and-gold Mogul carpets, where in the keen sunlight of early morning a vast throng awaited them. Delhi had never seen such crowds. Laughing and cheering, an ocean of brown figures clad in white surrounded the open landau as it drove them the short distance to the Council House, where the new Governor General would address the Assembly. As they left, the band played 'God Save The King', followed by the new anthem, *'Jana Gana Mana'*. The music was almost drowned by tens of thousands of voices lifted as one: *'Jai Hind! Jai Hind! Jai Hind!'*

Resplendent in his white uniform, with full orders and decorations and the dark sash of the Garter slung across his chest, Mountbatten spoke to the new Government of India. As he did so, he picked out faces in the crowd: Nehru; Vallabhbhai Patel, smiling for once; Prasad and Kripalani; his old friend and stalwart advisor, V.P. Menon. His voice was measured and grave, but in its tone there was a note that told them how he shared their triumph.

'From today, I am your constituent Governor General, and I would ask you to regard me as one of yourselves, devoted wholly to the furtherance of India's interests . . . . The tasks before you are heavy. The war ended on this day exactly two years ago. That was a moment for thankfulness and rejoicing, for it marked the end of six bitter years of destruction and slaughter . . . . But in India we have achieved something greater – what has well been described as "A Treaty of Peace without a war" . . . . What is happening in India is of far more than purely national interest. Not only Great Britain and the sister Dominions, but all the great nations of the world will watch with sympathy the fortunes of this country, and will wish it all prosperity and success.' He paused, remembering the man who at this moment must be in all their minds. 'At this historic moment, let us not forget all that India owes to Mahatma Gandhi – the architect of her freedom through non-violence. We miss his presence here today, and would have him know how much he is in our thoughts.'

At this, he was interrupted by the loudest applause and cheers. Outside, the sun shone down on the crowd, as many of them waved photographs of the Mahatma. The mounted cavalry, in their glittering ceremonial uniforms, lined the Great Place at the beginning of the Raj Path, the magnificent avenue which reached from Government House and the Secretariat Buildings down to the solidly imposing All-India War Memorial arch, a pale sandstone, monolithic arch of triumph guarding Princes' Park and the delicate, pencil-thin memorial statue to King George V. The superb horses, as disciplined as their riders, stood like statues themselves, only here and there the twitch of a tail or a harness-rattling shake of the head, with a proud snort, dismissed the too-insistent flies. And then, a fresh wave of cheering broke from the tumult of people as, out of the haze, and magnificently attired, the first outriders of the Camel Corps appeared, the stately beasts stepping with a measured, loping tread the length of the Raj Path.

'In your first Prime Minister,' continued Mountbatten; 'Jawaharlal Nehru, you have a world-renowned leader of courage and vision. His trust and friendship have helped me beyond measure in my task. Under his able guidance, assisted by the colleagues whom he has selected, and with the loyal cooperation of the people, India will now attain a position of strength and influence, and take her rightful place in the comity of nations.'

At his concluding words, the Assembly rose to applaud him.

Even for the short drive back to Government House, the host of impressions were almost too much for Edwina to drink in. She had hardly slept, but now any tiredness was forgotten. The crowd – almost impossibly – seemed to have swelled, and mingled with the cry of '*Jai Hind!*' they were shouting 'Mountbatten *ki jai!*', even '*Pandit* Mountbatten!' – bestowing on him a name of honour second only to Mahatma. She drew in her breath in admiration at the parade of elephants which they passed, in their impressive white-and-gold headcloths, and above the Council House, gracefully waving in the gentle breeze, the flag of the new nation unfurled. In a life it was given to few people to lead, she thought, this day must surely be the crowning moment.

And the day continued in a kaleidoscope of sound and colour. After a state luncheon, they attended a party for five thousand schoolchildren in the Roshanara Gardens, enjoying the side shows with the excited children and sharing their own daughter's delighted horror at a fakir whose trick was to appear to bite the head off a living cobra he held in his hands. They left, distributing candy and sweets in the traditional way, and returned to Government House with barely time to change before the last drive to the last ceremony of the day, which was also its climax: the official raising of the flag of India near the War Memorial Arch in Princes' Park.

All attempt at following the official programme of parades and speeches had been swamped by the enthusiasm of the people. The planners had reckoned on a crowd of thirty thousand and had been confronted by one approaching a million. On the dais by the flagpole Nehru stood waiting with Prasad and Patel. The band was playing with all its might, but even those closest to them could not hear them. In the throng of people sitting on the dusty ground around him, Nehru suddenly spotted Pamela Mountbatten, picking her way towards him. Everywhere the good-humoured Indians gave way to her, but now her way was blocked by the sheer density of people. She thought of a man on a bicycle she had just passed, unable to go forwards or backwards, or even to dismount! And everywhere she had witnessed the extraordinary sight of women holding their babies high above their heads to prevent them from being crushed.

'Come on, Pamela,' called Nehru at the top of his voice.

'I can't get across!'

'Just walk over them – they won't mind!' Seeing her hesitation, he laughed. 'Don't be a silly girl – just take your shoes off and come on!'

Gingerly, she began to move across the carpet of people as they reached up their arms to steady her and propel her forward. As she gained the dais and Nehru helped her up, the crowd gave an excited roar. The Mountbattens' state landau was approaching. But twenty-five yards from the dais, it stopped. The horses could no longer find a way forward, and would not tread upon the mass of humanity surrounding their hooves.

'Clear the way!' shouted Nehru angrily to his fellow citizens, but his anger faded at the sight of their beaming faces. Some had come from far outlying villages; some had walked all night to be present for this great moment of their country's history. They could comprehend nothing but their own happiness. Caste, race and creed were forgotten. And those who were too far away to come were celebrating at home. All over India, every town, every tiny village, was marking this glorious day.

'It's no good,' called Mountbatten. 'Just forget the speeches and get them to hoist the flag.'

Mountbatten stood to attention in his carriage as the soldiers at the base of the pole hoisted India's flag into the sky. With the approaching evening, a breeze had got up and the flag immediately rippled proudly open. It was banded in saffron, white and green, and at its centre was the wheel of Asoka, the last great king of India to unite his nation 2,200 years ago, whose wheel represented *karma*, destiny. As the flag flew the breeze brought with it a light shower of rain, and in the last rays of the sun a rainbow arched its way across the burning clouds, echoing the colours of the new national flag. The crowd roared like the sea breaking upon a rocky shore. After two hundred years, India had regained her freedom.

Nehru managed to conduct Pamela to the carriage.

'You'd better come with us,' Mountbatten advised, helping to hand them both up. 'We might be able to draw off some of the crowd.' He glanced over the thousands of people around them with an experienced eye. There was no less good nature in the crowd's ebullience, but although the rainbow had been a magnificent omen, it had thrown the crowd into a fever of excitement and people risked being crushed. With Nehru perched on the folded front hood and Mountbatten standing, responding to the delirious cheering, the carriage moved slowly off. By the time it reached Government House, it looked, as Edwina remarked, like Noah's Ark, for Nehru was not the only extra passenger. On the way, the Mountbattens had rescued from under its wheels four Indian women and their two children, the wife of a Polish diplomat and a left-wing Indian news photographer, who was later to say gratefully, 'Finally, after two hundred years, Britain has conquered India.'

If she had, then it was the Mountbattens' doing. But to the north-west, in the Punjab, the mood of celebration was tainted.

The railway station at Amritsar had been deluged for days by thousands of Hindus fleeing eastward from Pakistan's half of the Punjab. Although Sir Cyril Radcliffe's boundary lines had not yet been published the people knew roughly where they would cut across their homeland, and the trains had been packed with refugees, crowding not only the carriages, but clinging in hundreds to their sides and roofs. The platforms at Amritsar were crowded, too, with people waiting to meet the trains from Lahore, frantically calling out the names of lost friends, relatives and children as each train pulled into the station.

The express which arrived on the afternoon of 15 August was eerily silent. Nobody clung to the outside of its carriages, and the only people visible were the soldiers on the footplate with the driver and fireman. Their faces were ashen, and a bloody bandage had been hastily tied round the head of one of the men. The engine slowed with a violent hiss of steam from under its heavy wheels, cloaking those on the platform in a white mist. As it cleared and the noise of the train gave way to silence, they waited expectantly, but not a single carriage door was flung open. The people looked at each other in confusion, until one of them walked cautiously forward and opened a door, falling back a moment later with a strangled cry. As he did so, panic spread through the crowd, and calling out the names of loved ones they rushed along the train, opening other doors, to reveal the same terrible sight. The passengers had been hacked to pieces. Only a few badly mutilated survivors remained.

On the last carriage the Muslim *goondas* who had done the killing had chalked, 'This is our Independence gift to Nehru and Patel.'

That evening, as yet unaware of the horror that had taken place in the Punjab, the Governor General gave a garden party in the grounds of Government House. The trees sparkled with fairy lights, a small orchestra played by the Round Pool, and *khitmatgars* in immaculate white uniforms circulated drinks. The routine of the place had not altered at all in the past twenty-four hours: what had changed was the roles the principal characters were playing. Vallabhbhai Patel came smilingly towards Mountbatten in the company of an elderly, bald-headed, bespectacled Indian who might have been Gandhi's brother. Mountbatten only knew Chakravarti Rajogopalachari in passing, and was glad of the opportunity of meeting him properly at last.

'Rajaji has just accepted the post of Governor of Bengal,' said Patel. Mountbatten looked at the elderly man, aware of the problems he would soon be facing. The principal city of Bengal was Calcutta.

'The city authorities are afraid that Partition may bring even worse violence,' Rajaji was saying. 'Fortunately, Gandhi is still there, and his call for peace and unity has prevented all but a few isolated incidents.'

'We must pray that both sides there keep listening to him,' said Patel, seriously. A practical man, he had steeled himself to face the bloodshed which they all feared Partition would bring in its wake, as bewilderment and panic among the peasantry and the slum-dwellers found their focus on those who were felt to be to blame. The Muslim would strike down the Hindu, and the Hindu, the Muslim.

'At least by tomorrow the uncertainty over the boundaries will be over. Sir Cyril Radcliffe has completed his work and the new maps will be published tomorrow.' Mountbatten was speaking with an ease which in his heart he did not feel. He knew that whatever happened, the reaction of both Pakistani and Indian leaders to Radcliffe's boundaries would be angry.

'I shall be afraid to look at them,' said Rajaji, quietly. Mountbatten nodded to him, and, making his excuses, walked over to where Peter Howes was trying to attract his attention.

'I thought you might like to know at once. I've just completed the arrangements for Sir Cyril's flight home,' said Howes.

'Good. I don't want him here when the boundary awards are handed out.' He looked across the glittering assembly of people. On the other side of the garden, Edwina was talking with Nehru.

'I know you can do it,' she was saying. 'And now your hands won't be tied by London any more.'

He smiled. The events of the day were beginning to catch up with him and he was tired, his mood again turning sombre. 'That is a blessing – but it also a very great challenge. You see, the worst thing about the Raj was not that we were not our own masters, but that Britain only wanted our raw materials. It had no need to develop our industries, and at one time, as you know, we even had to import cotton goods from England.' He paused, thinking. 'At the moment we find ourselves in a position where we cannot compete in world markets. We cannot survive unless we industrialize, build up our exports, and improve our agriculture. It will take many years and – ' He interrupted himself, looking at her. 'I'm sorry. I have no right to lecture you in this way.'

'You don't have to apologize. I understand.'

He nodded and said, simply. 'That is what makes you . . . Edwina.'

She paused before replying. 'I should be apologizing to you, Jawahar. I don't really know a great deal about politics. I know what I feel is right and wrong, and that's about all. But I *do* know that, whatever's to become of India, the real responsibility will be yours. And I am very proud to know you, and to be your friend.'

In the crumbling house on Beliaghata Road, Gandhi was playing host to an incongruous guest. The plump middle-aged man in his expensive but ill-matched check sports shirt and shorts was sweating nervously. The wheel of destiny had turned in an unexpected direction for Shaheed Suhrawardy, the corrupt Muslim ex-Chief Minister of Bengal, who exactly a year earlier had interpreted Mohammed Ali Jinnah's Day of Direct Action so conscientiously in Calcutta.

'The city is like a volcano, Mr Gandhi,' he said, wetting his lips. 'It will erupt at any moment.'

Gandhi smiled calmly. 'A volcano is a force of nature,' he said. 'It is uncontrollable. The city is made up of human beings, each one capable of restraint, love and reason.'

'But you can't reason with people who have become fanatical!' Suhrawardy looked around as if for reassurance at the bodyguards who had accompanied him. When he had held power in Calcutta, he had made sure that the city police force was mainly recruited from Muslims. Now, half of them had fled. Too late he realized that in the mood of bullish confidence of one year ago he had released a monster which was now out of his control. And Independence meant that there were no longer even any British troops empowered to keep the peace. The Hindus were building themselves up to take a terrible vengeance for the Day of Direct Action. Now, with the anniversary at hand, they were at boiling point. Only Gandhi's presence in the Muslim quarter was preventing wholesale slaughter, and even so Suhrawardy wondered how strong the old man's hold over his people might remain. But Gandhi was his only hope.

'How long are you going to stay here?' he asked.

'As long as I am needed.'

'Do you guarantee that?'

'Until Calcutta is safe from communal violence, I will stay,' said Gandhi, quietly. 'Provided you stay here at my side and work with me.'

'Of course! I'll back you all the way.' Relieved, Suhrawardy started to get up to leave. It had been easier than he had expected.

Gandhi held up a hand, detaining him. 'I don't think you quite understand what I mean. I mean literally at my side. We will live here together, and we will have neither the police, nor soldiers, nor your bodyguards to protect us.'

Suhrawardy's eyes widened in their fat pockets in his face. 'But if the Hindus find out that I am here, alone, they'll tear me to pieces.'

'That is a risk you must choose to take,' said Gandhi implacably. 'We shall face them together.' He paused. 'Either that, or we lose Calcutta.'

The Muslim heaved himself from the floor and walked to the window. Cautiously looking out, he saw that a large crowd had already gathered, waiting in the darkness. Behind him, one of his men drew a heavy black revolver from the holster on his hip. 'Put that thing away,' he snapped. 'It won't help us now.' Then he turned once more to the Mahatma. His shoulders slumped. What demon had led him here to this terrible old man?

The crowd whispered expectantly at a movement spotted behind the windows of Hydari Houise. Moments later, Manu and Abha, each bearing a lantern, came softly onto the rickety verandah. Then a growl of anger broke from the people waiting in the garden as Gandhi walked onto the verandah in his turn, his right hand resting for support on Suhrawardy's shoulder. The Mahatma held up his hand for silence, stilling the furious muttering of the mob. Suhrawardy blinked as the sweat ran into his eyes. If this failed, he'd be dead and the whole Muslim quarter would be ablaze in a matter of minutes. In the darkness he could see the glint of the kerosene cans some of the people in the crowd were holding.

'My friends,' said Gandhi. 'I have decided to remain for the time being in Calcutta. And together, Mr Suhrawardy and I will work to bring back peace.'

'He's a murderer!' came a cry from the darkness.

'Get him! Muslim dog!'

The crowd surged forward angrily, but another gesture from Gandhi was enough to stop them in confusion. 'I have given him my word that he will not be harmed,' said the old man, sternly.

A young Hindu broke from the front of the mob. 'Why do you protect him?'

Shaheed Suhrawardy found his voice. 'Gandhiji can teach us all to be brothers. Let us rejoice in that good fortune!'

The young Hindu sneered. 'You talk of brotherhood now that it suits you. It was not so a year ago!'

'But we should not begin that insanity again now!'

'Who started the killing, Suhrawardy?'

Suhrawardy faltered, 'We all . . .'

A number of voices interrupted him from the crowd. 'Answer the question!'

The Muslim drew in his breath. On his shoulder, he felt the pressure of Gandhi's hand increase a fraction. Strength

199

seemed to flow into him. He bowed his head, but his voice was clear as he said, 'I did. I was responsible.'

The reaction of the crowd now was one of shocked silence. They could have dealt with a coward and a liar, but this was not the man they had come to kill. One whispered to another, 'What good would it do?' 'Would it bring back our loved ones?' 'No, it would take even more from us.' Gandhi waited patiently for them to fall silent again before speaking.

'This is a time to forget our past errors and build for the future. Do you want to lead your children into tomorrow with hands stained with blood? Or will not Muslim and Hindu greet the challenge of the coming years together? If the flames of communal riots envelop the whole country, how can our newborn freedom survive? But if Calcutta can return to reason and brotherhood, it will be a guiding light to show how all India can be saved!' It was so dark now that he could not distinguish the crowd beyond the glare of the lanterns his great-nieces were holding, but out of the warm night rose a chant which was almost a prayer.

'Gandhiji! Gandhiji! Gandhiji!'

The meeting in the Council Chamber of Government House was worse than Mountbatten had imagined. He was only thankful that the brooding presence of Mohammed Ali Jinnah was not there. On Independence, the Muslim leader had taken a vow never again to leave Pakistan.

Sir Cyril Radcliffe's Boundary Awards were certainly impartial, thought the Governor General, ruefully. Both Pakistanis and Indians seemed equally incensed at them. Two hours earlier he had handed the two groups of leaders copies of the new maps, asking them to reconvene when they had studied them to give their comments and opinions, and already the discussion had degenerated into a brawl. The Indians were furious that Chittagong and the whole of Sylhet had gone to East Pakistan. Liaqat Ali Khan and Rab Nishtar were equally angry that Calcutta was ceded to India, along with Gurdaspur, an unimportant little Punjabi town just to the east of the Ravi River. Gurdaspur had a small Muslim majority, but the Ravi had provided a natural frontier which Radcliffe had gratefully followed, thus placing the town in India. But it was not just the loss of Gurdaspur which infuriated the Pakistanis. Its possession provided India with that country's only possible land access to the still undecided state of Kashmir, with its predominantly Muslim population. Mountbatten had heard from London that Radcliffe was so disgusted by the botched job he felt he had been forced to make, that he had used the only sanction available to him and waived his fee. Well, there would have been this row even if he had had years to complete his task. He remembered the vivisection of eastern Europe thirty years earlier. What country was ever artificially divided except in pain?

'When we asked for Partition, I never expected it would create an East Pakistan unable to survive!' shouted Liaqat. 'We have the areas that produce the jute, but all the factories to process it, and the port to ship it, are in Bengal!'

'And what are we to do with factories with no raw materials to supply them?' Patel wanted to know, hammering the table in rage.

'What can I say for the Sikhs?' asked Baldev Singh numbly. 'We knew when we opted for Partition what the likelihood was, but it is as nothing compared with the reality. The boundary cuts through our heartland. It cuts off our irrigation canals from their source of water. Five million of our people are left in Pakistan, and five in India! What can I say?' He turned his eyes to the others, moist with tears. 'The Punjab was the granary of India. Now, the crops stand ungathered as men turn aside to destroy each other; and without cooperation, there may never be a harvest again. The united Punjab fed millions; now, divided, millions may starve.'

Patel, ever practical, broke the silence which followed. 'The monsoon's late this year, and that may be a blessing in disguise. There may yet be time to save at least some of

201

the crop – the wheat if not the rice. But first we have to decide how to put a stop to the violence.' He rose, glaring around the room as he emphasized his point. 'I tell you this: once these maps are made public, the destruction and the panic we have seen already will seem about as violent as a cricket match.'

'People who thought they were safe in India will find they are in Pakistan,' said Kripalani.

'And millions of others who rejoiced at the creation of Pakistan will find themselves trapped in India,' retorted Rab Nishtar.

'Did you say "trapped"?' shouted Patel.

'Gentlemen, please!' Mountbatten raised his hand for silence. 'Before we continue this discussion, I think we should have a situation report on the border areas from Field Marshal Auchinleck.'

Claude Auchinleck had sat listening in grim silence. Now he stood to deliver his report, but as he did so he knew that despite the Punjab Boundary Force, despite the Joint Defence Council which Mountbatten had set up between India and Pakistan, no power on earth would stem the violence until it ran out of momentum of its own accord. Well, that was not his business. As Supreme Commander his duty was the dismantling and dividing of the Indian Army into its Pakistani and Indian halves. Please God that the two new armies would not end up fighting each other. However, he confined his report to the facts he had received in dispatches from an increasingly beleaguered and despairing General Rees, whose fifty-five thousand men could not hope to maintain order over a terrain the size of the Punjab, with millions of people already on the move. He told them that there was scarcely a village for fifty miles on either side of the frontier that was not on fire, that Amritsar was in flames and that one-tenth of Lahore had been razed to the ground. He told them that it was common now for all the occupants of refugee trains to be slaughtered, and that crop-burning had become so commonplace that soon there would be no harvest left to worry about anyway.

'It is civil war,' whispered Liaqat into the silence that followed his report.

'Worse than that,' replied Auchinleck gruffly. 'It's an upheaval of nature.'

After the meeting, Mountbatten drew aside Pug Ismay, who had been present throughout. In a moment like this, he needed someone to sound out, if not to confide in, and Edwina had remained in Bombay where they had both been to see off the first contingent of British troops returning home. She had decided to make a tour of inspection of hospital and medical conditions in that teeming city.

'Was all this inevitable, Pug? Was there really nothing we could have done to prevent it?' he said, as he poured them both whiskies and soda in the privacy of his study.

Ismay answered without a moment's hesitation. 'Absolutely nothing, old chap. When we came here, India was a ship on fire in mid-ocean with ammunition in the hold. What we faced was a desperate need to put the fire out before it actually reached the ammunition. We had no other option.'

At the same time, far to the north-west, a young Muslim stood by the door of his grandfather's hut in his village in the eastern Punjab. His wife and two small children stood by him, surrounded by a few small bundles, containing all the possessions they could manage to take with them. The young couple kept looking around them in fear. The rest of the villagers had already gone. The young man appealed to his grandfather, who sat in front of his hut, placidly smoking his hookah for one last time.

'We can't stay here, grandfather! We'll be killed.'

Ahmad looked up at his grandson's worried face. 'Well, then, go if you must, and go with my blessing. But I have lived here all my life, and I am not leaving now.'

'Grandfather, Sikhs destroyed Fazilkhar last night. It is only two miles away. Today it will be our turn. We must try to get to Pakistan.'

'Go, then,' said Ahmad. 'I shall put my trust in Allah.'

His grandson hesitated only a moment longer. Then, slinging his bundles onto his back and taking his older child by the hand, he turned with his wife and started to make his way across the maize field, where already the corn was hanging heavy and neglected on its stalks.

They did not look back until they had reached the other side. The young man could feel the sun on his neck. The field was on a slight incline, and they could see over the whole village. To their horror, they saw that it was already burning. The blue-turbaned Sikhs must have arrived only minutes after their departure. Men were racing across the field towards them. They gathered their children to them and ran.

Ahmad was already dead. They had sliced his throat open with a *kirpan* and then cut off his penis, placing it in his mouth in a gesture of contempt.

The two lines of people stretched as far as the eye could see. Heads bent, backs bowed under their few possessions, the refugees tramped slowly along in the cloud of dust they raised. Here and there a more fortunate family drove a bullock cart forward, piled high with furniture and cooking pots. Many carried a sack of seed grain, the only legacy they could take to start a new life from the small farms they had been forced to abandon.

There was no difference at all in the two lines of people, except that one was marching east, and the other west. One was Hindu, one Muslim.

Earlier columns had shouted to each other as they passed on the road. Sometimes there had been flare-ups, but sometimes the marching peasants had called to each other the names of farms and villages, the ones they had been forced to abandon, hoping, in the helplessness of their humanity, to bequeath them to their fellow-sufferers, or to exchange an eastern farm for a western one. For the most part they were bewildered by what the politicians had done to their lives. The great migration was one of monumental futility. Now the columns passed each other in silence, heads bowed in the dust, mirror-images of suffering; the children in each tragic caravan passing each other wide-eyed, too tired to be curious or to offer to play. Only a few of them even showed any interest in the powerful car which crawled past them along the line, and was gone.

The car travelled many more miles that day before it stopped at the burnt-out village that had been Ahmad's home for seventy years. It was now some days since the Sikh raid, and the buzzards and the flies had done their work. Two grey-faced, shattered men climbed from the car, looking about them in a disbelief which none of the sights they had seen in their ghastly tour of the Punjab had been able to shake them from. One of them stooped to pick up something at his feet. It was a child's toy, a broken wooden horse.

'We never imagined anything like this when we agreed to Partition,' said Nehru. 'We argued, but we were brothers. How could this have happened?'

'Our people have gone mad,' muttered Liaqat Ali Khan, bitterly.

'Here perhaps. But not in Calcutta.'

'It is a pity there are not two Mahatmas,' said Liaqat, simply.

Not long afterwards, they drove into a neighbouring Sikh village. They were expected, and the village elders were waiting for them by the Council Tree at its centre. Nehru knew that in all probability it was the men of this village who had destroyed their Muslim neighbours. The Sikhs, always a proud warrior race, stood apart from Hindu and Muslim alike by their religion, which however owed far more in its origin to Hinduism than to Islam. Their militant leader, Tara Singh, a deceptively benevolent-looking seventy-one-year-old, had encouraged a merciless guerilla war against all Muslims on Sikh land in the Indian Punjab since Partition. Now, as he confronted the haughty elders of this village, Nehru trembled with anger. He had challenged them with the atrocity he had just seen the result of, at which the Chief Elder had shrugged, passing a hand over the net in which his silky white beard was rolled, and said, dismissively,

'We must protect ourselves.'

'Yes, you must protect yourselves! But there is a world of difference between that and going out and killing your neighbours' families!'

'Where are the Sikhs to live when they come here from Pakistan? Our people there go in fear of their lives. We do not need Muslims here!'

Nehru forced himself to continue to reason with the man. He remembered what Gandhi had said, that the only way to teach was by example. In fact, Nehru would have dearly loved to snatch a *lathi* from one of his bodyguards and beat this cold-hearted old man over the head with it. He restrained himself because he knew that they were all caught in a vortex of violence, and because he remembered the reports he had read of the ambushed Hindu and Sikh trains coming into Amritsar, running with blood.

'India is a democracy, not a communal state! Every citizen has equal rights, and the Government will protect those rights to the full limit of the law!'

The old men gazed back at him blankly. One of them ran his fingers along the hilt of his *kirpan*. He made no attempt to disguise his thoughts from Nehru: show me a Muslim, and I'll show you a dead man.

'Very well,' snapped the Prime Minister; 'since argument doesn't convince you, maybe this will. If I hear that one single Muslim village in this area is attacked after today – if I hear that one hair on their heads has been touched, I will have all of you brought to wherever I am – and I will personally give my bodyguards the order to shoot every one of you on the spot!'

The newspapers were calling it the Miracle of Calcutta. In the two weeks since Gandhi had asked Shaheed Suhrawardy to live at Hydari House with him, the Muslim and Hindu citizens of one of the most dangerous and violent cities of the world had lived together in perfect amity. The overpopulated, disease-ridden cesspit of a city was teaching India a love which had been forgotten in the lush, open farmlands of the Punjab. But Gandhi's message of amity and peace was not welcomed by everyone.

It was about midnight when Suhrawardy was awakened by the sound of running feet. Then there was a scuffling on the verandah as some of the homeless Muslims who had taken shelter there were roused from sleep. Somewhere in the house a door slammed, and there was the sound of a man moaning in pain. Suhrawardy was fully awake by now, and a clatter of stones hurled at the house, followed by a stream of obscenities, brought him to his feet. He made his way out of the room in which he was sleeping towards the front verandah. As he did so, two men scuttled past him into the rear of the house. One was nursing a bloody face, the other bleeding from a deep cut on the shoulder.

Shaheed Suhrawardy was not a conspicuously brave man, and now he was going out to face an unknown danger alone, without his bodyguards to protect him. But the last sixteen days in Gandhi's company had taught him more about life, and – more importantly – about himself, than he had thought there was left to know. He came out onto the verandah, where a handful of Muslims were still crouching in terror, and peered into the darkness. There must have been a dozen of them out there in the garden. In the light spilt from a lantern he caught a glimpse of an orange-pink armband.

'RSSS!' he thought, a tremor of fear running through his heavy body. But he had Gandhi to protect, and he was not the man to be pushed around by a gang of little fascist thugs.

'What are you doing here?' he bellowed into the darkness. 'Don't you know who lives here?'

'It's Suhrawardy – the butcher!' yelled someone. Immediately, a hail of stones shot out of the darkness and smashed onto the verandah around him. When he looked up again, the RSSS men had come closer, but at that moment a lamp flickered in the doorway and Manu came through it. Normally quiet and meek, this slight, nunlike girl who had devoted her entire life to the Mahatma was quivering with anger.

'Are you mad?' she shouted. 'This is the house of Gandhiji!'

We don't care whose house it is,' snarled the leader of the gang. 'We want the men who came in here.'

'What men are those, my children?' the Mahatma asked, as he appeared.

At Gandhi's arrival on the verandah the atmosphere changed. The Muslims there relaxed slightly, and Suhrawardy stood up to his full height. Even the RSSS men were cowed. But only for a moment.

'Two Muslim bastards! They attacked us and ran away in the dark.'

'If you mean the two men whose wounds I have just come from tending, I am surprised that the ten of you were not a match for them. But even if they did attack you, do you think that I would hand them over to you? Come back when you are less angry.' Gandhi finished speaking and was turning to go. Used as he was to the indignities of British jails, it had been over thirty years since any Indian had treated him with less than the greatest respect. He was quite unprepared for what happened next.

'Look at him! "Mohammed" Gandhi!'

'Muslim-lover!'

'Why don't you go to the Punjab and save some Hindus?'

The jeering words froze him on the spot. He was about to reply when the leader of the gang stepped forward quickly, hurling a half-brick at the old man's head. Shaheed Suhrawardy did not stop to think. He threw himself in front of Gandhi and the brick caught him on the temple, cutting a deep gash. Groaning, he stumbled at Gandhi's feet, as the other RSSS men began to pick up jagged stones to throw. Abha was hit as she came onto the verandah, but she was followed by Pyarelal Nayyar and some dozen or so of Gandhi's disciples. Seeing them, the RSSS rushed forward. Their leader was grasping a *lathi*.

Gandhi looked around him in confusion. How could these people never learn? A thousand might give the example of brotherhood, and then three would come and destroy it. Bodies, slashing and hitting at each other, whirled around him. He could not move. Above the noise he could hear police whistles, and Manu's voice, calling to him as if in a dream, warning him. Dazed, he turned to see her struggling to reach him; then another movement caught his eye. Suddenly beside him, his face contorted with hate, the RSSS leader was raising his *lathi*. He was young; he couldn't be much more than twenty. The Mahatma looked at him unflinchingly. He had lived and preached *ahimsa* all his life, and if his time had come to die, it had come indeed, and no raising of his hand against his attacker would save him from what was the will of God. For a fraction of a second, meeting the calm and steady gaze, the RSSS man faltered. Manu was just in time to snatch his arm and deflect the blow as he brought the *lathi* crashing down.

By now, police were rushing into the garden, and the Hindu extremists fled into the night. Pyarelal and Suhrawardy took Gandhi by the arms and gently led him back into the house. Outside, the noises of the chase gradually receded, and then there was nothing but the velvet silence of the Indian night.

# NINE

They sat together, the tea in its silver service on the low table between them untouched. Each of them was grey and drawn from a mixture of tiredness and anxiety, and they knew they had been right to stay on after the transfer of power, and that, despite what their enemies whispered, it had nothing to do with enjoying the benefits of high office with none of the responsibility or work. Yet they had not reckoned on the pressure being quite as great as it had become. Edwina had only that morning arrived back from Bombay, where not only had she driven herself through an arduous timetable involving visits to seven hospitals, clinics and dispensaries, three colleges, a remand home and a hospital for young women, and attendance at four social welfare committees, but also a gruelling tour of the notorious Bombay slums, where she had walked for hours in the mud and filth to see how best the sanitary conditions of the wretched inhabitants might be improved. All this in three days, and in pouring rain, for the first lourings of the monsoon were upon India. Mountbatten, his usual optimistic mood beaten down by the news which was coming in not only from the Punjab, but Calcutta, looked anxiously at his wife. If she continued to work at this pace, and in such extreme conditions, she could not hope to avoid a breakdown.

'Is it true about the Punjab? I heard Jawahar's broadcast on the wireless last night. Surely it can't be so bad?' Her voice was numb.

He reached out for his teacup, but still did not touch it. 'I'm afraid it is.' He looked at her again, carefully, and decided to tell her. If he didn't, she would only find out from somewhere else. 'If anything, it's worse,' he continued, cautiously. 'Quite apart from the killings, which just go on and on despite all the efforts of the Boundary Force, we already have two hundred thousand people in refugee camps, and all the reports indicate that another five million are getting ready to leave their homes.'

She looked up. '*Millions?*' They were barely a week into Independence.

'Whole populations are on the move. But that's not all. Gandhi's hold on Calcutta has broken.' He paused, thinking about it. Gandhi had performed an almost impossible task: for over two weeks his presence had maintained peace more surely than four military divisions might have done. The force of his spirit had been able to go where the soldiers never could, down the labyrinthine back alleys of the slums, into the little forgotten squares and tea-houses. Above all, into people's minds. But the pressure had been too great to be contained, even by such a man as the Mahatma. From the reports he had had, he gathered that Hindu extremists had started it. There had been an attack on Gandhi, and then Muslim houses and shops had been looted and burned. The Muslims retaliated, and terror had been unleashed. The miracle of Calcutta was over. He had seen an appalling photograph which showed a dead rickshaw *wallah*, his neck broken, twisted across the footboard and seat of his vehicle. He had not shown it to Edwina. He did not want the same image burnt into her mind, although he recognized the foolishness of his desire. She had seen far worse than that photograph, in reality.

'It's difficult to know where to turn,' said Edwina in desperation. 'To know where one is needed most.'

'You must rest.'

She laughed. 'I know, and so must you, but how can we? Look, things have improved considerably since Amrit Kaur took over the Health Ministry, but their resources are *already* stretched to the limit. Can you imagine what it'll be like, even by the end of August? No, I must go where I can do most good, and that means the refugee

211

camps in the Punjab. I can update that report I did in May. My God, that seems a lifetime away, now!' She paused, taking his hand. 'When I get back from Amritsar, then perhaps we both ought really to think of taking a few days off.'

Mountbatten returned the pressure of her hand, but said, 'I don't think you should go to Amritsar.'

'If I don't, we won't know for sure what they need up there – in the way of food, and medical supplies. Even if we can just get a shipment of antibiotics, of cholera serum, and train a handful of people to administer them – '

'Where you're proposing to go is at the very heart of the violence,' he interrupted her.

She looked at him in amazement. 'You're not going to forbid it?'

Mountbatten knew it was hopeless. He could control the destiny of millions more easily than he could this woman's will. 'How could I do that? But I want you to be aware of the danger. I'll give you what protection I can.'

'As little as possible, Dickie. I won't find out anything if I'm surrounded by armed guards. Besides, it's not the British they seem to hate. Only each other.'

'So far.'

'Well, I am Countess Mountbatten, the Governor General's wife.'

Mountbatten was silent, thinking. They had stoned Gandhi. 'Will you go over into Pakistan?' he asked.

'If I don't I'll only be doing half the job, won't I?'

'It might be harder to get the facts you need there. Don't forget that we are on one side now. We serve India's interests, not Pakistan's as well.'

'Even so, Dickie . . .' She smiled at him, gave his hand a final squeeze, and then stood up. Despite her tiredness she was looking radiant again, he thought. God, how she seemed to thrive on work. But how long would it be before her mind drove her body beyond its limits?

'Where are you going?'

'To telephone Amrit. She really ought to come with me.'

The monsoon refused to break in the Punjab. The unremitting heat bored into men's minds and the fury boiled there. Driving down the main street of Amritsar, Edwina was once again reminded of the worst days of the Blitz. But it was worse here. No air-raid had brought the havoc that everywhere met her gaze, yet the destruction was no less for having been caused by the simple, direct violence of the human hand. Shops and houses stood gutted by fire, still smoking after a night of violence. Bodies lay twisted like discarded rags, for there was no one to move them. The streets were deserted. 'It's like a city of the dead,' Muriel Watson, her personal assistant, whispered. They tied handkerchiefs round their faces to mitigate the stench. Edwina looked at Amrit Kaur, sitting behind the army driver, her eyes hollow with grief. It would be better to concentrate on practicalities. She touched Muriel's arm. 'Come on. We'd better make a list of supplies we need sent up from Delhi to the emergency hospitals here.'

On Monday, 1 September Nehru walked swiftly into the Governor General's study at Government House. He held a long cable from Chakravarti Rajagopalachari, now installed in Calcutta as Governor of Bengal. It did not take him long to communicate its contents to Mountbatten.

'A fast?'

'A fast to death.' Nehru paused briefly. 'He has said, "Either there will be peace in Calcutta, or I will die."'

Mountbatten assessed the news quickly. He knew that this was not an idle threat. Through his long years of fighting for a unified, Independent India, Gandhi had developed the fast as a simple tool for gaining his ends. Like all his ideas, the use of the fast as a weapon was one whose roots were to be found deep in Indian culture. Strict rules governed it: it could never be used for selfish purposes, but only in the interests of the common good. Mountbatten was well aware of the strength of Gandhi's will – years ago, he had fasted for twenty-one days in the same cause, of Hindu-Muslim friendship. But that had been in 1924. Gandhi was now approaching his seventy-eighth birthday, and years of severe abstinence had taken their toll of his body.

'He is in no condition to fast, Jawaharlal!'

'I know. Apart from anything else, his mental state . . . He is no longer sure that India needs him.'

'But if he dies – '

Nehru did not need to answer. They both knew what that would mean.

'Does he realize what would happen?' continued Mountbatten. 'He must be talked out of it!'

'Rajaji couldn't do it, and he is Gandhi's oldest friend. No, the Mahatma has decided; and it will be as he says. The violence will cease, or he will die.'

'Then we had better start praying. His death will start a fire which will engulf all India.'

'We have averted disaster before.'

'You mean Jinnah's threats in the past? They are like a boy blowing a toy trumpet compared to this!'

They called it a relief camp. To Edwina, as she wrote about it in her report afterwards, she was tempted to describe it as a concentration camp.

The local Pakistani authorities had been reluctant to let them cross the frontier, despite their mandate from the Joint Defence Council, but the shadow of the Viceroyalty still fell heavily across little bureaucrats and Edwina had prevailed. Together with Amrit Kaur, her ADC and her assistant Muriel Watson, she had made the short journey from Amritsar to Lahore. The two once-noble cities, formerly so close, not only in terms of distance but in terms of culture, trade and language, were now a world apart. The camp for non-Muslims just outside Lahore was little more than a cattle-pen, its overcrowded population of refugees sitting stinking and apathetic in their stockade, with little food and water, and no shelter from the pitiless sun.

Guarded by armed soldiers, jumpy young men ready to fire at the slightest sign of disturbance, they looked at the visitors with eyes that were already empty of curiosity or hope.

Edwina remembered the immaculate and suave Pakistani officers, a captain and a major, who ran the camp and who had greeted her with a studied indifference just this side of politeness. The captain had seemed embarrassed and kept fiddling with his new uniform, the colour of whose tunic was barely discernible as olive green under the crowd of brightly coloured badges sewn onto it. It was the major, in whose face, with its silky black moustace and liquid brown eyes, Edwina found it difficult to read anything but self-regard and a total lack of interest in his charges, that she had to confront. Any appeal to his humanity was, she quickly realized, futile. She had established one thing. Food and fresh water had been delivered to the camp, but they had not been distributed.

'Why not?'

'We are undergoing some difficulty in locating them,' replied the major, blandly. 'When, and if, we do, they will be handed out.'

'But these people are starving!' Amrit Kaur had protested.

He had not even looked at her. 'They are refugees . . .' He shrugged, wiping imaginary dust from his brass-and-bamboo swagger-stick. 'Since they've decided to leave Pakistan, they must be prepared to put up with a little hardship until it can be arranged.'

Even at the recollection of this, Edwina became so angry that her pen trembled as she continued to write her report.

'Do you know to whom you are talking?' she had said. She had not shouted. Her voice had remained level and firm, but there was an edge to it that would have worried a king, let alone an arrogant, provincial army officer. 'Rajkumari Amrit Kaur is Minister of Health in the Dominion of India Government. She is here at the express request of the Joint Defence Council.'

The major was on his guard now. He had stopped polishing his baton and looked at her guardedly, but still attempted to fight. 'Of course I know. My orders were to show you round.'

'Then you also know that I am Countess Mountbatten of Burma. Now, you will locate and distribute the supplies that have been delivered, and you will undertake to arrange immediately a permanent and adequate water supply.' Her voice had carried to the young soldiers, who had neglected their guard duties and turned to stare. 'Unless you have done all this within two hours,' she continued, 'I will personally telephone your Governor General, Mr Jinnah, in Karachi, and demand to have you arrested for corruption, and deliberate obstruction. Do I make myself clear?'

The major all but buckled physically. His captain had been looking at his own feet for some time. Now they both stood stiffly to attention. 'At – at your orders, Your Excellency!' One or two of the soldiers had lowered their rifles completely, positively gawping by now. The major rounded on them. 'Come with me! Get my jeep! Move!'

He had scurried away with his captain and half a dozen of the guards. Well within his time limit, Edwina had been gratified to note, he had brought up the supplies and had had two of the standpipes from his own barracks diverted to the camp. She felt that the threat of Jinnah's wrath would be enough to keep this bully at least in line for the future, but privately she wondered what she would have done if the major had called her bluff.

On the other side of the continent, the crowd of Hindus and Muslims that had gathered in the garden of Hydari House was growing. Gathered in brotherhood, some prayed, some wept, and some simply stood in mute appeal as they watched the figures seated on the verandah. Suhrawardy and Rajagopalachari had called a meeting there with other Hindu and Muslim leaders. In a room inside the house, Gandhi lay still on his straw pallet, gently attended by Manu and Abha. For twenty-seven hours now he had

taken nothing but water and bicarbonate of soda, and he
was growing steadily weaker. His two grandnieces watched
over him anxiously. His breathing was so light and shallow
that only the occasional flicker of his closed eyelids betrayed
the fact that he was still alive.

Under the broken roof of the verandah, one of the
Muslims was saying desperately, 'Gandhi is our only shield.
What will become of us if he dies?'

'The Hindus have heard his appeal,' answered a lean
man clad in a *dhoti*. 'We beg him not to risk his life any
further.' But even as he spoke, they could hear the sounds
of gunfire, and anguished shouting two streets away. A
ripple of tension ran through the waiting crowd.

'The guns answer for him,' said Rajaji, slowly. The old
man's face was serious, intent. 'The Mahatma has lit a
candle for all to see, but still he cannot reach the hearts of
the mindless thugs who are looting and rioting.'

Voices called from the crowd. 'We will swear brotherhood! We pray for Gandhiji night and day!' Shaheed
Suhrawardy heaved his bulk upright and answered them
sternly.

'What use are your prayers here? You should go, and fill
the streets of the city with them! All of you, Muslim and
Hindu – join together and go out onto the streets: warn the
people that he is on the verge of death!'

Rajaji stood too, adding his voice to Suhrawardy's.
Strange, he thought, they see us together in friendship who
have been enemies until now, and yet they do not follow
our example. 'Tell them that he is dying to save all of you,
as he saved thousands in the Bihar. You, and only you, are
his life or death!'

For a long moment the crowd stood silent, uncertain.
Then, at the front, a young Muslim in an astrakhan cap
linked his arm with his Sikh neighbour. The two men
smiled to each other, and turned, arm-in-arm, to walk out
of the garden and along the street in the direction of the
fighting. Gradually, others followed their example, Hindu
with Muslim, Muslim with Sikh, in twos and threes,

linking arms and marching out of the garden; and as they did so, they said to each other '*Ek ho* – unite – Hindu, Muslim, *ek ho!*', their voices growing bolder as more and more of them followed each others' example.

At the gate, the young RSSS leader whom Manu had so narrowly prevented from killing the Mahatma only days earlier, stood with his gang and watched in disbelief.

Ahmad's grandson came over the rise in the land in front of him cautiously. For a week now he and his little family had been wandering through the devastated countryside, sheltering in fields during the day and struggling as far as they could at night, eking out their meagre supply of food with maize from the unharvested fields. Several times since they had escaped from the Sikhs who had burned his village and murdered his grandfather had they almost fallen foul of other marauding gangs, once only escaping notice by covering themselves with fallen maize stalks and lying flat, hardly daring to breathe. They had been forced to abandon most of their belongings, and his younger child would not stop crying, but now his eyes widened in hope. Ahead of him, on the road beyond the ridge he stood on, the refugee column crawled along in its shroud of dust. He turned to beckon urgently to his wife, crouching with their children in the gully below him. As she struggled up the slope, he reached out his hand to her, smiling reassuringly. They would be safe now.

The third day of the fast, Gandhi lay on the verandah, his eyes closed, his skin soaking up the gentle warmth of the early morning sun. Soon it would be too strong, and they would have to carry him inside, but now it was a friend to his exhausted body. He could sense the sheltering presence of Shaheed Suhrawardy, seated near him. The Muslim was quietly, hesitantly repeating half-remembered verses from The Koran. Behind him, he knew, Manu and Abha would be sitting, spinning cotton as he had taught them.

The anxious crowd, now double its original size, had

returned to watch over him in the garden. Now, there was a sudden disturbance in its ranks. He felt Suhrawardy tense beside him and forced himself to open his eyes. At first the sunlight dazzled him and he could only see dark, blurred forms separating themselves from the people at the front, and making towards him. As his pupils adjusted to the light he saw eight or nine young men standing near him. One of them was speaking. His words seemed to come from far away.

'Remember us? . . . Do you recognize me?'

The voice was not threatening – but taut. Frightened. Gandhi blinked again in the sunlight which flashed on the metal rims of his glasses.

'Yes,' he said slowly, looking up at the intense young face. It would have been handsome, had it not been for the smallpox scars etched deep into the cheeks. 'You are the children who attacked us here.'

The RSSS leader hesitated, glancing briefly at his men for his reassurance. 'Is that why you started this fast?'

Gandhi spoke slowly. 'It was to stop the killing.' The effort of conversation was tremendous. He closed his eyes. He heard the voice almost snap off its next anxious question, to Suhrawardy.

'What's the matter with him? Is he going to die?' Gandhi felt the big Muslim shift his weight by him, caught the sharp aroma of his body, as he replied,

'Nothing is more certain. If he goes on for another day, he will be dead.'

'We didn't want that!' The voice was pitiful now. 'We didn't want that! You're not to die, do you hear?' pleaded the RSSS leader to the man whom a week earlier he had tried to maim. The Mahatma's eyes flickered open again, and he moved his lips, but the only sound he made was a gentle sigh.

'Tell him we didn't mean it . . . .. Look!'

For a moment the hair stood up on Suhrawardy's neck as the young man reached inside his shirt and pulled out a gun. It was a type he recognized: a black .38 Biretta.

Hundreds of them had been captured from Italian prisoners in North Africa and smuggled back to India by returning soldiers after the war. Then the young man simply dropped the gun onto the floor of the verandah. Head bowed, he reached into his pockets and dug out three or four cartridge magazines, which he let fall too. Then, stepping back, he motioned to his men. One by one they came forward, following suit. By the time they had finished, an untidy pile of metal lay at Gandhi's feet: switch-blades, sheath-knives, home-made pistols, blackjacks and razors.

The RSSS leader had fallen to his knees. Again, his men followed his example.

'Gandhiji – please – forgive us. Don't die! Tell us what to do. Forgive us . . . please.' Tears poured down their cheeks, as they looked at the little old man lying prostrate before them imploringly.

With a great effort of will, the Mahatma summoned up his last remaining strength. 'I forgive you,' he said, though his voice was barely audible, and they had to strain forward to hear, 'on one condition. Your punishment . . . your only punishment from me . . . will be to go to the streets of the Muslims, and help protect them.'

He raised his hand weakly, and the RSSS leader took it, bending over it gently. Gandhi felt his tears fall on it.

The hospital in Sialkot was like an antechamber in hell. The less seriously wounded stumbled along the corridors, doing what little they could to help the handful of doctors and nurses who moved like sleepwalkers in their exhaustion from the overcrowded wards to the overcrowded corridors, where men, women and children lay jumbled together on stretchers, and where the linoleum floors were slippery with blood.

Edwina hurried along the first-floor corridor with Amrit Kaur, Muriel and a worried nurse. The nurse had lost her cap, and her hair was streaked with blood. A man with a bandaged head moved out of their way and stumbed over a stretcher where an elderly woman lay staring at the ceiling.

Her scream joined the demonic babel of pain around them. The nurse did not even pause: she had more urgent cases to attend to.

'Many were killed. There's so little we can do,' she told the others as they walked. 'We're nearly out of swabs and bandages.'

'Then we must make them – from sheets and towels,' said Amrit, urgently. Nodding to Edwina, she hurried away with the nurse, as two orderlies came along the corridor bearing yet another body on a stretcher. Quickly, they transferred their load onto the last vacant mattress of the many lining the corridor wall. Edwina now saw that it was a young man, alive, but badly wounded in the leg. A sword had laid it open to the bone. 'Get some antiseptic, Muriel,' she said quickly. 'Iodine, soap and water – anything!' She knelt by him, taking a pair of scissors from her pocket and cutting away the cloth of his trouser leg around the wound. It was Ahmad's grandson. 'Quick, give me your apron. Apron!' she snapped at the young nurse who was hurrying past with a steel kidney-tray. Impatiently she tugged at it as the girl untied it, and, wadding it into a ball, pressed it against the thigh wound to stop the spurting blood from a severed artery. She guided the man's hands to the wad she had made.

'Press down on it! Press down.' The young man did as he was told. His eyes were open, bewildered, not seeing her. 'Good! Now keep pressing down.'

His eyes met hers, and held them. 'They attacked the column! I thought we would be safe . . .. But they attacked the column! My family . . .' He wept.

Edwina stood up. There was nothing she could say to him, but she had to find that iodine, quickly. She would comfort him as best she could when she returned.

Five minutes later Muriel and she hurried back, with a quarter-full bottle of iodine and an improvised swab made from a cotton sari. A young woman and two children squatted by the man. The older child with a head wound which had already been treated, but the bandaging was coming loose. Muriel secured it with her handkerchief, while Edwina tended to the young man. He was quiet now, holding the woman's hand as she helped him press down on the wad. He smiled to Edwina. 'Allah be praised. They are safe.'

She paused, struck by the warmth of his look. What must this one little family have been through already, she wondered. But there was no time to stop and talk. She soaked the swab with iodine. 'This will hurt very much,' she said, 'but it will clean the wound. Then we'll see if we can't organize some food for you all.'

Day gave way to night and still she was working. She helped them distribute bowls of *dahl*. When the quinine and iodine ran out, she cleansed the wounds with soap and water. Late in the evening, she entered a ward she had not visited before, picking her way among the mattresses laid down on every available inch of floor space between the beds. Most of the people here were sleeping, but in one corner an old woman was tossing fitfully. Edwina made her way over to her and managed to find space to squat down next to her, supporting her head as she gave her a little water to drink. She had one last clean handkerchief, and she dampened it in the water-bowl, gently wiping the old woman's cheeks and forehead. Slowly, her patient quietened down, her breathing becoming more regular.

'That's better,' Edwina whispered. She laid the old woman's head gently back on the mattress, and stood up to go. 'You'd better keep this,' she said, putting the handkerchief into her hand. The old woman caught her hand in her own, and, kissing it, pressed it against her cheek like a child.

Crouching there in the dark, in her blood and sweat-stained uniform, and feeling the old woman's soft breath on her hand, Edwina felt her eyes fill with tears.

Edwina and Rajkumari Amrit Kaur returned to Delhi in a state of almost total exhaustion, but also one of triumph. During their tour of the Punjab they had visited and worked at twelve camps and seven hospitals. Amrit Kaur shared Edwina's indomitable will: within twenty-four hours of becoming India's first woman Cabinet minister she had been confronted with a task of almost insurmountable difficulty, and she had risen to meet it. But an additional concern weighed on her. Amrit was a practising Christian and a close disciple of Gandhi. With all India she waited, poised between hope and fear, for news of him, though for her the tension brought even greater agony of mind.

Despite the penitence of the RSSS, he would still not take any food until he had had assurances from all the religious leaders in Calcutta that they would maintain peace between their communities. He would settle for nothing less than a signed declaration. Finally, on 4 September 1947, he got what he wanted. At 9.15 pm the Mahatma, nursed in Suhrawardy's arms, broke his seventy-three-hour fast by accepting a little lime-juice in water. By his strict rules, lime-juice constituted food, and it would be one or two days before his emaciated body could once more sustain solid nourishment.

After he had drunk, he smiled at the people gathered around him and said simply, 'It feels good to be alive.'

Mountbatten was at a briefing for a meeting of the Joint Defence Council, when Edwina got back to Government House. The Council was increasingly embattled, since the Pakistani and Indian delegations to it could not reach agreement on the administration of the Punjab Boundary Force. Increasingly, the little peace-keeping army was coming under criticism from both sides, and its future seemed to be hanging in the balance as its ability to cope with its overwhelming task became more and more questionable. Indeed, Edwina had herself sent back reports that there seemed to be no confidence left in it. Restless, and filled with an urgent desire to talk to somebody, Edwina told her driver to take her to York Road.

She found Nehru working at a table on the rear verandah of his house. He was deep in thought, toying abstractedly

223

with the rosebud in his buttonhole. At her approach, he looked up with pleasure and came down the steps to meet her.

'It's a relief to see you back safely,' he said, taking her hand in his. 'I was worried about you.'

She smiled to him. For a moment, her tiredness seemed to slip away. 'Why should you be worried? It was an official tour of inspection. I couldn't come to any harm.'

'You were going into a madhouse,' he said seriously. 'The ordinary rules no longer apply there.'

'Well, the only bad thing to happen to me was that I nearly got sunstroke!'

Smiling at her strength of spirit, he led her back towards the verandah. His concern at the continuing horror of the Punjab was balanced for the moment by news of what Gandhi had achieved in Calcutta. Now, he shared it with her – and sharing it with her doubled his joy.

'The city of dreadful night, your poet Kipling called it. But now it has become a place of hope for us all. Rajaji tells me there is an incredible will now in all Bengal to make sure the truce is never broken.'

'"Lead us from darkness into light," he said,' Edwina answered, and then her voice faltered. 'I was beginning to – to be unable to believe in anything. After all that we heard and saw in the Punjab.'

Nehru held a chair for her to sit. Serious again, he could see what a great strain this wonderful woman was under. Quietly, he sat down by her.

'How much worse is it going to get? How much longer can it go on?'

'We must hope and pray that the worst is over,' he said. 'The reports you sent back shocked everybody, but thanks to you much more help is now being given to the injured and the dispossessed.'

'But it's never enough, Jawahar – and it's always too late!' She rose, tensely, moving away from him. He followed her.

'Don't walk away, Edwina. Come and sit with me.'

224

'I can't sit still! There is so much to do!'

He was shocked to realize that she was far closer to a state of nervous collapse than he had thought. 'You must rest,' he ordered her gently. 'You owe it to yourself, and to the rest of us. Come, we'll sit quietly for a little. Then we'll talk.'

She turned to him, her eyes filled with panic. 'But people are dying! And more and more refugees are on the road!'

'Edwina . . .' He took, her in his arms, holding her tense, fragile body as he would a child.

'I have to make you understand!'

'I do, my dear,' he said softly. 'Believe me, I do understand.' He went on holding her close, until gradually, shuddering as the tension ebbed from her, she sank her head onto his shoulder, and closed her eyes. After a moment, he continued, quietly, 'What we are doing may not seem enough, but it is all that we can do. And you have done far more than enough.' She started to raise her head but he gently pressed it back to his shoulder. 'Just listen to me. You have been driving yourself too hard. Please . . . For everyone's sake – for my sake – you must rest.'

Later, having taken her home, the Prime Minister waited alone for the Governor General in his study. Outside, the heavy, brooding silence of the night heralded the long-awaited monsoon. Nehru hoped it would not be long before it arrived. The rain would in some ways add to their problems, but the lower temperatures and the release of natural tension it would bring with it might possibly also help to stem the tide of violence.

The door clicked open softly and Mountbatten entered.

'She's in bed now,' he said, seating himself at his desk. 'I'm grateful to you for bringing her back . . . . She's not as strong as she appears to be.' He paused, hesitating. A strong bond of friendship had grown up between the two men, but Mountbatten was aware that an even closer one existed between Nehru and his wife. 'She is much more affected by suffering than she lets anyone see,' he finished.

He thought of her, lying upstairs, racked by neuralgia. He was lucky that Pamela was with him to look after her. Poor girl, she had had to grow up fast, but she was doing sterling work in the Delhi medical dispensaries.

'The people of India saw behind Edwina's shield some time ago. She is greatly loved,' said Nehru.

'I think I'd realized that.'

The two men sat in silence. Both sensed they were close to a more personal conversation than either of them was yet ready for.

'She told me more than was in her official reports,' Nehru said, finally, breaking the mood. 'Most worrying is the panic among the refugees. They don't trust our promises, but then, why should they, when they know that the situation is getting worse and worse, and that we're unable to do anything about it?'

Mountbatten tapped his fingers on the desk. 'Is it because of me?' he asked suddenly. 'Because I rushed everything through?'

'You must never think that. Maybe it's the price we have to pay for freedom. It's certainly the price we have to pay for Partition. But we all accepted that.'

'Only we never imagined it would be so high . . . .'

Nehru looked at the tired, lined face opposite him. The last few months, and especially the weeks since Independence, had aged them all.

'You, too, should rest,' he said.

'I can't. I'm flying to Lahore tomorrow to chair a meeting of the Joint Defence Council.'

Nehru saw the opportunity and seized it. 'Then why don't you take Edwina with you? Depending on what is decided at the meeting, you could stop in Simla for a week or so on the way back.'

'Are you trying to get rid of me?' Mountbatten smiled to him.

'Of course not, but you are much too valuable to us to have you out of action through exhaustion.' Nehru paused. He wished fervently that they could all go up to Simla for a month, and talk about England, and forget the whole thing. 'Seriously, Dickie, I insist that you consider it. We'll be in constant touch, and there's nothing we can't handle by telephone or by messenger.'

After Nehru had left, Mountbatten pondered his proposal. After all, he wasn't going to be there for ever, and for Edwina's sake . . . At least he could take her and Pammy with him, and see how things transpired.

Above the entrance of the Governor General's residence in Lahore the flags of India and Pakistan flew side by side to welcome the members of the Joint Defence Council. Mountbatten was in the anomalous position of chairing the Council despite his being, as her Governor General, strictly speaking of the Indian party, but both countries had requested that he take the chair: it was a reflection of their respect for his former disinterest as Viceroy. Now, dressed in a formal lightweight uniform, he waited in an ante-chamber of the Residence with the key members of his staff, Ismay, Menon, his Conference Secretary Erskine Crum, and the tough, stocky commander of the Punjab Boundary Force, Major General Pete Rees. Liaqat Khan would be joining them as leader of the Pakistan delegation, and Sir Claude Auchinleck was expected to report on his meetings with the powerful Sikh leader, Tara Singh, whose followers had been arming and mounting organized attacks in all the border districts.

'Let's hope Auchinleck has been able to talk some sense into them,' said Erskine Crum.

'As long as he's here for the final session,' replied Mountbatten. 'We'll have to expect a lot of stick from both sides over the PBF.'

'If they spent less time giving us stick, and more on cooperation, we'd be better able to do our job!' snapped Rees.

'I wasn't criticizing you, Pete.'

'And I'm not making excuses, sir. We're doing our best, but we're like a matchstick dam against a river in flood.'

227

'The Defence Minister assured us you have enough men to control the situation,' put in Ismay, carefully.

'With all respect, sir, he's talking rubbish. Don't they realize yet in Delhi and Karachi what's happening here?' Rees paused for breath, and then thought – to hell with it: if he was going to drop a bombshell, now was as good a time as any. 'I know we're only talking about an area the size of Wales, but there are ten million people on the move in it!'

Mountbatten rounded on him in shock. 'Is that a reliable estimate?'

'It's not an estimate, sir. It's the lowest positive number. The actual number could be anything up to fourteen million.'

Menon was on the verge of asking another question as the others absorbed this critical new piece of information, when the door opened suddenly and a Pakistani colonel strode into the room, his hand resting on the butt of his revolver. Behind him four armed guards in dress uniform flanked the entrance and came smartly to attention.

Immaculate as ever, the gaunt figure of Mohammed Ali Jinnah walked into the room. His monocle dangled from the high-necked tunic he wore, and on his head was a black astrakhan cap. Between his long yellow fingers, a cigarette burned in the ever-present jade holder. This was the second surprise in the space of a minute for Mountbatten. Jinnah had not announced his intentions of being present at the Council meeting at all.

The two Governors General bowed stiffly to each other. 'Welcome to Lahore, Your Excellency,' said the Qaid-i-Azam in his crisp, toneless voice.

'This is an unexpected pleasure,' replied Mountbatten, evenly. 'I'm sure you know everyone here. But you may not have major General Rees?'

'I met His Excellency in Karachi, sir,' said Rees. Jinnah nodded to him curtly, and turned back to Mountbatten.

'We must talk.'

'Certainly, but the Defence Council meeting is due to start at any moment.'

Jinnah smiled. 'I am sure these gentlemen will excuse us if we keep them waiting for a few minutes.'

Ismay was the first to realize that the Governor General of Pakistan had dismissed them. 'We'll wait in the Council Chamber,' he suggested. His slightly self-conscious bow to Jinnah reminded the others to bow also as they left.

Once they were alone, Jinnah indicated two armchairs in the corner of the room. He waited for Mountbatten to sit down, and then sat carefully himself, lowering his body as if it were made of glass. As he did so, the deep, hollow cough which racked him so often now shook his frame. He took a silk handkerchief from his sleeve and dabbed at his lips fastidiously.

'If you'd announced your arrival, we might have arranged a reception,' said Mountbatten.

'Nonsense. In any case, in Pakistan it is I who should be the host.' Jinnah gave his faint smile again. 'I came purely to see you. Now that we are on absolutely equal terms, I can tell you that you are the only man I have ever truly admired.'

Mountbatten was taken aback. What was Jinnah leading up to? 'That's very gracious of you,' he said.

'I am merely stating a fact,' said Jinnah, tonelessly, as he took out another Craven 'A' and fitted it into his holder.

'You wanted to talk.'

'Yes. About many things. But for now I shall confine myself to the essentials.'

'Well then – fire away.'

Jinnah looked at him, inhaling hungrily. 'Something must be done about the attitude of the present Indian Government to Pakistan. Their unhelpful manner, their lack of communication, is nothing less than a crude attempt to interfere with the efficient running of my country!'

Mountbatten had expected this. Despite his imperious manner, Jinnah was in trouble. His desire to be Governor General of Pakistan himself had cost his new country several million rupees, for by making it impossible for Mountbatten to be Joint Governor General of India and Pakistan, he had sacrificed the opportunity to have a detached arbiter of the division of the assets of British India. Mountbatten had been strenuously fair, but nevertheless he had accepted the Governor-Generalship of the new Dominion of India, and thereby made it his duty to put the interests of that country first. Jinnah had thrown away the chance of a powerful ally. Moreover, his economy was in chaos. The Hindus who had run Karachi's banks had all fled, and although Pakistan was capable of producing enormous amounts of jute, cotton and tobacco, she had no factories to process them in, and no money to build them. Two hundred million rupees had already been paid over to Pakistan by India, but the balance of five hundred and fifty million remained to be paid. Mountbatten knew that Auchinleck shared Jinnah's view that the Indian Government was being disruptive, as he himself occasionally suspected also – yet he was no longer the master of that government, but its servant.

'I'm sure there's been no deliberate interference,' he said mildly.

'The share of assets we agreed before Partition either has not arrived or arrives in such small quantities that I cannot plan ahead! Goods scheduled for delivery either go astray or simply disappear. And I am not compensated for their loss!'

'I'll see what I can do about speeding up delivery, but with the Punjab still in turmoil I can do little more than that.'

The muscles in Jinnah's cheek twitched angrily. 'You must order them to fulfil their obligations!'

Mountbatten remained calm. 'I can make suggestions. I cannot order.'

'You are Governor General of India!'

'Yes. That is what you made me by refusing to accept a joint Governor General. It means that I am now an Indian, and that is how you must deal with me. Furthermore, I do not have the special powers that you have granted yourself to make your power in Pakistan absolute. My position remains strictly constitutional.'

It was clear that Jinnah did not believe him. He bent forward, stubbing his cigarette out impatiently. Then he spoke icily. 'I see that you refuse to discuss the matter. Very well, let us move on to something for which you cannot deny a certain responsibility – indeed, it is why you are here. I refer to Joint Defence.'

'Very well.'

Jinnah drew himself up. 'I came here to see you, but that was not the only reason. I also came to insist upon the immediate disbanding of the Punjab Boundary Force. I have serious doubts about its effectiveness, conduct and impartiality.'

Mountbatten demurred. He knew that the behaviour of the PBF, hampered as it had been by difficult terrain and poor communications, had been impeccable. It was a credit to Rees's leadership and to the discipline of its Hindu and Muslim units. 'What is more,' he added, 'Field Marshal Auchinleck has said he will resign if the force is dismantled.'

'I shall be sorry to lose him,' replied Jinnah evenly.

Mountbatten stared at him in disbelief. Was there no limit to the man's ego? Did he believe he had the power of a god, to throw away one of his staunchest allies? He made a final attempt to dissuade him. 'Mr Jinnah, without the intervention of the Force, the risk of an increase in violence becomes considerably greater. That means Muslim refugees will suffer as much as Hindus.'

'The Pakistan Army will be enough to keep law and order, at any rate on my side of the border. I have every faith in Generals Messervy and Gracey.'

Mountbatten barely hesitated before replying. From the sniping criticisms it was receiving from both sides, it was clear to him that the PBF was going to hell in a bucket, anyway. Jinnah's unilateral rejection of it put the last nail in its coffin. 'Very well. The Force will be disbanded,

231

providing the decision meets with the full approval of the Joint Defence Council.'

'I have little doubt that it will.' Jinnah was surprised. He had expected tougher opposition, and his devious mind was already on its guard again. What was Mountbatten up to?

'Nor I. Actually I'm grateful to you, Mr Jinnah. You see, my authority over the Boundary Force was my last remaining executive responsibility. Now that I'll no longer be directly involved in the affairs of the Indian Government, I suspect you have done Mr Nehru a favour, too. He won't need to feel that he's got me looking over his shoulder any more.'

Jinnah stiffened, but said nothing more. Mountbatten sat back. As Governor General, he had one last not-quite constitutional duty to perform: Pug Ismay was due to travel on from Lahore to Kashmir to take a much-needed holiday. Mountbatten would ask him privately to try to persuade the vacillating maharajah, Hari Singh, finally to accede to the Dominion of India. The position in that state was dangerously unstable, and he did not want suddenly to find himself with another Punjab on his hands.

He himself would take Nehru at his word and go up to Simla with Edwina, where he prayed that they would finally have some time to themselves.

Nehru looked up from the table where he was working on the rear verandah of his house. There was a slight commotion in the road outside, which he noticed had attracted the attention of one or two of his servants. They were making for the garden gate, where a group of young men had gathered.

'Hey, Panditji! Jawaharlal! Can you spare a moment? We've got a present for you!'

Smiling at the sound of their friendly voices, he stood up and, still uncertain, waved to them. On the lawn, his servants hesitated. He nodded to them reassuringly and made his way to the gate himself. As he approached it, the

232

men outside pushed it open to reveal that they had with them a young Muslim woman, tightly enveloped in her traditional *burqa*. Because of it he could not see her face, but she seemed to be crouched forward, as if in pain. His smile became puzzled, but still he moved forward.

'You like Muslims, don't you?' said one of the young men, still smiling politely. They looked as if they might be students.

When he was about ten yards away they pushed the woman towards him. Something flared in the hands of one of them, and he threw it after her. Too late Nehru smelt the kerosene. As the woman fell to the ground the match caught in the folds of her *burqa*, turning it in an instant into a sheet of flame. Nehru plucked at it, tearing it away, shouting to his servants as the woman screamed. The gold-and-black leather mask fell away from her face and he was looking into the eyes of a terrified girl of no more than sixteen. There were blue welts on her cheeks and her chin was caked with dried blood. Pulling her to him, away from the burning clothes, as his servants ran up to beat out the flames, Nehru held her close to him, feeling her whole body shudder as she sobbed in terror.

The young men had long since fled, but he would remember the horrible sound of their laughter.

# TEN

Independence had changed very little in Simla. The only outward signs were Indians walking freely on The Mall, and the Indian flag above the entrance to the Viceregal Lodge replacing the Union Jack. Mizzen bounded about the lawns, rediscovering the sights and smells he had found there on his first visit, and chasing the monkeys, who scampered off high into the pine trees, shrieking their defiance.

Mountbatten had given his staff the day off to be with their families. He himself was spending the morning playing croquet with Pamela, pleased to see that Edwina had given herself over completely to rest. She lay on a lounging chair in the sun, dozing, a neglected book on the grass beside her. He had had no cause to regret his decision to remove himself from the centre of things for a while. It was high time that the people of India should see and understand that it was their government which ruled them now, not an English ex-Viceroy.

He might not have been so sanguine had he known how events were turning in Delhi. The sudden influx of so many embittered Hindu refugees had sparked off a chain of anti-Muslim demonstrations of which the outrage in Nehru's garden was one. The following day, the Prime Minister had been driving through Connaught Circus in the smartest quarter of New Delhi, when he had been shocked to see an excited mob attacking two shops. A glance at their names confirmed the reason, Khan and Ismillah. The Muslim owners could not be seen, but the crowd was gaily looting the shops, men and women streaming out of one carrying bolts of brightly coloured cotton and silk, while from the other, chairs and stools and cushions were being thrown out and grabbed by the people outside. The atmosphere would have been one of grotesque carnival, were it not for the fact that already the Hindus were beginning to fight amongst themselves for the goods they had stolen. But it was not the looters which most appalled Nehru. It was the sight of four Hindu policemen standing by, their *lathis* holstered, smiling and watching what for them was obviously 'fun'.

Shouting to his driver to stop, Nehru leapt from the car and ran over to the policemen. Cursing them, he seized one of their *lathis* and waded into the mob himself, laying about him in fury as he did so. Recognizing him, and cowed, the ugly knot of people began to break up and move away, as the policemen reluctantly moved forward to help him.

That same evening, V.P. Menon's car, driving north away from the Council House up Queen Mary's Avenue, was attacked. Angry faces appeared like goblins in the headlamps of the car, and a solitary policeman who was doing his best to restrain them was swept aside. The mob closed in on the car, hammering at its sides, roof and windows in rage, and rocking it violently. It was a nightmare of a situation. The car's engine had stalled and the terrified driver, too urgent with the ignition, came close to flooding it. Menon hastily dropped the locks on all the doors, and looked straight ahead, refusing to let the mob see the fear in his own eyes. Finally, the motor fired and the car shot forward, displacing two men who had climbed onto the bonnet. The crowd howled furiously at the loss of their prey.

This was in New Delhi. In the Old City, with its crowded labyrinth of ramshackle streets and dark alleyways, matters were far worse. To add to the tension that was building in the city, thousands of Muslim refugees had been coming in from the countryside around, thinking that in the capital, with its civilizing influence, they would be safe. They were terribly wrong. The simultaneous arrival of greater numbers of Hindu refugees had been like pouring petrol onto a fire. While the peace in Calcutta and Bengal held, Delhi was fast developing into a Punjab.

'It's getting out of control,' said Nehru. Tired and strained, almost overtaken by the rapid escalation of the violence, he had called an emergency meeting of his chief ministers.

Patel's face reflected his. For all his assumption that Partition would bring violence in its wake, he had been prepared for nothing like this. 'We'll have to proclaim martial law – a curfew from dusk until dawn.'

'We'd need a twenty-four-hour curfew to control this, but in any case how can we?' asked Nehru. 'Half the police force were Muslims, and they've all left for Pakistan. The ones that are left can't be relied on to be non-partisan themselves!'

'Then we'll have to call out the army,' said Prasad.

'No, that's no good,' put in Patel. 'We've sent most of the garrison to the Punjab. We've less than nine hundred men left to guard the city.'

They fell silent. None of them had foreseen this. They had assumed that Delhi stood apart from the rest of the country. The problem was that the rest of the country had come to Delhi.

'We'll be lucky if we can contain it for more than a day,' Patel warned.

Nehru bit his lip, looking at V.P. Menon. Still shaken by his experience of two hours earlier, he found he was unable to make any constructive suggestion at all. He knew that, bereft of many of its efficient Muslim administrators, the machinery of the city's bureaucracy was in a state of collapse. He knew too that if Delhi collapsed into anarchy, the government would effectively be finished.

Something had to be done.

In Simla, the Mountbattens emerged from the dining-room into the heavily decorated two-tiered hall of the Lodge.

For the first time since arriving in India, the three of them had been able to dine simply *en famille*.

'I enjoyed that,' said Mountbatten. 'Lovely just to wear a plain old comfortable dinner jacket to dinner, too. Dougie Fairbanks used to tell me I ought to have become an actor, but I don't think I could take it. It's such a relief not to be on show all the time.'

'But it's all right for just some of the time,' commented Edwina, drily.

'Well, I hate it,' said Pamela.

Mountbatten laughed. 'Well, I must admit, compared to you two shrinking violets, I'm a positive glutton for the limelight!'

They paused together at the foot of the stairs. Edwina, who had lost much of the tension around her eyes already, said she was going to make the most of her rest, and turn in immediately.

'I think I'll take a walk round the garden before I go to bed,' said Pamela.

'Good idea,' smiled her father. 'Good night.'

'Good night, darling,' said Edwina, kissing her, and then turning to climb the stairs.

Mountbatten watched as one of the armed guards at the main door opened it to let Pamela out into the cool night air. Beyond her, he could see the few twinkling lights of the little town, and some of the heavy scent of the night came to his nostrils. He let his daughter go, and then nodded discreetly to the guard, who followed her out. Simla certainly seemed peaceful, but it was barely 150 miles east of Amritsar, and he was taking no chances.

He went upstairs to his small study. There, ready spread out and waiting for him on the ample desk, were his reference books and his beloved genealogical tables. He knew he really ought to catch up on some sleep himself, but he had not yet been able to wind down sufficiently to sleep for more than five or six hours anyway, and it had been a long time since he had been able to indulge his hobby. He had hardly had a chance to do so since the

237

near-disastrous meeting with Nehru here in Simla at the beginning of May, four months and half an age ago. He switched off the main light, leaving only a standard lamp to cast a pool of warm yellow onto the desk. He took off his jacket, selected a handful of differently coloured pens, and settled down with pleasure.

The telephone's raucous bell roused him from deep concentration. He had been buried in a reference book, seeking the birth-date of Princess Eleonore of Lich, an aunt by marriage. He looked up from the book and blinked, glancing at his watch.

'Damn,' he said, briefly, picking up the receiver.

The line crackled and then a voice identified itself.

'Hello, V.P.,' said Mountbatten. 'Still working? It's very late'

V.P. Menon hunched over his own telephone. The line was not as clear as it might have been. He prayed they would not be cut off. 'I am sorry to disturb you, Your Excellency, but I am afraid it is essential for you to return to Delhi at once.'

'What on earth for? Look, if it's something for me to sign, why don't you send it up by messenger tomorrow?'

'I don't know if you've heard of the trouble that's broken out here,' insisted Menon, urgently.

'I know there's been some isolated rioting, but I thought that was pretty much under control.'

He sat up in his chair as he heard Menon's next words. He knew that the tough Indian was not a man given to over-reaction or exaggeration. Now Menon was telling him that whole sections of the city were out of the authorities' control. There were some quarters of Delhi which the police dared not enter – or would not. 'Both Mr Nehru and Mr Patel are afraid that this is only the beginning. I do urge you to return as soon as possible.'

'V.P., on whose authority are you making this call?'

Menon hesitated for a fraction of a second. If he told Mountbatten the truth, the Governor General would almost certainly refuse to come until the appeal had been made official. He could not risk that. 'I'm sure Mr Nehru and Mr Patel will be very anxious to have your advice, sir,' he said, which was, after all, no more than the truth.

Mountbatten considered. 'Look here, V.P. – I think the worst thing I could possibly do is to come haring back to Delhi now. I'm sure the last thing the Government wants is for me to start interfering.'

The intensity of Menon's reply surprised him. 'Is that final, sir?'

'Both Mr Nehru and Mr Patel are perfectly capable of dealing with this on their own. They know where to contact me, if they want my backing.'

Menon's mouth was dry. 'Very well, sir, I'll tell them that. But if you do not change your mind within twenty-four hours, it will be too late. We will have lost India!' Trembling with untypical emotion, and at his own audacity, he hung up.

At his end, Mountbatten jiggled the telephone cradle up and down in annoyance, but the line was dead. He sat quietly for several minutes, pondering. If Menon had, as he suspected, telephoned without Nehru's authority, then it would cause more harm than good to ring the Prime Minister now. And Menon was not a man given to easy panic. He remembered the civil servant's integrity when the unstable young Maharajah of Jodhpur had pointed the little pistol at his head, no less deadly for being a toy. If Delhi were in turmoil, then it was something which Nehru and Patel had no experience of controlling. It was ironical that their *forte* had until now been in organizing civil unrest, against the British! Whereas he knew exactly what would have to be done. Despite himself, he was already planning it. He stood up. At least he could drive down and see for himself what the situation was like, and if it looked as if he were interfering, he could always take a back seat again. He picked up the telephone and dialled another number.

'Hello Peter,' he said as the sleepy voice of his ADC answered. 'I'm sorry to wake you at this hour, but I want the Rolls ready at 6.00 am. Something's come up in Delhi and we've got to go back.'

At his desk at Government House the following day Mountbatten confronted a dispirited Nehru and an angry, frustrated Vallabhbhai Patel. They had described the situation to him in the plainest terms, but he was still reluctant to take over from them. For one thing, despite the fact that he knew he needed help, Patel would resent it. For another, Mountbatten would have to proceed very carefully. Whatever line he took, all decisions would have at least to appear to emanate from the Government. He would have to put the advice which he was constitutionally allowed to give in such a way that they could convert it into direct orders.

'I can see that it's bad here, but I don't see why you need me! You're perfectly capable of coping with this yourselves.' He was still sounding them out.

'Given time,' said Nehru impatiently. 'But the right steps have to be taken at once! We find ourselves in a war situation, near enough, and we cannot deal with it. We don't have your experience, and we need it.'

This was the opening Mountbatten needed. 'Then I take it you would be interested in my advice?'

'That's what we're here for!' Patel almost exploded.

'But you are the Government, and I can only take my orders from you.' He paused. 'Well then, first of all there must be a central authority to combine all our efforts. We'll need to set up an Emergency Committee – if you agree.'

'We do,' said Nehru, brusquely, but he was looking at Mountbatten with more hope now.

'I'm prepared to head it – if you invite me to.' Mountbatten was at his crispest and and most decisive, yet his passion for detail dictated that, once established, form should be observed in all its finest points. He knew exactly the procedure he would follow, one which he had tried and tested both as Head of Combined Operations and as Supreme Commander, South-East Asia Command.

Patel feared that the Governor General might run away

with them. 'Now please don't misunderstand me, Lord Louis,' he said. 'I agree that we need your experience. Yet I can't help feeling that, less than three weeks after Independence, you and not the Government will be seen to be running the committee – and that might suggest that you are still running the country.'

Mountbatten smiled briefly, appreciating his reservation. 'I have no desire or intention to run the country, Mr Patel. But in a situation like this, someone has to take command. However, I shall only head the Emergency Committee *at your request.*'

The words sank home. 'We invite you,' said Patel laconically.

'Good. Now, you'll want to know how I propose to run it. When I make a decision, I shall ask both of you to agree to it. In that way I shall be deferring to your judgment and the decision will be, in effect, yours. However, there will be no time for argument. I shall expect you both to agree at once.'

Nehru and Patel were surprised for a moment, then Nehru smiled. Patel cleared his throat and shrugged.

'There isn't time to pussyfoot around if we're going to get the situation under control. If we go down in Delhi, we are finished.'

'When shall we call the first meeting?' Nehru asked.

'As soon as we can get everyone together. We'll need Erskine Crum to organize it. Campbell-Johnson and Ismay from my staff. I'd suggest Rajkumari Amrit Kaur, and we'll need Baldev Singh and Maulana Azad to represent the Sikhs and the Muslims.'

'The Chief of Police?'

'Yes, and someone to represent Auchinleck. Oh – and we can use Pete Rees as our military advisor, now that the Punjab Boundary Force is gone.' Mountbatten looked at them.

'Perhaps Edwina, too,' suggested Nehru. 'She has become an authority on the refugee problem.'

'Very well, since you wish it. Above all, gentlemen,' he

241

warned, 'let us observe the forms we have agreed on. Without them, the Government will risk losing its standing, and we cannot afford that possibility.'

At the beginning of the meeting the Prime Minister invited Mountbatten to take the Chair, which he did on condition that the fact be kept secret. He would not take the slightest risk of control appearing to be out of the hands of the new Indian leadership. His organization had been so efficient that already a system had been set up whereby Erskine Crum's minutes would be typed up by relays of stenographers straight onto duplicator 'skins', so that they could be run off, collated and distributed by special motorcycle messengers within two hours of the end of the meetings. The time saved by this system would, Mountbatten hoped, bring matters to a speedier conclusion. Those members of the Committee given special tasks or assignments would have to be prepared to give progress reports at each succeeding meeting. This, too, was a device to keep people on their toes. Mountbatten knew that the sense of emergency alone should be enough to do this, but he also knew that now he had effectively taken over there would be a risk of some committee members thinking that they could safely leave it all to him, and this was only natural. He had had years of experience in the exercise of power: the Indians had not yet had a month. Rees had been enjoined at the first meeting to organize the return of certain units of troops from the Punjab to police the city. The Governor General's bodyguard was also put at the disposal of the Delhi garrison. This *corps d'élite* was completely reliable, but to make assurance doubly sure, Mountbatten suggested that it patrol in sections each of two armoured cars, one manned by Muslims and one by Sikhs or Hindus, but operating in unison.

'Now,' said Mountbatten, briskly. 'Communications. At all costs the telephone system must be maintained, and a radio link with the Punjab.' He turned to the Deputy Prime Minister. 'Would you agree, Mr Patel?'

'I'll take responsibility for that, Governor General,' said Patel, his tension making him look more like an ancient Roman senator than ever.

'Thank you. Mr Campbell-Johnson, I would like you to liaise with the army and the ministry of Information.'

'Very good, sir.'

'Good.' Mountbatten sat back, looking at the intent faces around the table in the Council Chamber where they sat. 'And now to the main problem – the refugees themselves.'

The Delhi camps had long since been swamped, and it was proving increasingly difficult to maintain an adequate supply of food and water to all the refugees. Amrit Kaur had reported that the risk of disease, particularly cholera, increased with every day that passed. Two hundred thousand homeless Muslims were already housed in the Purana Qila, the Old Fort, and at Humayun's Tomb, buildings which ironically were relics of the golden age of an Islamic Mogul empire which had had its centre here. Initially, there had been only two standpipes of water at the Purana Qila, and religion added its difficulties too. The Muslims, herded together in conditions of sanitation which would have disgraced a concentration camp, refused to defile themselves by cleaning their latrines.

'We must make arrangements to resettle as many as possible in new areas, and to transport as many as wish to go to Pakistan,' Mountbatten said.

'We cannot cope with the numbers we expect to arrive,' said Amrit Kaur. 'In a few days' time, the refugee population of Delhi is expected to be about three-quarters of a million. We do not have enough food or medical supplies, and far from enough doctors and nurses.'

'In that case, we'll have to find them,' Mountbatten told her.

'The RAF squadrons still here could fly in the most urgent vaccines and medicines,' Nehru suggested.

'Would you like me to contact the Commander-in-Chief about that, Prime Minister?' Mountbatten asked.

'Would you please, Your Excellency?'

Mountbatten made a note. The mood of the meeting was changing under his positive drive. Despite the enormous tasks confronting them, the men and women round the table were exchanging their expressions of despair for ones of determination. 'Additional transport will be needed to ship in staple foods, grain and rice, from wherever we can get them. Trucks must be made available by the Ministry of Defence. Your Ministry, Mr Singh.'

'I will take care of it,' said Baldev Singh, writing on the pad in front of him.

Mountbatten had turned back to Nehru. 'If you agree, we can get the RAF planes to drop leaflets warning looters and would-be attackers that they'll be arrested or shot on sight if we catch them. I'd also suggest that train guards should be subject to immediate court martial if they bring in ambushed trains and show no sign of having tried to defend them. Would you like the Information and Defence sub-committees to look into that?'

Nehru agreed, while Patel added, 'As a matter of priority.'

'I'd like to get back to the refugee problem,' said Edwina, who had been writing busily for several minutes. 'I know medical staff are in short supply, but there are many additional welfare organizations. They are all doing excellent work, but it would be much more effective if there could be more cooperation and coordination between them.'

'Could we ask you to take charge of relief measures, Your Excellency?' Nehru asked. 'You have more experience of handling refugees than any of us here.' She had had so little rest, and now he was asking her to do more work, he thought with regret.

'I would be very happy to, Prime Minister,' Edwina said. She was frowning in concentration, already assessing how much of her Burmese experience she could apply to this new situation. Nehru need not have worried for her. Like her husband, her fire was up and her spirit would carry her through until the job was done.

Maulana Azad raised his hand. 'The difficulty will be –

if I may say – that the organizations were founded by different religious and political groups to serve distinct communities. They will never agree to work together.'

'Perhaps they never had to face such a crisis, Mr Azad,' Edwina replied, crisply. 'All we can do is put it to them.'

'Well, we leave that to you and Rajkumari,' Mountbatten said. 'No doubt, Prime Minister, you would like us now to pass on to such questions as the banning of weapons, and the larger subject of martial law.'

'I would like us to discuss that,' Nehru said.

'I agree,' Patel added, with a slight smile.

A table had been set for tea on the terrace of the Mogul Gardens and the servants waited with the duty ADC, watching the Prime Minister walk slowly along the long central path of the gardens with the Mountbattens.

The first meeting of the Emergency Committee had lasted several hours and, although it had achieved much and the atmosphere among those taking part had changed from worry and dismay to something more positive, Edwina had been aware of a certain strain developing, as a result of Dickie sweeping forward at such a speed. Especially when he had announced, without reference to Nehru or Patel, that meetings were to be held every morning from now on until the crisis was past and that everyone was expected to attend. It demonstrated without doubt who was in charge and the polite fiction of deference to the Prime Minister and his Deputy had suddenly seemed very hollow.

From the unusual silence as they walked, she knew that Nehru had been conscious of it and that the two men were at the danger point of what could become a conflict of personalities. She looked from one to the other. 'The meeting really went very well, wouldn't you say?' she prompted.

'I agree,' Nehru replied formally, as if that was all he was permitted to say. When she glanced at him, he smiled and shrugged very faintly.

245

'I'm sorry I had to go ahead so fast,' Mountbatten said. 'There really was no other way.'

Nehru had taken a cigarette from his small leather cigarette case and lit it. He knew that they were waiting for him to respond, yet it was not easy. At moments it had felt like being back under the direct control of the Raj, at its most autocratic, and he had had to fight the demon of rebellion in himself. Fortunately, he had realized that that was an emotional reaction, when what was needed was an attitude both positive and practical. 'My advisers warned me,' he said, 'that by virtually handing over power to you, I would feel threatened. But today I am even more certain I made the right decision.' They stopped, as he paused. 'I was very impressed – we all were – by your ability to move straight to essentials. You took a group of people who were bewildered, near despair, and in a few hours turned them into a working team.'

Mountbatten was grateful, knowing what it had cost him to step down deliberately into second place. 'Thank you. But I'd say you were the one who deserved admiration – for having the courage and the stature, in your position, to allow youself to ask for help.'

As they smiled to each other, Edwina was proud of them both. But it was best not to let it become too solemn. 'Perhaps we had better adjourn this mutual admiration society and have tea,' she said lightly, and they laughed.

Mountbatten and Nehru turned with her and they walked back to the table on the terrace. The servants stepped in to hold their chairs.

'You'll excuse me, if I only stay for a minute,' Edwina went on. 'Elizabeth's waiting for me.'

'What are you up to?' Mountbatten asked.

'We're going on a tour of the hospitals. I thought it might be as well if I checked conditions before this get-together with the welfare groups.'

She left them shortly afterwards and ordered her car. To brief herself on the kind of information she would need to convey to the welfare organizations when she spoke to them, she had arranged an exhaustive tour of Delhi's clinics and hospitals, and a survey of the nearest refugee camps. Experience had taught her that such a vast daily increase in the number of refugees would lead to uncontrollable chaos, unless a firm system of organizational routine were not quickly imposed. Although she objected, Mountbatten insisted on her being accompanied by Major Gilliat and her Indian ADC as bodyguards.

As she approached her car with her joint assistant, Elizabeth, she was pleased to see her favourite driver, Gurdial, a Sikh, smiling to her from the wheel. At least he is still all right, she thought. Indeed, most of the servants who had remained on the staff at Government House had continued to live and work peacefully together. If only the rest of the city would follow their example, she thought, then realized that if her servants were suddenly to be dispossessed and thrown onto the road, an anger similar to the refugees' could seize them.

As their car turned into the forecourt of the tuberculosis hospital, Edwina saw with horror that it was strewn with bodies. They must have been lying there for some time, since they were already bloated. The car drew up at the hospital entrance, where a doctor and a handful of nurses were standing nervously. Indifferent to the sudden crackle of gunfire in a nearby street, Edwina climbed out of the car. She looked at the bodies, registering to herself how quickly she was becoming hardened to sights of such ghastliness, but she noticed that many of the corpses were wearing white medical coats or tunics. She turned to the Hindu doctor who had hurried out to meet her. He kept ducking his head at the gunfire.

'What happened here?' she asked.

The doctor spoke hastily, unhappily. He would not move far from the hospital entrance. 'They came last night – *goondas*. They demanded all our Muslim domestics and orderlies. We could do nothing.'

She closed her eyes in momentary grief. 'Why haven't you removed the bodies?' she asked more gently.

'They told us, if we did anything at all to help Muslims, they would burn down the hospital. We are all afraid.' He glanced round the tops of the buildings surrounding the forecourt. 'There are still snipers around.'

Gilliat came forward briskly. 'We should get inside, Your Excellency.'

'No,' said Edwina. She took out a handkerchief and tied it over her mouth and nose. Muriel Watson was already following suit. She had been with Edwina in the Punjab and knew what was expected of her. Together the two women began to lift the nearest corpse. Gilliat grimaced, then motioned to Gurdial and the ADC who had accompanied them. They all started to carry bodies to the hospital entrance.

The doctor watched them for a moment, before beckoning to the nurses inside the hospital to follow him as he, too, moved forward to help.

A map room had been set up in the anteroom of the Council Chamber and was fully operational within forty-eight hours of Mountbatten's first meeting with Nehru and Patel. Army clerks and officers bustled over the maps showing the refugee columns spread over the large map-tables, and those of the city which covered the walls, altering the positions of a complex assortment of red and black pins, and the small flags which indicated army units. In one corner, a miniature telephone exchange had been set up and, in another, General Rees worked with his assistant, a young Indian Army major, and his new secretary, Pamela Mountbatten.

Nehru paused on the threshold of the room as he entered with the Governor General. He was deeply impressed, and revitalized by the knowledge that now they were doing something positive. It had needed Mountbatten's experience and expertise to set it in motion, but the work was being done – and done well – by Indians.

Rees was reading a message which Pamela had just torn off the teleprinter and handed to him. Still holding it, he

248

came over to the two men at the door, his expression set, serious.

'It's a report of an attack on the Victoria Zenana Hospital in Old Delhi,' he said.

'Is it bad?' asked Mountbatten.

'It doesn't give details. Some staff and patients killed.'

'You'd better make sure your mother hears about this before her Relief Committee meeting,' said Mountbatten tersely to Pamela. Edwina had managed to call together all the disparate welfare organizations in the city, and was to address them later that day.

'It is always the weak, the defenceless, who are attacked,' muttered Nehru. He looked at one of the wall maps. A black flash affixed to Wingfield Airport indicated a massacre which had occurred there that same morning. As he scanned the map, he saw a number of other, similar black flashes.

'They all show the trouble spots,' explained Rees. 'These other markers indicate the latest reported outbreaks of fighting; these show the location of the existing refugee camps, and these the ones under construction.'

Nehru turned to the map-tables, pointing to long lines of red pins with directional arrows beside them.

'And these?'

'The refugee columns moving to and from India, sir.'

In several places along the red lines, Nehru noticed that black pins had been affixed. 'Are these marking attacks on the columns?'

'Yes, sir. But only the main incidents. They're exposed to constant hit-and-run raids. We can't plot them all with any certainty.'

Nehru looked at the neat rows of little pins. He could see what they represented in his mind. Wretched, exhausted men, women and children suddenly panicking, and trampling each other under foot as gangs of mounted Sikhs bore down on them, whirling their deadly swords. Or Muslim snipers cruelly aiming at oxen, or following the rear of the column to beat up and rob the elderly or infirm stragglers.

'As if they had not suffered enough . . .' he said.

'If we are to offer them any degree of protection I strongly request, sir, that you give me permission to move army units into these areas,' said Rees. 'We can put armed jeeps at the end of the columns to protect the stragglers, too.'

'Yes,' replied Nehru. 'Do all that you consider necessary.' He looked at Mountbatten, knowing what he was thinking. The situation was appalling, but at least the violence had been confined to one area. He should be grateful for that, and to Gandhi, once more, for ensuring that Bengal had not become a mirror-image of the Punjab. 'I want as many people as possible off the roads,' he continued to Rees. 'I'll see to it that more trains are provided to take Muslim refugees to Pakistan, and they can bring back Sikhs and Hindus to India. But the tracks must be well guarded, and the trains themselves must be heavily armed.'

'Very good, sir.' Rees turned to go back to his desk.

Nehru continued to stare at the maps. He was sure that the attacks were the work of a few extremists, who wanted only to stir up fear and hatred, and he could not blame people for hitting back. He knew that in the end nothing could be won by violence, and that in time it would cease. The emergency measures they were taking would hasten a return to normality, and perhaps then the India he had dreamt of for so long would finally emerge. But it might take years to recover from the damage that had been done, and leave a whole generation who would remember Independence not as a time of glory, but of horror.

Edwina looked around the Council Chamber of Government House. The fifteen representatives of the welfare organizations had all taken their places, and she now faced one of the most daunting tasks in her career. But surely they could be persuaded. She smiled briefly to Amrit Kaur,

250

sitting next to her, and stood up to address the meeting. There was nothing in her manner to suggest any of what she had been through. She summoned up all of her charm, and began.

'In my experience, lack of information adds greatly to the fears of the refugee. One of our most important jobs through this Relief Committee will be to let them know that with your help and cooperation we shall soon have an organization whose only object is to solve their problems. I should like to invite your reactions and comments.'

'While we applaud the aims you put forward, Your Excellency,' said an elderly Sikh, 'it would seem more suitable for them to be undertaken by a government department, rather than by charitable and welfare groups such as ours.'

'Our job is to serve the needs of our own communities,' put in a young Hindu, earnest and bespectacled, who sat near him.

'I agree that cooperation is of the essence. Indeed, we have an opportunity here to demonstrate something which stands at the centre of the Christian ethic.' Another young man, wearing a tan jacket over his black shirt and dog-collar, was speaking. 'We do not turn anyone away, regardless of race, creed and denomination. But we are already operating at the limit of our resources.'

'Your greatest resource, ladies and gentlemen, is the bond which already unites you,' replied Edwina, 'your willingness to care for the needs of others.' She paused for a moment, looking round the room again and forcing them to meet her eye. 'Let me remind you of what we are facing. Three-quarters of a million refugees, hopeless, starving, are centred in Delhi alone. Daily, the death-toll rises, from riots, malnutrition and disease. We are nearing a state of anarchy, when none of you, individually, will be able to carry out the very work your organizations were formed to do.'

'Delhi has food supplies for two more days,' added Amrit Kaur, urgently. 'As for medical treatment, facilities are already stretched beyond the limit. More appalling than anything are the attacks on hospitals: police and soldiers have to be taken from other essential duties to guard them . . . .' She had spoken quietly, simply, but the emotional force of her words bore down upon the men and women around the table. The old Sikh covered his face with one hand. Near him, a woman sobbed. Everybody present knew what Edwina and Amrit had done and what they had seen. Everybody admired the example they had set.

'We do not tell you these things to make you despair,' said Edwina, 'but to make you aware of the task which faces us. It is too great for any one group, too great even for any government. It can only be tackled by all of us working together.'

Out of the silence which followed, the young Hindu spoke. 'Tell us what you want us to do, Your Excellency.'

'I want you to unite your separate organizations into a single team, working together.' There was an immediate reaction round the table. Despite everything, Edwina still sensed hesitation and reluctance. 'If necessary,' she continued firmly, yet losing none of her charm, 'I am prepared to keep this meeting going all day; but by the end of it, I want your unanimous agreement to the formation of a United Council for Relief and Welfare. I beg you to accept this, and I warn you that it is our only chance.'

Only the small crowns on the front and rear bumpers identified the shabby old black Buick 8 as a Government House car. Campbell-Johnson, still in his dinner jacket, sat in the back seat with Major Martin Gilliat, peering through the dusty side-window into the murky Delhi night. They had watched a dismal Joan Fontaine melodrama after dinner in the Government House cinema, and afterwards Gilliat had invited Campbell-Johnson to accompany him and Inspector Elder, Mountbatten's personal security officer, to inspect the guard that had now been mounted at the Victoria Zenana Hospital. The staff and patients had seemed greatly reassured at the presence of the Gurkha troops, and now the men had decided to make a detour on their way home to the district of Pahargunj, one of the worst-hit trouble-spots.

As the Sikh driver, Gurdial, wove his way slowly through the dimly lit streets, the two young members of Mountbatten's staff discussed Her Excellency's success that day in forming a unified Relief Council to administer work in the refugee camps and to pool the resources of the various welfare organizations. Both of them had been present at the meeting when she had done it, and both were filled with admiration.

'Just to get them all together in one room was a tribute to the respect they have for her,' said Gilliat, laughing. 'And after that, well, I don't think they knew what had hit them!'

Gurdial had reached the wide approach road to the large over-bridge near New Delhi station, and had accelerated slightly, but was still travelling at no more than thirty miles an hour. There was no other vehicle in sight. Gilliat reached into the breast pocket of his tunic for his cigarette case.

'Want one?'

'No thanks.'

The gunfire hammered out of the night ahead, shattering the windscreen as the car slewed violently round. The two men in the back threw themselves to the floor as bullets ripped into the metal of the old Buick. Elder had grabbed the wheel as the car continued its swerve. The side of the bridge loomed up beyond the broken windscreen and for a split second the Inspector thought that he would be too late, and that they would all be hurled over the edge. The tyres shrieked as he managed to pull the car round. Its left wing ripped along the concrete of the bridge wall, as Elder seized the handbrake and, forcing himself not to hurry, eased it on. The Buick juddered to a screaming standstill.

The Inspector had drawn his pistol and was out of the car in one movement. 'Stop shooting!' he bellowed, too furious to be afraid. 'Government House!'

In the back of the car, Alan Campbell-Johnson looked down at Martin Gilliat. Everything had seemed to happen at once, and yet the ten seconds since the shooting started had taken an eternity. Blood was pouring from Gilliat's head, but slowly, so slowly. Campbell-Johnson eased his arm under his friend's shoulder to support him, and watched, momentarily fascinated as the blood soaked into the sleeve of his white dinner jacket.

The Inspector had returned to the car. He was breathing hard.

'Whoever the bastards were, they've gone.'

'Major Gilliat's been wounded,' said Campbell-Johnson, urgently. 'We'll have to get him to a hospital.'

'Right!' Elder climbed back into the car and nodded to Gurdial. 'Let's see if you can get this thing started.' Gurdial did not move. 'Come on, man!' He shook Gurdial's shoulder and the driver's head fell back. He was dead, shot through the forehead.

The hospital assured Campbell-Johnson that Gilliat's head wound was superficial, and he returned to Government House in some relief, though now it was tempered by his doubts about what kind of reception he would get from Mountbatten. The diversion to Pahargunj had not been authorized, and both Gilliat and he were lucky to be alive.

He need not have worried. Mountbatten greeted him with sympathetic concern, and having assured himself that Gilliat was in no real danger, he poured his Press Attaché a stiff whisky. Edwina had come down in her nightclothes to see him, and sat down to hear the story.

'I can't blame you for wanting to see for yourself what's going on, but I can't do without you, Alan. Be more careful in future,' growled Mountbatten.

'Yes, sir. It's odd . . .'

'What?'

'It's 9 September. I had another near miss exactly seven years ago tonight. The Germans dropped a 500-pounder just outside our flat in Westminster. About the same time, too.'

Mountbatten scratched his chin. 'Then you'd better remind me to keep well away from you on 9 September 1954,' he said, drily.

'I'm sorry I wasn't here at the beginning of your story.' Edwina said. 'Was anybody hurt apart from Martin?'

Campbell-Johnson looked at her. 'The driver was killed, I'm afraid, ma'am. Died instantly. I was sitting just behind him.' He paused. It had just occurred to him how close he himself had been to death. 'Inspector Elder was unhurt. A very brave man.'

'Who was your driver, Alan?'

Campbell-Johnson hesitated. 'I'm afraid it was Gurdial Singh.'

Edwina caught her breath, deeply distressed. 'Oh, no . . . He was going to be married soon . . . .' She looked down, feeling the tears pricking at her eyes. The death of her favourite driver was one among many thousands, but it was the first of a person she knew well. For every death, she thought, there were people who felt as she did now.

At the meetings of the Emergency Committee, Mountbatten cracked down so hard on any sign of dragging feet that few dared attend without having made every effort to set their individual assignments in motion. Through the Relief Council, Edwina was managing at last to stem the tide of disease and tension which had been mounting up at one of the worst of the refugee camps, in the Old Fort of Purana Qila. There, starving and without adequate water, the homeless Muslims had further been a prey to Hindu *goondas*, and to disaffection and fighting within their own ranks, the direct result of intolerable overcrowding. But the Committee had yet another, new crisis to contend with. Government personnel had been attacked in their offices, and now clerks and secretaries were staying away, in fear of their lives. As a result, vital work was being done sketchily, or not at all. To counter this, Rees proposed the deployment of yet more troops to guard Government offices. The only problem was that the supply of soldiers, even drawing heavily on Gurkha regiments, was not unlimited.

'We must issue orders for all Government employees to return to duty, on penalty of dismissal,' suggested Nehru.

'And we should do it at once, even on just the promise of troops to protect them,' added Patel. 'I also think we should cancel all leave, including public holidays and Sundays, until the state of emergency is past.'

Mountbatten agreed. He was secretly pleased that the Indian leadership was gradually gaining confidence and taking a greater and greater control of the Emergency Committee. He knew that they were not yet ready to do without his support, but he was gratified to think that the time when they could was not far off now. Slowly, there were signs that the situation in the Punjab was beginning to ease. The battle was not over yet. Delhi was a bomb which they had not yet managed to defuse, but he dared to hope that they would succeed.

And help was on its way from a much-needed quarter. Mahatma Gandhi had announced his intention of travelling to the Punjab. In preparation for this second great undertaking in the name of peace, he was even now journeying from Calcutta towards Delhi.

# ELEVEN

The long, low, marble-fronted mansion stood well back from the brick wall which separated it from Albuquerque Road. Its wide lawns were always the lushest green, even at the height of the dry season, and everywhere hung the scent of magnolia and rhododendron.

Birla House was the Delhi residence of the industrialist and disciple of Gandhi, G.D. Birla. One four-roomed wing had been put at the Mahatma's disposal for his stay in Delhi. The old man, still weak from his fast, had been greatly annoyed at the arrangement, and had at first tried to insist on living as he had done before in the sweepers colony. His disciples listened to him politely, but remained firm. As Sarojini Naidu, the poetess and politician who was one of Mahatma's closest followers drily remarked, 'Sometimes it is just too costly to keep Gandhi in poverty.' Gandhi's vision remained strong, but like all great men, he did not always find it convenient to grasp practical realities. If he had gone now to the sweepers' colony, crowded as it was with refugees, and the centre of one of Delhi's grimmest trouble-spots, he would have needed a regiment to protect him. Here in Delhi there were many embittered people who saw him not as a saviour of his people, but as a traitor to the Hindus.

If he was to be forced to abandon his beloved *harijans*, however, he was not going to be seduced by the luxurious appointments of the rooms in Birla House which had been set aside for him. He wandered through them, briefly looking at, touching, wing armchairs covered in silk brocade, low rosewood tables, and deep, comfortable sofas. He was followed by Amrit Kaur and Vallabhbhai Patel,

257

who had met him at the station, and by Pyarelal Nayyar and Manu and Abha. Among the rest of his entourage, one stood out incongruously: Miraben, who was the daughter of an English admiral and who had formerly been known as Miss Madeleine Slade.

What Gandhi enjoyed most about the rooms was the coolness of their marble floors. He slipped off his tattered sandals and pressed the soles of his leathery angular feet against the smooth stone.

'I am not sure,' he said.

'Gandhiji, it is the most convenient place for those who wish to see you,' urged Patel.

'What? Here? In this luxurious district? My place should be at Purana Qila.'

'You do not understand. People coming in from the Punjab bring such stories of bitterness and hate that nowhere is safe.'

'God is my protector, so how can I not be safe?'

'You would not be able to work. Things have become so bad in the city that even the Muslim servants at Government House have been allowed to bring their families in to protect them.'

Gandhi smiled. He would have expected no less of the Mountbattens. 'I do not know if I could work here, though. I could not even sleep here,' he said to Patel.

'Muslims and Hindus can come to you in peace here.'

'It is far too grand for me, Vallabhbhaiji.'

Amrit Kaur stepped forward. Her plain, noble face was haggard with exhaustion. 'Bapu, please accept the offer. It was kindly meant.'

Gandhi hesitated. He disliked feeling in any way pressured, but he also saw what they were proposing was reasonable. At any rate he could stay here for a time. After he had learnt something of the situation here at first hand, perhaps then he would move. And there was much to plan for his journey to the Punjab. He would go there the way of the refugees, on foot. He smiled to Amrit.

'Very well. Birla is an old friend and I cannot refuse a kindness. But I do make one condition.'

'Of course, Bapu.'

He swept his arm round the room. 'I want all of this furniture removed.'

Two hours later found him sitting quietly alone on his old straw mat on the verandah overlooking a little side-garden. He was spinning thread on his *charkha*, and as he did so he quietly sang his favourite Christian hymn, 'When I Survey The Wondrous Cross'.

His visit to the Map Room both moved Gandhi and alerted him to the extent of the work still to be done. He had kept in touch with events as best he could from Calcutta, but he had imagined nothing like the scale of confusion and misery which arched across the countryside of north-western India from Delhi to Lahore.

'Oh my children, my children, what demons drive you?' he muttered sadly, scanning the maps with their many, many black pins.

'At least you were always against Partition,' said Mountbatten quietly. The Governor General had been shocked to see how emaciated the Mahatma had become, but never ceased to wonder at his spirit. There seemed to be an aura about the man now, which communicated itself to everyone around him. In his presence, the staff of the Map Room had fallen silent, respecting the greatness of his heart, and of his feeling for his suffering people.

'Partition, yes,' Gandhi smiled faintly. 'India clamoured for it, voted for it. I prayed that, when the time came, she would show her maturity by accepting it.' He ran his hand along a long, long line of red pins. 'What is this, General Rees?' he asked the stocky general who stood by him.

'A column, sir. Refugees from Pakistan.'

Gandhi was shaken. It seemed impossible. 'How long is it?'

'At the latest estimate, over fifty-seven miles.' Rees let his words sink in before continuing. 'We're keeping it

259

under constant air surveillance. No one can calculate how many people it contains.'

Gandhi looked again at the ragged line of little red pins. 'Fifty-seven miles . . . of suffering, of despair . . . Fifty-seven miles . . .' The pins covered almost a quarter of the distance between Delhi and Lahore on the map. 'There must be millions there . . . how many will even reach the end of their journey? *Hé, Ram* . . . .'

'We are seeing the beginning of what could be the greatest mass migration in history,' said Mountbatten. 'And only here in Delhi, at the centre, can a possible resolution of it be found.' As Gandhi looked doubtful, the Governor General urgently pressed home his point. 'I know that you want to go on to the Punjab, Gandhji, but I also know that Mr Nehru has asked you to remain in Delhi. I add my voice to his. It is here that you can do most good.'

Gandhi paused for a long moment before answering. 'I cannot promise. I am not yet certain what is the right thing to do. God is silent. My conscience has not yet spoken to me.'

A hundred miles to the north-west, two figures stood by a dust-covered Government Staff Rolls which was parked well off the road on the lip of a steep rise which climbed some twenty-five feet above it. A little apart, the driver and an ADC attended them. Time was passing. The driver shifted from foot to foot, and finally squatted more comfortably upon his haunches in the dust.

For an hour, the attention of the two people standing at the edge of the little rise had been focused on the procession passing on the road below. The people down there all shuffled along at the same tired pace, set by the rhythm of the cooking pots clanging on the sides of the oxcarts to which they were tied. It did not seem possible that there could be so many people. Women carried tiny children, too tired to cry, looking about them with wide, bewildered eyes. Men bore elderly fathers and mothers on their backs. Pale straw-coloured dogs trotted along the flank of the column, forever looking up and looking back. Goats, donkeys, and cows jostled unwillingly along at the ends of lengths of rope. On the tops of the jumbled piles of belongings on the oxcarts more children and old folk sat, jogging with the motion of the carts and staring out over the countryside with unseeing eyes, their thin hands twisted together in their laps.

On and on they marched, their silence only broken by the clattering of their cooking pots: not a child, not an animal made a sound. Terrified of resting, of being left behind, they ground on numbly, to pile up at the few bridges over the Sutlej, over the Ravi, over the Beas, where the bottleneck would be so severe that they would have to wait a week to cross. Not one of them turned his eyes up to the two figures watching them.

'I don't think I ever fully believed it,' said Edwina, quietly breaking their silence.

'Neither did I. Just rows of red pins, until now, seeing it for myself . . .' Jawaharlal Nehru was desperately tired, bowed down by the unending problems he had to cope with, and which seemed to him to be symbolized by this column. He managed a smile for her. 'Thank you for coming with me, Edwina, So much misery . . . Merely the thought of what was happening – at one time I didn't think I could go on.'

She laid a hand on his arm. 'I can't see you ever giving up.'

'No, you're right. I couldn't. Somehow I had to cope, although each day was torture. That I came through at all was thanks to you, and Dickie, and to Gandhiji. I was always aware of him, and his spiritual support helped me to find my courage again.'

They looked at each other in silence, remembering that moment in Nehru's rose garden so many months ago. 'I thank God that Dickie and I did not leave India on 15 August,' she said.

'I give thanks, too.' He hesitated. 'Through you, I have rediscovered the meaning of friendship, and what it is to

261

love.' His eyes tried to tell her what he most dearly wanted to say, but could not. And her eyes answered him.

'We both have our duty, Jawahar,' she said, softly. 'Sometimes . . . it is very unkind.'

They turned to look at the column again, disappearing around a rise in the road ahead, and stretching as far as the eye could see in the direction of Pakistan.

'We can do nothing here,' said Edwina.

'No . . . .' He turned, almost reluctantly, towards the car. 'It is time to go back.'

That evening, a formal dinner was held in the State Dining-Room at Government House in honour of Lord Listowel, the last Secretary of State for India, and his departmental head, Sir Gilbert Laithwaite. The chandeliers shone bright over the great silver dinner service and centrepieces which graced the enormous table. Mountbatten sat opposite Edwina at the centre, she in a damask silk evening gown and he in dress uniform, surrounded by their principal guests and Nehru, his daughter Indira Gandhi, Vallabhbhai Patel, Dr Rajendra Prasad, and Rajkumari Amrit Kaur. Outside on the terrace, a small orchestra was playing Viennese waltzes.

Listowel and Laithwaite had just arrived in Delhi, and as yet no one had warned them of the new regime of austerity that Edwina had imposed on Government House. As long as food remained in such short supply in the city, she was determined to ration severely what was used at her own table, and this occasion was no exception. The silver covers of the soup tureens were removed to reveal the first course, a soup made from cabbage water. Listowel just managed to cover the look of surprise on his face when he caught Edwina turning to him, smiling sweetly as she explained.

Although he applauded the motive, Lord Listowel had to admit that he was disappointed. Instead of the splendid Indian feast he had been looking forward to, he had to make do after the soup with a thin slice of spam and a potato, followed by one biscuit and a small piece of cheese. The regal splendour with which this fare was served did nothing to lift his spirits.

Mountbatten had seen Listowel and Laithwaite off on their continuing tour of India and managed to seize the opportunity to take a swim with Pamela in the pool at the rear of Government House. As he completed a length, swimming with strong, even strokes, he saw Pandit Nehru approaching the side of the swimming pool. The Indian Prime Minister still looked tired, as he sank into a deckchair.

'Why don't you come and join us?' called the Governor General, laughing.

Nehru smiled. 'No, thanks. I've just come from a six-hour Cabinet meeting. I don't have the energy!'

Mountbatten laughed again, and hauled himself up onto the side of the pool. Nehru leaned across to hand him a towel.

'Did something crop up? Is there something on your mind?' asked Mountbatten, drying himself and shaking the water out of his hair.

'Just a thought . . . It occurred to me that there is now no reason why the Emergency Committee can't be phased out, and the country return to its normal government.'

Mountbatten looked up. 'No reason at all. I'm not sure about Delhi yet – but we could appoint a small committee to handle the situation here, while you and the Cabinet get back to the wider issues.'

Nehru looked at him with relief. 'You mean you don't object? Patel swore I'd have to talk you into it.'

'When is that man going to realize that I have no desire to take over the Government?' Mountbatten's amused tone was tempered with a touch of impatience, but Nehru relaxed visibly at it, stretching back in the deck-chair and closing his eyes for a moment to enjoy the sun. As he did so, Edwina emerged from the pool house, wearing an attractive two-piece sun-dress. Still drying her hair, she waved and walked over to them, nodding to Nehru as he stood up to greet her.

'You really should have a dip, Jawahar. It makes a world of difference.' She, indeed, was looking fresh and reinvigorated.

'I would go in, truly, Edwina, if I thought I had the energy.' He sat down again, turning to Mountbatten. 'As it is I wonder if I'll ever get back to leading a normal life again. Jinnah keeps up his diplomatic attacks on us, but I cannot yet give full priority to the transfer of assets to Pakistan. Not until the refugee question is settled.'

Mountbatten looked surprised. 'Jinnah keeps assuring me that his only wish is for peace between you.'

Nehru's only answer was to laugh drily.

'In any case, there are still some very urgent questions to be settled between you. Not least, over Kashmir and Hyderabad.'

'It is unfortunate that Lord Ismay wasn't able to get an unequivocal answer out of Hari Singh,' said Nehru. 'And the Nizam of Hyderabad is as slippery as a squid. But they must both decide soon whether to join India or Pakistan – certainly by the end of the year. And there is still the question of Junagadh to be settled.' He paused, considering. Although his little state was entirely contained within the frontiers of India, and although even within Junagadh there were pockets of land belonging to the Dominion, the Muslim Nawab still flirted with Jinnah over taking his country with its Hindu majority population into Pakistan. His great bargaining point was his little strip of coastline, and Jinnah was supporting him. Nehru knew that Jinnah had not the troops, the transport or the money to move a Pakistani army there, which is what he would need to do to enforce any claim to the state, but he also knew that Jinnah was using Junagadh to play for higher stakes: Kashmir, with its Hindu ruler and Muslim majority. If India forcibly took Junagadh, Jinnah would have the moral justification to take Kashmir. The question was, for how long could they outface each other? The thought of Kashmir, his family's homeland, falling into Jinnah's hands, was unbearable for him. To Nehru, it seemed inevitable that in the long run Junagadh and Hyderabad would have to accede to India. Although both had Muslim rulers, their populations were Hindu, and Junagadh was too small to withstand India, and Hyderabad too far from Pakistan, and landlocked. Still, the risk of losing Kashmir to Jinnah weighed on him.

'I gather you've pipped Dickie at the post,' Edwina was saying. Nehru looked at her blankly. His thoughts had been far away. 'He was going to suggest running down the Emergency Committee himself!'

'No wonder you gave in so easily!' Nehru smiled to Mountbatten.

'Great minds think alike, Jawahar. No, the Committee has done good work, but nobody could be more pleased than me to say goodbye to it. Why don't you announce it tomorrow morning?'

'I think it will mean more to all of us if we hear it from you,' said Nehru delicately.

'Certainly a return to normal government should reassure everybody,' said Edwina. Across the pool, Pamela had got out and was making for the house. 'Shall I get Pammy to order some tea or coffee?'

'Not for me,' said Nehru. 'I hope you're right about people being reassured by a return to normality. Gandhi seems to think that the violence in Delhi has only been driven under the surface.'

'At least he's agreed to stay,' said Mountbatten. 'He might not have been able to repeat the miracle of Calcutta here yet, but his presence is certainly a calming influence.'

'Is he any stronger?' asked Edwina.

'He says he is,' replied Nehru. 'Yet I worry about him. He will be seventy-eight next Thursday, but every day he visits the camps, and holds his prayer meetings at Birla House in the evenings. He's like you two, he doesn't know how to stop.'

Edwina was thinking. 'Could we visit him on his birthday?' she suggested.

Nehru was pleased. 'It will be a great celebration that day, and I am sure he would be delighted to see you. Many will be coming to him to receive *darshan*. But,' he looked at Mountbatten, doubtfully, 'I think it could be awkward, politically, for the Governor General himself to go. Matters are so finely balanced at the moment, the slightest mark of favouring one side or the other . . .'

'Well, there's nothing to stop me from going,' smiled Edwina. 'After all, I've been to see him before.' She caught a look of mild warning from her husband's eye. 'Oh, come on, Dickie. I do think one of us should go.'

Gandhi rose slightly earlier than usual on his birthday. He had awakened with a start, the noises of his dream still beating in his ears. But all was quiet in the cool bare room in Birla House, and at his side he could hear Manu sleeping peacefully. He sat up and stared out of the window, where the night sky reflected the first pale hint of dawn.

He had been dreaming about the train. The incident had happened shortly after his arrival in Delhi, and was what made him decide to stay. He shuddered at the memory, so freshly conjured up in his mind by the nightmare. He had gone down to the main railway station, where many Hindu refugees were crowding the platforms, waiting for relatives to arrive on the next train. The platforms were crammed with people and the authorities were powerless to move them on forcibly. Partly for their own protection, they were hemmed in on the platform by coils of barbed wire.

As the train approached, the great black iron engine releasing a deafening hiss of steam as it slowed, the crowd surged forward, as it always did. Two young women were almost hurled from the platform beneath the huge prow of the locomotive, and they would not have been the first to die in this way; but people managed to catch their hands and haul them back to safety. The density of the crowd was such that any real movement on the platform seemed

266

impossible, yet as the train drew up, the people fell back, the babel of shouting voices and the overriding shrieking of the women fading into shocked silence.

It must have been one of the last death trains out of the Punjab, and one of the few to reach Delhi itself. The twisted bodies of the dead soldiers hanging out of the locomotive's window and lying on the coal in the tender told their own story. The badly wounded driver managed to stagger down from the footplate before he collapsed into the arms of the young man who stepped forward to catch him.

Along the train, people were opening carriage doors to reveal the mangled dead. A few bold men in the crowd climbed into the carriages to search for survivors, as it was by no means unusual for refugees to sham death to escape their attackers. Others ran to fetch water, and to call the police and ambulances. But from the majority of the people on the platform a dreadful howl of rage went up.

'Muslim dogs! Murderers!'

The crowd had become a mob, and it was confronting Gandhi. He had come to the station directly from a visit to the Muslim refugee camp at Humanyun's Tomb, and a handful of his brave Muslim devotees had accompanied him there.

'Get them!' The people at the front of the mob surged forward, pushed by the press of people behind them.

Gandhi raised his hand to them, and they hesitated, growling with rage. He was swaying with shock at what he had seen on the train, and now he realized with grief that the violence alone would once more breed upon itself unless he could stop it. Inwardly he prayed that God would give him the strength he needed to do so.

The mob was still, its attention focused on him. The Mahatma had closed his eyes, and when he opened them they could see that his cheeks ran with tears.

'Has there not been enough death here already?' he cried. 'Have you not seen enough horror? Would you really kill these people, these innocent people who could not possibly be responsible for the deaths on the train?'

'They're Muslims, aren't they?' yelled someone from the crowd.

'They are people who suffer, like you,' replied Gandhi. 'And India is their home as well as yours. You are all my brothers and sisters, and my children – and yet you have learnt nothing from my teaching. You turn your hand against your brother only because he calls God by a different name. Is this how you show yourselves worthy of the freedom we have won after such a long struggle?' He paused, glaring at them, as they bowed their heads in shame.

Gandhi sat thinking, reliving the moment as he watched the dawn break behind the pipal trees in the garden. He had calmed the mob, and they had even worked shoulder to shoulder with his Muslim friends in helping carry the wounded survivors from the train to the ambulances. But Gandhi knew that if he had not been there the story would have been different, and had come to see why no Muslim would show himself alone in this city, which had been built by Muslims, and which three hundred years ago had been the cornerstone of a Muslim empire which had stretched right across northern India.

Manu was stirring, smiling at him sleepily as she rose.

'Am I late, Bapu?'

'No, child. I am early.'

She brought him water to drink, and to wash in. Abha rose and went outside to the verandah, where already the first Indians had arrived to pay their respects and offer birthday gifts to the Mahatma.

He sat cross-legged on a simple *charpoy*, nodding and smiling as the people filed past him, depositing their presents of money, fruit and flowers in an ever-increasing pile in front of him. Someone had placed a garland of jasmine flowers around his neck. Another had smeared his chest with saffron powder, and a *tilak* had been placed on his forehead. Beside him on this day of celebration, the Prime Minister of India, Jawaharlal Nehru, sat humbly on the floor.

Although the sun was high in the sky by now, the marble room remained pleasantly cool, and Gandhi was grateful for it. He began to long for the seemingly endless procession of visitors to be over. His eyes lit up with pleasure, however, when he saw who was entering the garden room now.

'My dear Lady Louis,' he said, smiling as he placed his palms together, returning her *namaste*. 'You will forgive my not rising, but it has been a tiring day.'

'Of course. Many happy returns, Gandhiji.'

'You honour me by your presence.'

'My husband asked me very particularly to bring you his warmest wishes. He is very disappointed that today of all days his schedule prevents him from coming to see you.'

Gandhi smiled at her formality, glancing briefly at Nehru. 'I received his charming letter. That is more than kind enough.'

'You've never seen so many letters!' said Nehru excitedly. 'And telegrams and cables from all over the world.'

Gandhi's face became sad. 'Why do they congratulate me? My heart bears nothing but anguish.'

'I am certain that through your influence bad will give way to good,' said Edwina. 'And you still have so much to do. Didn't you say you would need to live to be a hundred and twenty to achieve all you wanted to?'

'Ah, that was in what seems now like another world, my dear friend. Now, I have lost all desire to live long. I will never give up hope, but I do not wish another birthday to come upon me in an India in flames.'

Fifty miles north of Rawalpindi, in that part of Pakistan which had been the North-West Frontier Province of British India, a line of trucks came to a halt near the bridge over the Jhelum River which marked the border with Kashmir. The night was dark and moonless, and the only

269

sound was the rushing water of the Jhelum, crashing down its rocky bed far below. The men in the trucks had counted on the noise to conceal the sound of their motors, and they had taken care to switch off their headlights two miles further down the road. Now, they cut their engines, and sat waiting in the freezing night, looking across at the few lights of the little town of Muzaffarabad a couple of miles beyond the frontier post.

Led by a young member of the Muslim League's militant Green Shirts, the men in the trucks were all Pathans. Owing allegiance to no one but themselves, they nevertheless fiercely upheld the Koran. Now they waited for the signal from across the river which would tell them that the Muslim troops of Hari Singh's frontier garrison had overpowered their Hindu officers and taken the frontier post. It had all been very carefully arranged. The telephone lines to Srinagar would be cut. The capital of Kashmir lay not a hundred and fifty miles away along the mountain road, and it would be undefended.

Suddenly the green flare from a Verey pistol, its dull report clearly audible through the thin air above the roar of the river, arched high into the sky, bathing the bridge for an instant in lurid light. The trucks' engines fired into life, and the column moved forward into Kashmir.

Mohammed Ali Jinnah could wait no longer. So confident was he of his surprise attack that he had already moved to the town of Abbotabad on the Pakistani side of the frontier, from where he planned to make a triumphal entry to Srinagar, the beautiful mountain city on its enchanted lake, within days. He had decided to use Pathans rather than the Pakistani Army for two reasons: if he used the army, the British officers who commanded it would resign as soon as they realized what was going on; and if the manoeuvre went wrong, he could disclaim any involvement on the part of Pakistan. The whole business could simply be dismissed as another Pathan raid. Everyone knew the Pathans were lawless plunderers, quick to take advantage of any unstable situation.

Jinnah smiled to himself in the modest house he was staying at in Abbotabad. His arrival there had been a triumphal one. '*Hamchelya Pakistan, Lar ke linge Hindustan!*' the people had shouted. He had covered himself well, not that he expected to fail. He knew that he had no hope of keeping the operation secret, but by the time his British officers got wind of what was going on and reported to Delhi, it would be too late.

The direct-line telephone rang on General Sir Robert Lockhart's desk in New Delhi in the late afternoon of Friday, 24 October. He picked it up immediately, and tensed as he listened to the report from his counterpart in Pakistan, General Douglas Gracey. Gracey was able to give the size, armament and location of the Pathan force. They appeared to have been in Kashmir since the Wednesday night, but unaccountably were not yet anywhere near Srinagar. As soon as he had set the phone down, Lockhart picked up another phone and dialled the Governor General's number.

'*Kashmir?*' said Nehru, stunned.

'The report we have says that they've been there for two days. Apparently the tribesmen say their aim is to liberate their fellow Muslims from the Hindu maharajah,' said V.P. Menon.

Nehru had gone white with anger. 'Oh, yes, I am sure,' he snarled. 'But we all know who is behind this! Well, he isn't going to get away with it. I want our troops sent in at once!' He had stood up, making a tight ball of his fist. Now he subsided once more, shaking. The Punjab was barely under control, Delhi was still a powder keg, and now this! Jinnah could certainly pick his time. He glared at his fellow members of the Defence Council.

'Please believe that I understand exactly how you feel,' began Mountbatten carefully, 'but I must tell you that the greatest possible harm could be done, politically and militarily, by acting too fast. In any case, we can do nothing

271

until we have heard General Lockhart's full report.' He turned to the Scottish soldier sitting on his right.

'As far as we know,' said the General, glancing at his notes, 'the invasion was carried out by approximately five thousand Pathan tribesmen. They are heavily armed, and they have taken the cities of Domel and Muzaffarabad.'

'Can the maharajah's army hold them off?' asked Nehru, despairingly.

'It's unlikely, sir. Its rank-and-file is Muslim, and the whole Muslim population is disaffected.'

'An invasion on this scale must have needed a great deal of preparation,' put in the Defence Minister, Baldev Singh. 'Why have we not had any earlier intelligence reports?'

'The only reports we have had regarded defence preparations along that border. To confuse matters, General Messervy, Mr Jinnah's C-in-C, is on a mission to London. I had the news from the acting C-in-C, General Gracey. None of the general staff at Rawalpindi knew of any preparations for an invastion.'

Vallabhbhai Patel rapped his knuckles irritably on the desk in front of him and exchanged a look with Nehru. 'Obviously, Jinnah planned all this under the noses of his British advisors, and made sure that when it happened his C-in-C was out of the way!'

'That's an assumption, Mr Patel, not a fact,' snapped the Governor General.

'It's one we have every right to make,' the Deputy Prime Minister shot back.

'But until it's proven we must act under international law, or the consequences will be disastrous.'

'In my view the consequences are already disastrous,' stormed Nehru. 'We must send in troops at once!'

'Are we to sit idly by and let Jinnah take Kashmir?' Patel wanted to know.

'The point is, gentlemen,' said Mountbatten, raising his voice just enough to override the furious Indian politicians, 'that Mr Jinnah is *not doing so* – at least, not openly. He has been clever enough to disguise his actions behind the

Pathans. Obviously he hoped that by the time we got to hear of it, the invasion of Kashmir would be a *fait accompli* and Srinagar would be taken. But as things stand we still cannot send Indian troops into a neutral state. And that is what Kashmir remains, despite everything. If we did, it would be an act of war, and would give him the only excuse he needs to commit the Pakistani Army. Do you really want – can you *afford* a full-scale war?'

'If it is unavoidable,' muttered Patel, stubbornly.

'We must avoid it, Mr Patel!'

Nehru was calmer now, but it was still an effort for him to speak without emotion. 'What do you suggest, Your Excellency?'

Mountbatten exhaled deeply in relief, and then continued. 'We are still legally bound by our Standstill Agreement with Hari Singh. He must decide whether he is ready now to make a formal Accession to India. But I must stress that whatever decision he makes must be confirmed later by a referendum of the people of Kashmir.'

'Agreed,' replied Nehru urgently. 'And now I propose that we send our representative immediately.' There was no need for him to stress the importance of prompt action. As soon as the maharajah had signed even a provisional Instrument of Accession, Kashmir would be part of the Dominion of India, and they would have the right to move Indian Army troops into the new province to protect it quite legitimately aganst the depredations of the Pathans.

'I propose that we send Mr Menon,' suggested Mountbatten.

'Seconded,' rapped out Patel.

Menon had already risen.

'Get his agreement, V.P., and get back here with it as soon as you can,' said Mountbatten, tersely but warmly. If anybody could do the job, this was the man. And after three months of vacillation in the faint hope of hanging on to his independence, the vainglorious maharajah should now be in no condition to argue. It was almost pathetic, thought Mountbatten, how quickly the old feudal princes of India were being swept aside by modern power politics and the march of history.

'General Lockhart, detail two military advisors to go with V.P. to report back on the exact disposition of the Pathans and whatever part of the maharajah's army that remains loyal,' he continued.

The General and Menon hurried out.

'You realize it may already be too late?' said Nehru, quietly.

'I can't answer that, but the information Lockhart had was pretty fresh. I must say I can't understand why the Pathans aren't in Srinagar already, unless they've been inside Kashmir for a shorter time than our information suggests.'

Patel suddenly looked up, his expression clearer, more hopeful. 'Of course! They are looting!' Nehru turned to him, as, almost laughing, he went on. 'This time Jinnah's been too damned clever for his own good! He thought he'd covered himself by using Pathans, but the whole plan's rebounded on him. The Pathans are hopelessly undisciplined – they answer to no one. Oh, he might have told them to make straight for Srinagar, and offered them all sorts of rewards to do so, but if he sent them in virtually on their own, they'll have forgotten all about it. My guess is they'll stay at least a day in every town and village they pass along the way, and they won't move on until they've picked it clean.'

'Well, if that's the case,' said Nehru, beginning to hope, too, 'we might just have time.'

Peter Howes had entered the room, and crossed to Mountbatten briskly, passing him a handwritten note. The Governor General scanned it quickly, and looked up. 'Will you excuse me, gentlemen? I've been summoned to an urgent meeting with Field Marshal Auchinleck.'

The others did not demur. There was in any case little they could do until Menon reported back to them. Mountbatten hurried down the long corridor from the Council Chamber to his study on the upper basement floor of Government House. Grim-faced, he held the note crumpled in his hand.

Sir Claude Auchinleck dispensed with preliminary greetings in a matter of seconds and came straight down to cases.

'There's no diplomatic way out of this Kashmiri mess, Dickie. There's going to be fighting, and a lot of it.'

'That seems only too likely, Claude,' replied Mountbatten with equal brusqueness. 'But what's your point?'

'There are a lot of retired Britons in Kashmir – ex-army, ex-ICS, and so on. Hundreds of them, in fact, especially up around Srinagar.'

Mountbatten hedged. 'That's hardly surprising. It's one of the most beautiful spots on earth.'

'Well, it won't be once the Pathans get there. You know as well as I do that there'll be a massacre.' Auchinleck drew himself up. 'I want permission to lift a brigade into Srinagar now to protect and if necessary evacuate our people.'

'You mean *British* troops?'

'I'll command them myself.'

'Claude, I know how you feel, but I can't bring British troops into this.'

'Why not?'

Mountbatten struck the desk in exasperation. 'Haven't you got it into your head yet? These countries are *independent*! We have no mandate for military operations here!'

It was Auchinleck's turn to be astonished. He looked at the younger man keenly. 'You mean to say you're just going to bloody well stand by and let your people be slaughtered? Have you any idea what Pathans *do* to people?'

Mountbatten had gone grey, but he stood his ground. It was not just a question of upholding any principle. It was the principle of free government that was at stake. Put like that, Auchinleck saw his point. 'But it's damned hard to have to watch and do nothing,' he muttered.

275

'It's the hardest lesson I've had to learn.' Mountbatten told him. 'But there is something you could do.'

'What? Anything!'

'Get in touch with Jinnah. He'll listen to you. Tell him what a disaster a war between his country and India would be at this stage. Spell it out to him.'

'He'd lose half his officers for a start! His British commanders would resign on the spot.'

'Then tell him! For God's sake go and tell him that!'

Glad of the chance to bury frustration in action, Auchinleck left immediately. Mountbatten was left pondering the state of Jinnah's mind, that he could not see what he was so obviously risking. Had the megalomania that had seized him from the moment he had won Pakistan now totally conquered his devious but rational mind?

After the Defence Council meeting had ended, Nehru sought out Edwina in the private drawing-room. Now it was he who had an urgent need to unburden himself to a sympathetic listener.

'I have tried to think like Gandhiji,' he exclaimed. 'I have preached non-violence for years! But this is Kashmir!'

Edwina had never seen him so moved. 'Dickie is right though – we must act within the law,' she ventured.

'I know!' Nehru paced up and down behind the sofa on which she was sitting. 'Yet all the time I am asking myself if really all I am doing is making Jinnah a present of Kashmir? I could not face the future if that were so. I could not face the people of India!' He wheeled round nervously as the door opened to admit Mountbatten. 'What did Auchinleck want?' he demanded, as the Governor General poured himself a whisky.

'Nothing,' replied Mountbatten. 'He's trying to arrange a meeting with Jinnah. Make him see sense.' He sipped his drink.

'Then I wish him luck most sincerely,' said Nehru.

Edwina heard the bitterness in his voice. Like him, she was puzzled by her husband's lack of positive action. 'Are

276

you just going to do nothing, Dickie? Nothing until V.P. returns?'

'I wouldn't say that.'

'Then what?' Nehru asked.

'Well, if there's going to be any kind of showdown we'd better be ready for it. And since it seems pretty clear that we're going to need more transport than the Air Force has available, I would suggest that you issue an order to all the Indian civil airlines to put their passengers off at the nearest airport and head for Delhi.'

For the first time that day, Nehru laughed.

V.P. Menon, haggard after his turn-around flight to Srinagar, stood once more before the emergency session of the Defence Council. His report was grave.

'. . . the city of Srinagar is in total panic, and the maharajah completely demoralized. I should say that he was confused and unnerved; overtaken by events. He is ready to sign an Instrument of Accession on any terms we propose.'

The relief around the table was palpable, not just at the success of Menon's mission, but at the fact that Srinagar had not yet fallen. Patel's secretary handed him a folder.

'Here is the document for Hari Singh to sign,' said Patel.

'He won't go back on it, V.P.?' Nehru was still jumpy, suspicious.

'No, sir. In fact it is now extremely urgent that I return. I advised the maharajah to move to his winter palace at Jammu, in order to ensure his safety. He has done so, but he has given his bodyguards orders that if I do not return by dawn, it will mean that India has abandoned him, and they are to shoot him in his sleep.'

Nehru looked at the dapper little bald-headed civil servant. It hardly seemed possible, sometimes, that this man lived through such dramas.

'Then you'd better go back at once – before his unusual alarm clock goes off.'

'With pleasure, sir.'

'Just a moment, V.P.,' interrupted Mountbatten. 'You said you'd had him move south to Jammu. What's the military situation in Srinagar?'

'I was going to mention that. The advisors will give you a full report, but the essence of it is this: the Pathans have reached Baramullah, and that's only thirty-five miles from the capital. I'm afraid they've raided a convent there. Once they've finished looting, Srinagar will be their next stop. That's why I asked the maharajah to move south.'

'How many men did he leave to defend the city?'

'Only one squadron of cavalry,' Menon told them bleakly.

Nehru was on his feet. 'Srinagar has the only airfield big enough to take transports. Whatever troops we send must be flown in immediately.'

Mountbatten turned to General Lockhart. 'Are your preparations complete, Rob?'

'The First Sikh Regiment is standing by, sir.'

'Right. As soon as we hear from V.P. that Hari Singh has signed, I want the airlift to Srinagar begun. We can start sending up reinforcements by road via Gurdaspur at dawn, but the Sikhs must hold the airport at all costs.'

Menon took the folder from Patel and hurried from the room. Mountbatten turned to Nehru. 'I had a message from Auchinleck half an hour ago. He's had a meeting with Jinnah, and it sounds as if it didn't go too badly. But Jinnah's in Abbotabad, waiting to make a triumphal entry into Srinagar himself.' He paused, allowing himself a faint smile. 'If we can only move quickly enough, he may have to wait a little longer than he thinks.'

In his study in Abbotabad, Mohammed Ali Jinnah, his thin form taut with fury, stood looking out of the windows which faced towards Kashmir. He was smoking in small, jerky puffs. Liaqat Ali Khan, his prime Minister, sat at the desk, keeping as still and as quiet as possible.

'Those tribesmen had two days to reach Srinagar,' Jinnah raged. 'They could have done it in as many hours! A hundred and thirty miles of undefended road . . . . The Muslims there would have risen to support them – and we could have annexed Kashmir in the maharajah's palace, itself!' He swung away from the windows and began to pace. 'But what did they do? They stopped to loot every town and village on the way – and gave Nehru time to fly in his soldiers!'

Liaqat was still holding the transcript of the radioed report and laid it on the desk. 'Tragic, Your Excellency.'

'To think that we risk losing Kashmir because of the greed of a few hillmen for bazaar trinkets and women!' Jinnah broke off pacing and glared at Liaqat. 'And now they are being forced back!'

'They'll make a stand as soon as the surprise of the Sikh attack is over,' Liaqat said, reassuringly. 'And we can move our own troops in to support them, long before Indian reinforcements arrive.'

'Don't talk nonsense!' Jinnah snapped. 'We daren't order our regulars in. You heard Auchinleck. Until we have trained enough commanders of our own, our army would fall to pieces without its British officers.'

He stubbed his cigarette out in the ashtray on the desk and turned to the window again. It was a bitter fact to face, that his army was not yet ready to stand on its own. The maharajah would accede to India, of course. There would be no Muslim rising and so he would have no excuse to move his troops in, even if it were possible. All he could hope for was that the Pathans would be able to hold on at least to some part of Kashmir, long enough for him to negotiate some kind of deal with Delhi. Even if it meant splitting the state in two, like the Punjab. Or perhaps . . . Liaqat had given him the germ of an idea. Perhaps he could dress one or two of his crack battalions as hillmen and send them in secretly. Either course was shabby, ignominious, compared to the triumph which had so nearly been his.

It was night outside. Through the windows he could see only blackness and the vast wheeling night sky with its countless tiny points of fire. Some men were inspired by the stars. He had always found them cold and bleak, their remoteness and lifelessness a mockery of all human aspiration.

'The "K" in Pakistan stands for Kashmir,' he said. Liaqat had to strain to hear him. 'It was my last dream . . . to possess it. Have you any idea how it feels to win – and then lose – your dream?'

Edwina was at her desk, working through a pile of reports, appeals and statistics, far too busy to stop for lunch she said to Dickie, when he came to find her.

However, that was not why he had come. 'I thought you would want to know,' he told her. 'Nehru's doctors are worried about him.' She laid down her pen. 'He's had too many problems, made do with too little sleep. From the Defence Council this morning, he went straight to a Cabinet meeting, and afterwards had to be put to bed.'

They drove at once to the villa in York Road, where Indira met them. She told them that her father was resting. 'It is mainly tiredness, strain,' she said. 'But I am sure he'd want to see you.'

She took them up to the bedroom, where Nehru lay, weak and drawn. They were concerned to see him so ill and, when he tried to thank them for coming, Mountbatten stopped him. 'I don't think you should talk. We want you to get your strength back.'

Edwina moved a chair nearer the bed and sat by Nehru, taking his hand. 'You must recover,' she said. 'You must get well, now when there is so much need of you.'

His head moved in denial, his voice little more than whisper. '. . . I am not a war leader. Even the anger of these last days has taken all my energy.' His tiredness made him low-spirited, a prey to depression. He felt useless lying here. 'I cannot stop thinking, cannot rest – for the thought that my homeland may be lost to India for ever.'

'Then there's something you should hear,' Mountbatten told him. 'We have had a report that the Sikhs have held

Srinagar – and begun to push the tribesmen back. Sadly, their Commanding Officer was killed, but apart from that there were very few casualties.'

Nehru lay gazing at him and his eyes moved to Edwina.

'It is true,' she confirmed. 'The report came just as we left Government House. I have seen it.'

Mountbatten smiled. 'As soon as our reinforcements arrive, they will clear the Vale of Kashmir – and they will keep it clear.'

Nehru was too weak to react, but the relief made his tense body begin to relax. 'That is news I had not dared to hope for,' he whispered. He lay back and his eyes closed. His hand was still in Edwina's and she did not let go.

Mountbatten watched them for a long moment in silence. 'I have a great deal to do,' he said. 'Maybe you'd like to stay for a while.'

She looked at him, but did not answer. As always, she was grateful for his understanding. She could not leave now. He went out, closing the door.

Edwina sat quietly by Nehru, holding his hand as he fell asleep.

# TWELVE

Jinnah had been checked, but not defeated. Indian spies working in the Pakistani administration were reporting within days that the Muslim leader had deployed units of his soldiers, disguised as tribesmen, to help the Pathans at least to keep their foothold in Kashmir. They were commanded by one of the best officers in the Pakistani Army, General Akhbar Khan, himself masquerading as a Pathan chieftain under the name of Tariq.

At the same time, Jinnah made another, more direct approach to the Indian Government. Nehru, still easily cast down by his illness, was depressed when Mountbatten and Patel gave him the first piece of news, but rallied when he started to learn about the second. He pulled himself more upright as a servant adjusted his pillows, and looked keenly at the two men sitting one on either side of his bed. Although his face was still drawn and grey, his eyes had regained some of their usual brightness.

'Jinnah's reaction to the Accession is very much what you might expect,' Mountbatten was saying. 'He's denounced it as "based on fraud and violence", and so not to be accepted by Pakistan.'

'*He* accuses *us* of fraud and violence!' spat Vallabhbhai Patel.

'Yes, but it's bluster. The real point is, Jawahar, that he wants a top level meeting to discuss the problem. He wants you and me to meet him in Lahore.'

'Don't do it! There's nothing to talk about!' insisted Patel.

Nehru's eyes narrowed slightly as he weighed the possibilities. The problem had been all of Jinnah's making, and

India had gained Kashmir by it. On the other hand, if they could push home their advantage through diplomacy it might be possible to avoid further bloodshed. Nehru was well aware that the state had a mainly Muslim population, and it would be better to woo them into wanting to be part of India than to hold them by force. The former course would not be accomplished by turning Kashmir into a war-zone, something which Jinnah would probably be prepared to do if only to swing popular Muslim feeling there against India. But even if he had the money, Jinnah dared not commit his army openly.

'In any case how dare *he* summon *us* to Lahore,' continued Patel. 'He should come here, if there's to be any meeting.'

'You know he won't leave Pakistan,' said Mountbatten.

'Then it's a trick of some sort. He knows Jawaharlal's too ill to travel! His doctors would not allow it.'

'Well,' replied Mountbatten, 'Liaqat Ali Khan is unwell, too, at the moment – so much so that he won't be able to travel from Karachi to Lahore.'

'He is a cipher, merely Jinnah's shadow,' Patel pointed out, quickly.

'The Qaid-i-Azam may have appropriated more power to his Governor-Generalship than I have to mine,' Mountbatten said, mildly, 'but nevertheless it would not seem strange for the two Governors General to have a first meeting alone on this, without their Prime Ministers. And I have no objection to going alone, if you would like me to. I am quite prepared to go to see anyone, anywhere and at any time, if it will help the public interest.' He looked at Nehru, who had closed his eyes.

He was not sleeping. He had followed the brief discussion between his two friends, and was weighing their opinions. Much was in his favour. On Accession, the pro-Congress Muslim leader of the Kashmiri popular front, Sheikh Abdullah, who had only recently been a guest in one of Hari Singh's prisons, had been appointed Prime Minister of Kashmir. Abdullah was a close personal friend of Nehru.

Jinnah might well object that, under these circumstances, in any plebiscite the Muslim population would be afraid to vote for Pakistan. Well, let him, thought Nehru. On the other hand, if he allowed a referendum and the vote did go for Pakistan, he would have lost Kashmir. And he could not bear the thought of even risking that, especially now that he was in such a strong position. He opened his eyes and looked at them both.

'Really, the decision is up to me,' he said.

'I expect you to back me on this,' Patel warned. Relations had been strained between the two men, at the best of times uncomfortable allies, and there was a note of warning in his voice. Nehru was certain that Patel's ambitions would not tempt him to split the party at a time like this, but he was equally aware that the danger was there.

'I am sorry, Vallabhbhai, but I agree with Lord Louis,' he said. 'I will do anything I possibly can to prevent this from becoming an all-out war.' He turned on his pillow to face Mountbatten. 'If my health permits, I will come with you to Lahore. And don't look so worried, Vallabhbhai. At least Jinnah's request for a meeting tells us that, in his heart of hearts, he knows his invasion cannot succeed.'

The long line of women queued patiently in the hot sun at the refugee camp at Panipat. In the past weeks, the camp had swelled to take on all the appearance of a sizeable shanty town. Those arriving at the two trestle-tables set up outside the medical tent received cholera injections from two overworked nurses. Beyond them, through the awning of the large hospital tent, two doctors could just be seen working among the women patients crowded in there.

Edwina turned to the Nursing Sister who was showing them round. 'I'm glad you got the supplies we sent.'

'Two days ago, Your Excellency, but already they are nearly used up. Almost a thousand new people come here every day.'

'Well, we'll just have to try to keep supplies coming as fast as we can. Though we'll never get ahead of ourselves.'

284

They were entering the hospital tent, followed by Muriel and an Indian ADC. For a moment, Edwina stood looking around at the wretched women, some wounded, some already suffering from the tuberculosis which would kill them, others heavily pregnant. She turned to the Sister. 'The other thing I should tell you is that the Relief Council has put out an appeal for blankets and warm clothes. We ought to be able to send up the first consignments at the end of the week.' To add to the misery, the cruel Punjabi winter was coming.

Edwina moved further into the tent, now and then stooping to talk to or help a patient. Her assistant, Muriel Watson, watched her worriedly. Edwina had been pacing herself a little more sensibly since the Relief Council had begun to operate smoothly, but now Muriel recognized all the signs that Her Excellency was gearing herself for another marathon of back-breakingly hard and selfless work. Faced with such a cliff-face of suffering, it was difficult for Her Excellency to react otherwise, Muriel knew. Yet it was a daunting prospect.

'You haven't forgotten you have a speech to make to the relief workers, have you?' Muriel asked anxiously. 'We should be going.'

As she spoke a junior nurse came up to the Nursing Sister and spoke quietly.

'Excuse me, Your Excellency,' said the Sister. 'There's a telephone call for you in the Dispensary Tent.'

Edwina looked up but did not move from where she was standing. 'See who it is, will you, Muriel?'

'It's a personal call for you, Your Excellency. From Delhi.'

'Very well.' Edwina left the tent, followed by her little retinue, and crossed the hot square where the mudcakes created by the monsoon rains were already drying in the sun. As they reached the shade of the Dispensary Tent the junior nurse handed her the heavy field telephone receiver and stood back. The walls were piled high with cardboard boxes of medical supplies, everything available from cholera serum to ordinary aspirins and bandages, but most of the boxes were nearly empty of their contents.

'Edwina Mountbatten,' she said abstractedly. The phone responded with a buzzing rattle. 'Sorry, this is a terrible line . . . .' She looked across at the others, frowning comically. 'Oh it's you, Dickie . . . What's the problem? . . . What?' Her expression changed to one of delight, and she laughed. 'But that's wonderful! To tell you the truth I've been so busy I'd almost forgotten she was pregnant! No, no, I'm not being serious! . . . Yes, I'll be back tomorrow – you can tell me everything then . . . .'

She turned smilingly to the others. 'I have some lovely news and you can both congratulate me. My daughter Patricia's just had her baby. I have a grandson!'

The cork popped and he quickly poured the cold champagne into two fluted glasses. 'Here you are,' he smiled. 'For the year's most glamorous grannie!'

'Don't, Dickie,' she laughed, accepting the drink. 'I certainly don't feel like one.'

'You and me, both. It feels distinctly odd to be a grandfather.' He was joking, yet it was unbearable to think of his beloved daughter going through a whole pregnancy, childbirth and motherhood – and he had not been there. He paused, looking down at the bubbles winking in his glass. 'Well, we'd better have a toast. What's it to be?'

'I think we ought to drink to him, don't you?'

Mountbatten raised his glass. 'To our first grandson, to Norton!'

'And to his generation,' Edwina added, raising hers. They drank, and she continued, 'I can't wait to see him.'

'Well, you should be able to, quite soon,' he told her, 'when we go home for the wedding.'

'Wedding?'

'Elizabeth and Philip's.' He was surprised he had to remind her. Naturally, they had been invited to the marriage of his nephew to the twenty-one-year-old Princess Elizabeth. He could not think of missing it.

Edwina was troubled. Dickie was quite capable of accepting the invitation out of family pride. But it was not possible. 'I don't know whether we should go,' she said.

He was reaching for the bottle to top up their glasses, and stopped. 'It would be noticed if we weren't there.'

'How can we go to England?' she demanded. 'I mean, there's so much to do here. It's out of the question!'

Mountbatten saw that she could become upset and said soothingly, 'It's only a suggestion. We don't have to decide anything yet.'

'The situation's far too critical. We can't even think of leaving! You'd be accused of being irresponsible – just walking away from all the problems here.'

He saw that he would have to play it very carefully. He took up the champagne bottle, but she shook her head and covered her glass with her hand. He refilled his own. 'As I said, we don't have to decide now. And I'll be in a better position to judge after tomorrow, once I've had my meeting with Jinnah.'

'Is he going with you?' Edwina asked.

'Nehru? No, his doctors have forbidden him to travel.'

'How is he?'

'Weak as a kitten still,' Mountbatten said. 'But on the mend.' He sipped his champagne. And wished, not for the first time, that he was the sort who could happily get drunk. He had had to convince Edwina it was right for them to stay. Now she was objecting to leaving even for a few days. She was not the only problem. 'I wish he *was* coming with me. I'm not looking forward to this meeting.'

Given his emotional attitude to Kashmir, perhaps it was better that Jawaharlal was still too unwell to travel. However, Mountbatten did not relish meeting Jinnah alone. The Qaid-i-Azam was ageing rapidly and had begun to show all the classic symptoms of what happens to those who have absolute power. Once it had been interesting, even fascinating, to cross swords with him in argument, but now he would not brook argument or contradiction from his own people and could barely tolerate it from

287

others. Mountbatten could not count on the tenuous and inexplicable affection the old man appeared to have for him. It was of flimsy construction and one frank statement too many, or one really serious dispute, could bring it crashing down like the little piggy's house of straw.

In addition to the glittering guard of honour and a military band, two lines of the Governor General of Pakistan's personal bodyguard, their automatic rifles at the present, stretched up the steps of Government House in Lahore to where, flanked by two Pakistani generals, Jinnah stood at the apex of a deliberately impressive and theatrical triangle. It was meant not only to show honour to Mountbatten, but also to demonstrate the power and importance of Jinnah himself.

Gaunt and more skeletal than ever, he was wearing his immaculate white Muslim jacket and tight trousers, an astrakhan cap, his gold-rimmed monocle hanging at his breast, as he waited for Mountbatten to ascend the steps with Lord Ismay and the uniformed Peter Howes. For a moment, Jinnah's eyes burned with fury. He had been looking forward to a meeting alone with Mountbatten, equal to equal, a true summit conference. He savoured the phrase. His anger was at seeing Ismay. He respected him and out of courtesy could not exclude him from the discussions, yet it was not how he had imagined them, or wished them to be. He was more curt in greeting Mountbatten than he had intended, while he was abrupt with Ismay and ignored Peter Howes.

Concealing his displeasure and his rage at events in Kashmir behind a screen of frigid politeness, he conducted them to the garden of the residence, where he refused to be drawn into anything more than the blandest of social conversation as they strolled on the lawn. While they paused to admire a display of gold and orange lilies, he observed, 'Summer has lasted a remarkable length of time this year.'

Mountbatten saw his chance. 'Yes, but the nights are cooler now. It will be a bitter winter in Kashmir.'

Jinnah was lighting another Craven 'A'. 'Bitter everywhere, I expect.' He fitted the cigarette into his holder, as they talked. 'My sister Fatima sends her cordial regards, by the way.' He smoked as heavily as ever, and the jade holder was yellowed and blackened at its mouth.

As long as Ismay was with them, Jinnah refused to indulge in anything but small talk, ignoring Mountbatten's pointed hints in the direction of more serious discussion. An enquiry from Ismay after Liaqat's health prompted the scathing comment that he, at least, was not shamming sickness.

'If you mean Pandit Nehru, Your Excellency, I assure you that he literally collapsed,' said Ismay, mildly. He was rewarded with a glacial look, but no reply, as Jinnah turned once more to Mountbatten.

'Yes, I deeply regret that I have been unable to meet Lady Louis on any of her visits to Pakistan. Her tireless work has won her golden opinions,' he remarked. Without waiting for a reply, and perhaps he did not truly expect one, he snapped his fingers at a pair of servants who were following him with a drinks tray. They hurried to pour him a Scotch and ice, but he invited neither Ismay nor Mountbatten to join him. It would not have occurred to him to do so. An extraordinary meanness had entered the heart of the old man. He continued to live well himself, but his miserliness affected all those around him. He had not even allowed his personal aircraft, idle for weeks in its hangar at Karachi, to be used for the evacuation of Muslim refugees. The two Englishmen exchanged a quick glance: what the hell was going on? Then Ismay shrugged, pointing to himself, and moved his fingers as if walking away. After a moment's consideration Mountbatten nodded briefly, turning to Jinnah.

'Perhaps we should have a word or two on our own, Mr Jinnah?'

Jinnah had not yet touched the drink waiting for him on

the tray. 'I would not wish to seem discourteous to Lord Ismay.'

'As a matter of fact I was hoping you'd excuse me,' countered Ismay. 'I wanted to catch up on a couple of things with General Gracey, as I'm here.'

'I think you will find him in his office.' Jinnah snapped his fingers once more at the servants, dismissing them, and, nodding to Mountbatten, made off towards the house. Left alone, Ismay looked at the untouched Scotch. He beckoned to the servants as they, too, prepared to leave.

'If no one wants that drink, I think I'll have it.'

Alone in his study with Mountbatten, Jinnah unwound slightly. But he had called the meeting and he did not see that a conciliatory attitude would help him. He had by no means given up his fight for Kashmir.

'I stand by my stated position,' he said, sitting down opposite Mountbatten in the careful way that he had, his body now so shrunken that even his beautifully tailored clothes hung on it in ugly folds. 'Kashmir's accession to India was brought about by violence and fraud, and Pakistan does not recognize it.'

'The violence came from an invasion of Pathan tribesmen – for whom Pakistan is responsible.'

Jinnah waved his arm impatiently. 'Nonsense. As you very well know, the frontier tribes are a law unto themselves. The violence lay in India's illegal action in sending in troops!'

'Forgive me, Mr Jinnah, but as a servant of the Indian Government I must tell you that their action was perfectly legal. No troops were sent in until after Hari Singh had signed an Instrument of Accession. The Indian Army is in any case only there to drive off what appears merely to be a large raiding party of Pathans . . . .' Mountbatten was just as inscrutable as Jinnah. Neither of them showed the slightest expression. 'It's obvious that their sole interest was loot,' continued the Englishman, blandly. 'Or they wouldn't have wasted so much time on it. They might have had an easy victory, if they'd been bent on invading

Kashmir, but they threw it away. Now they've lost all hope of reaching Srimagar.' The words were intended to goad Jinnah, but still he kept himself under control. 'Incidentally,' Mountbatten added, 'fourteen European nuns were raped and killed at the Baramullah convent. I shall be registering a formal protest to your Government in due course.'

Jinnah bent forward, coughing, to stub out a cigarette. 'In the circumstances, I propose that both sides should withdraw at once, and at the same time.' His voice remained neutral.

Mountbatten registered mild surprise. 'But you said yourself that the Pathans are a law unto themselves. How can they be talked into leaving?'

'If you agree to my proposals I will call the whole thing off!' snapped Jinnah, interrupting. Immediately he realized that he had fallen into the trap Mountbatten had set for him. He went rigid with fury at once again being out-flanked. 'That is, I will use my influence to get the raiders to withdraw,' he corrected himself. But it was too late.

Mountbatten was careful not to let the slightest sign of triumph show on his face. He appeared to remain worried and preoccupied, even solicitous. In his present mood, back pressed to the wall, Jinnah might do anything. For a man who had lived all his life by constitutional principles, he had begun to behave with frightening irrationality.

'If you are able to induce them to leave, that will be the best solution,' he said, cautiously. 'Then the people of Kashmir can decide by free vote whether to join Pakistan or India. The maharajah's signature is only binding on a temporary Instrument of Accession, don't forget; to be ratified or rejected by the people.'

'An independent vote?' Jinnah all but sneered.

'I assure you it will be.'

'Never.' Jinnah was going to amplify, but suddenly his whole body was caught in a massive fit of coughing. It seemed as if a giant hand seized him and shook him in his chair. It left him wracked and breathless. He heaved his body forward and rested his elbows on his knees, sinking his head down and catching his breath in painful, wheezing gasps.

Mountbatten was genuinely concerned. 'Can I get you a glass of water?'

'No . . . No, thank you. The cigarette smoke . . . irritates my throat sometimes.' Jinnah straightened, touched by Mountbatten's concern for him. For a moment, the two men reached a point of human contact that had nothing to do with their political enmity. Jinnah picked up his gold cigarette lighter and turned it over and over in his hands. When he began to speak again, it was almost to himself. 'A few days ago, there was another attempt to assassinate me, at Government House in Karachi. They were young Muslims . . . Young Muslims, for whose future I have given my life . . .. They blame me for accepting the Partition of Bengal and the Punjab. They cannot see that, without compromise, Pakistan would never have become a reality.' His mask was down and revealed an old, sick and embittered man.

'You once told me, better a moth-eaten Pakistan than no Pakistan at all,' Mountbatten said, gently. 'Surely you still believe that?'

Jinnah's voice was a dry whisper. 'I believe it. I must believe it. I will always believe it. With all its faults, however imperfect, it is my monument.'

The little Morris saloon car drove through the main gate set into the high, massive red sandstone walls of the Purana Qila, and came to a halt. Gandhi had been told that Hindus and Sikhs in Delhi were becoming increasingly angry at his visits to the Muslim camps. He had even been warned against the Muslims themselves, who, constantly attacked and harried by Hindus, had begun secretly to arm themselves. In such a teeming mass of humanity as the one gathered at Purana Qila, it was difficult for the police to maintain effective control.

Gandhi's answer had been simple. 'How often do I have

to say that I go where I am most needed? The Muslims live here in fear, surrounded by neighbours who have become enemies. I must give them what comfort I can.'

A Muslim passing the car recognized the old man in the back and turned to call to a group of his fellow refugees squatting crowded into the shade of a single ragged banyan tree.

'It's Gandhi!'

The Mahatma smiled to the man, raising his hand in greeting. He was appalled to see the man spit in his direction, shaking his fist.

In the front seat, Pyarelal Nayyar assessed the situation in a moment. 'Drive on,' he commanded the driver. By now, a considerable crowd was gathering round the car, shouting angrily.

'No,' said Gandhi. 'Stay where you are.'

Pyarelal turned round in astonishment. 'Don't you hear what they're saying? "*Gandhi murdabad*"!'

'If it is God's will that I die now,' replied Gandhi calmly, 'there is nothing I can do to change it.' He opened the door and climbed out, blinking in the sun.

The crowd had left a space around the car, and as he stepped out their shouting gradually ceased. They glared at him in angry silence, waiting for him to say something. Gandhi looked around them.

'I have come to pray with you, my brothers and sisters.'

'What use are your prayers?' someone screamed.

'Every day we pray,' came a woman's voice. 'Every night more of our people are killed.'

'We must fight!' cried another. The crowd shouted its angry agreement.'

'If you were all to die, blessing your enemies, you would become immortal,' said Gandhi, raising his voice above theirs. 'I tell you what I tell the Hindus and the Sikhs. We are all one – all children of the same God. What man wounds his brother and sister?'

The muttering of the crowd was becoming louder again, and Gandhi strained to make himself heard. 'If your brothers attack you, offer yourselves as willing sacrifices. Overcome their rage with love! Die, if die you must, with God's name on your lips, but do not lose heart!'

The crowd was not listening to him. They had had enough of the Mahatma's doctrine of non-violence. The old man might have done some good in Calcutta, but it was obvious that his day was past. And he was a Hindu. By what right did he keep coming to bother them with his blandishments and his meaningless prayers? He would be better dead.

Gandhi looked around him, shaken and disbelieving, as the chant rose to drown his voice. *'Gandhi murdabad! Gandhi murdabad! Gandhi murdabad!'*

Gradually, Nehru's health was improving, and Edwina was delighted to see him sitting up in an armchair in his bedroom when she called to see him on a bright morning early in November. She had been so anxious for him in his illness that his recovery had made their relationship lighter and easier. She hardly dared admit to herself the degree of relief she felt at not having lost him.

'Are you sure you should be up?' she asked, taking his hand.

'My doctor permits it. Though every day I sit a little longer than he knows!' His smile was mischievous as she drew the collar of his dressing-gown tighter round his neck.

'You must be careful.'

'I am careful! You're not going to bully me, are you, Edwina?' He looked at her reproachfully. It had been long since he had the leisure simply to enjoy someone's company as he enjoyed hers.

'That little-boy look doesn't work on me,' Edwina told him, with mock severity.

He smiled. 'No, believe me, I feel better. I improve every day – like the news from Kashmir.'

'Ah, *now* I believe you. Have you taken my advice and stopped smoking?'

His shoulders hunched, apologetically. 'Strictly speaking

294

– not stopped. But I have cut down.' He showed her his small leather cigarette case. Each of the untipped cigarettes inside had been neatly cut in half. 'I smoke at the same intervals, but only half as much, you see.'

Edwina laughed and sat by him. 'You're incorrigible! You must still take care of yourself.'

'Oh, I do. Or rather, Indira makes certain that I do. She keeps an eye on me. She is so like her mother. Long ago, when I first made a name in politics, I was for a time a sort of popular hero. The people called me things like "Jewel of India" and "Embodiment of Sacrifice".' She smiled. 'You are not to laugh. It is true. I can remember it turned my head. I was in danger of getting too big for my boots – if one wears boots on one's head. Anyway, at mealtimes, Kamala and Indira would bring me back down to earth. "O *Bharat Bushan*," they would say, "pass me the butter." "O *Tyagamurti*, what's the time?"' They laughed. 'Poor Kamala . . . It is hard to believe that it is nearly twelve years since she died.'

As always, the memory of his wife softened and saddened his expression. He reached for his leather case to take one of his half cigarettes, but remembered Edwina and smiled an excuse. He put the case back in his dressing-gown pocket.

'What was she like?' Edwina asked quietly.

'Kamala?' He paused. This was something he rarely talked about. The bright room seemed to have grown just a little darker. 'Delicate. Frail. Sensitive. She wanted very much to help me in my political life. But she was never very strong and her health began to fail quite early – consumption. When I was in prison, she carried on my work. We were apart for long periods.' He paused again, thinking. 'Her last years were . . . hospital, prison, hospital again. But she was always cheerful, for me, to raise my spirits.'

'She sounds wonderful,' Edwina said softly.

'I only realized she was dying when they let me leave prison twice a week to visit her.' It was the most painful of his memories. 'You know – the British said, if I would give an assurance to stay away from politics, I would be released and could be with her. She whispered to me, "What's this I hear about you giving an assurance to the Government? Don't do it."'

They sat in silence for a while. 'I wish I'd known her,' Edwina said.

'She had great courage. Even in her long dying, she never lost courage,' he said. 'In many ways, she was like you. You, too, are not as strong as you seem – yet you will never submit, never give up.'

She was gazing at him, conscious of the honour he had done her by comparing her with his wife. She did not want him to have a false idea of her. 'I don't claim any special courage. I only suffer from headaches. And sometimes I get sick before I have to make a speech.'

'Yet you still make speeches. And in spite of the headaches, you never stop working.'

'I am perfectly well,' Edwina said. There was much about herself that she did not like to think of him analyzing. 'And I think I have stayed long enough. I don't want to tire you.'

She was starting to rise, but Nehru stopped her with a slight smile. 'No, you don't escape so easily.' He held out his hand. Edwina hesitated, then placed hers in his. He held it gently. 'I want to ask you, most sincerely, to take care of yourself,' he said. 'You have become very precious to . . . all of us.'

Gandhi sat alone in his garden room in Birla House, spinning his *charka* and thinking. Manu and Abha squatted on the steps outside, ready to answer if he called. Several poor families sat under the arbour, watching him, following every move he made, like silent worshippers. One of their children, a small boy, had come forward until his nose was almost against the window, gazing in at the little old man in a white *dhoti*, steel-rimmed glasses slipping from the end of his nose, spinning tirelessly. His parents had said the old man was holy. The boy smiled, seeing how his ears stuck out.

Gandhi was aware of none of them. The violence in Delhi had never decreased, despite what people said. It had merely gone underground and now threatened to erupt again. There were fewer open attacks on a large scale, much of the Muslim vegetable market had been reassembled after the attack on it by fire, and hospitals and public buildings were no longer under direct threat. Yet he had been forced to break off some of his prayer meetings once more as people objected to his using texts from the Koran, and death still stalked the streets of the city in the form of snipers' bullets, knifings in narrow alleyways, and petrol bombs. A Muslim shopkeeper whom he had personally persuaded to take down his shutters and open for business again had been shot. *Hé Ram* . . .

No. The Mahatma would not leave Delhi for the Punjab until he had defeated death and brought his children to reason. He sat, patiently spinning, waiting for God to tell him what to do.

Mountbatten rose expectantly from his desk as his Indian Duty ADC opened the door of his study to admit Vallabhbhai Patel.

'Good evening,' he began. 'Thank you for coming so – ' He broke off as another figure, moving more slowly, entered the room behind the Deputy Prime Minister. 'Jawaharlal!' he said delightedly. 'I don't believe it!'

'I have been an invalid long enough,' Nehru smiled, easing himself into a chair.

'I told him we were managing perfectly well without him,' joked Patel, 'but he simply wouldn't accept it!'

Mountbatten thought he saw a flicker of annoyance cross Nehru's face at Patel's comment, but he let it go. A *khitmatgar* entered with coffee and as they drank it Patel, always eager to get straight to business, spoke approvingly about the agreement Mountbatten had wrung out of Jinnah over Kashmir. For the moment, at least, matters seemed rather more under control than they had been for some time, and if Mountbatten had privately felt that Patel's action over Junagadh had been precipitate, he acknowledged to himself that he had to stay his hand and let the Indians rule their own country as they thought fit. As far as Kashmir was concerned, the coming winter in that mountain country would literally freeze any possible military activity until the spring. Already the higher passes would be blocked with snow.

There remained the problem of Hyderabad. For months the Nizam had dithered and prevaricated, sending first one delegation, and then another, composed of entirely different officials, to Delhi. The greatest danger lay in Kazim Razvi, a militant racist who headed the Muslim extremist organization in the state, the Ittehad-ul-Muslimeen, and their quasi-military offshoot, the Razakhars. Razvi had great influence with the Nizam, but his extreme views had isolated him, and the Nizam himself, for all his miserly eccentricity, had a sharp brain and would not be dictated to. As an overture, he had offered a loan of twenty *crores* of rupees to Pakistan, as the new country was trembling on the verge of bankruptcy; but, like Kashmir, Hyderabad had secured a Standstill Agreement with the Indian Government. The Nizam was simply holding onto his own independence for as long as he could. It could only be a question of time. Vast as its land area was, Hyderabad had no coastline and was geographically far away from Pakistan, in central southern India. No violence threatened there, and for the moment Nehru and Patel would have to be patient and sit it out, thought Mountbatten. Sipping his coffee, he wondered how patient they would be.

'What was it you wanted to see me about, Your Excellency?' asked Patel.

'The Royal Wedding. If my wife and I are going to attend it in London we must leave soon. I have been concerned about whether it would be right for me to be absent from India at this time.'

'Surely you must be there?' said Nehru.

'Normally I wouldn't hesitate. Philip is the closest I will ever have to a son, and Elizabeth is the daughter of one of my best friends.'

Nehru smiled at the easy casualness with which Mountbatten could talk about the British Royal Family. Well, after all, he was a member of it himself. 'I think there's no question,' he said. 'You must attend, not only for your own sakes, but to represent the Dominion of India.'

'Apart from that,' added Patel, bluntly, 'a lot of people have been beginning to wonder who actually runs this country, you or us. If they see you can be spared, their doubts would be allayed.'

Mountbatten had often found it difficult to like Patel's manner, but he took his point absolutely. He looked across at the rough-edged seventy-two-year-old, the tough peasant farmer's son who had had to fight hard to win rewards Nehru had gained by privilege. Nehru was anglicized and an Anglophile, whereas Patel was an Indian through every inch of his body. He found Mountbatten's continuing presence increasingly difficult to tolerate, although he appreciated his personal capabilities.

'I have no doubt of that, Mr Patel. However my wife is concerned that she should not leave her work with the refugees even for a moment at such a critical stage.'

Nehru, with his great love of foreign policy, had been much taken with his idea of the Mountbattens as representatives of India at the wedding of a future Queen of England. He was determined that they should go. And although he would not dream of undervaluing Edwina's contribution, Amrit Kaur and the Relief Council had learnt so much from her that he felt confident that they could well manage without her, certainly for the month or so that they would be gone. He put this to the Governor General, who still looked doubtful that Edwina would agree.

'Then it seems to me that you need some extra help in persuading her,' smiled Nehru.

Gandhi had always admired her. She was the practical embodiment of everything he had tried to instil in his people, mending instead of breaking, and tireless in the cause of others. At Nehru's suggestion, he had roused himself from his private musings, and made his way to Government House.

'It will be a joyous occasion, Lady Louis,' he told her as soon as she had welcomed him into her private sitting-room, where her husband and daughter had joined her for tea. 'And I shall be happy to know that you will be there representing the people of India. I hope you are easier in your own mind about it now?'

'My husband and Mr Nehru have been trying to persuade me – but it is you who have finally convinced me,' she said. Gandhi smiled warmly at her charm. She looked at her husband. 'I'm sure he intended to go all along.'

'My uncle Bertie – who also happened to be Edwina's godfather, *and* King Edward VII of England – always said that kings are members of the smallest trades union in the world. Well, I believe in supporting my union,' Mountbatten chuckled.

'I hope you are also going to be at the wedding?' Gandhi asked Pamela.

'Yes,' she smiled back. 'I'm to be a bridesmaid.'

'Ah, that's a very responsible position.'

They all laughed, and then, almost shyly, Gandhi drew something wrapped in tissue paper from the folds of his shawl.

'I had a special reason of my own for coming to see you,' he said. 'I know you are taking an official wedding present with you from the Government but I have brought a very small gift of my own for the Princess and your nephew.' Still shyly, he handed the package to Mountbatten, who carefully drew aside the tissue paper. Inside was a delicate lace cloth.

'It was woven from yarn which I spun myself,' said Gandhi. 'I hope that, amid all the pomp and circumstance, it may remind the royal couple to think now and then of the little people.'

Mountbatten was deeply touched. 'I'll give it to them personally, Gandhiji,' he said. 'I know they will treasure it.'

As he was leaving, Gandhi turned to Mountbatten with a familiar twinkle in his eye. 'By the way, I am so pleased they have recalled C.R. Rajagopalachari to be Acting Governor General while you are away. There could not be a more suitable choice than him. And – with no disrespect – although they could have found no greater contrast to you, I think they will find that Rajaji is also a strong man.'

Their month in London passed quickly and in a mood of total unreality. Edwina could not take her mind away from Panipat and Purana Qila. Chester Street and even Broadlands seemed to have nothing to do with her. She almost found herself disliking their comfortable English opulence. She thought about the thousands of Britons who had made India their home and who had, with the coming of Independence, been forced to return to uncertain futures on this damp little island far away to the north. Surely it must seem alien to them here, among these grey-faced people in their green landscape?

The Royal Wedding had passed brilliantly, and the warmth of the cheering crowds lining the Mall to wave to the state coaches and share the joy of the day did much to soften Edwina's heart towards England. In Westminster Abbey, she prayed for the refugee columns which in her mind's eye she could still see vividly in their never-ending march, in the straggling fire-lines of their night-time camps, in their bent, human misery under the monsoon rains and the remorseless Indian sun. The marriage of Princess Elizabeth and Philip, youngest son of her sister-in-law Princess Alice of Greece, seemed to be a dream. The splendour, the red and black and gold of the uniforms, the Guard of Honour, the golden and the black coaches, the dapple-grey horses, the rain-washed red tarmac of the Mall, the great, grey, Palladian façade of Buckingham Palace and the Gothic glory of the Abbey, the entire panoply of English state and tradition, in which she was now privileged to play a major role, seemed to dwindle to nothing beside her vision of that unending, ragged line of humanity.

Under the night sky of the Punjab, a column had bedded down for the night. Under the great sweep of the heavens, in which a million stars shone bright and cold, small fires flickered into life beside makeshift shelters of sticks and rags. By one, two small children, a brother and sister, huddled down for warmth close to their pet goat, their only possession. Two other figures sat near them, an old Sikh and a young Hindu. The Sikh began to shiver as the night chilled him.

The young Hindu was called Sunil. He had been with the column for ten days, and was beginning to be more hopeful now that the end seemed to be in sight. Waiting at the river bridge had been the worst, night after night in fear of attack. Now he took off his own coat and walked over to the old man, settling the coat around his shoulders. He would forage for some more wood and make the fire bigger. It had been stupid and lazy of him not to bother before. As the old man smiled in gratitude, Sunil raised his head, listening tensely. He could hear horses, many of them, galloping towards them. The old Sikh was beginning to rise. Sunil pushed him down, covering his head with the coat, as he picked out a brand from the fire and whirled it at the chest of the first horse. Its hair shone chestnut and orange in the flame and then it reared away into the darkness, but there were so many horses, and he could see the swords of the riders slashing and stabbing as they screamed, '*Allah akhbar! Allah akhbar!*'

Sunil glanced round at the children. The boy had pushed his sister almost under the goat, and had his own arm round its neck, holding it down strongly as it struggled to rise in panic, shaking its shaggy grey fleece and twitching

302

its long ears, the strange, bar-like pupils of its amber-green eyes glinting in the firelight.

In that moment, a *khaksar* swordsman was upon him. Sunil felt the sword hit him in the chest and then slide on, through him. Transfixed, as the Muslim leant down to withdraw his blade, he pushed the firebrand into the man's face with all his force. Screaming, the man fell from his horse and staggered away into the darkness.

The little boy watched, his wide brown eyes huge in the night firelight, as the brave young man who had tried to protect them toppled forward and lay still. From his back, the blade of the sword rose like a finger of silver flame as it reflected the light of the fire.

# THIRTEEN

'Your Excellency, I am glad and relieved to see you returned safely, and soon.' Chakravarti Rajagopalachari smiled his greeting as he entered the Governor General's study. It was mid-December, and the weather in Delhi had become fresh.

'Thank you, Rajaji,' replied Mountbatten. 'It's good to be back. I hope you enjoyed your stint as Governor General?'

'"Enjoy" is hardly the word I would have used. It was a great honour to be recalled from Calcutta for the task, and I have learnt a great deal in a very short time.' The elderly statesman hesitated for a moment, and his manner became more serious. 'One thing I have observed from the height of this office which has disturbed me.'

'Yes?'

'It is what appears to be a growing split between the man of feeling and the man of power, Jawaharlal Nehru and Vallabhbhai Patel.'

'But is it that serious? They've worked together as a perfect team for years.'

'Indeed. For so long that we all take their differences for granted.' Rajaji adjusted his steel-rimmed glasses. 'They had a common aim – Independence. Now that battle is won, the differences in their thinking are becoming more apparent, and are driving them slowly apart.'

Mountbatten was silent, thinking.

'Sadly, too,' continued Rajaji, 'they are moving away from the true but unofficial leader of the Congress Party.'

The Governor General looked up sharply. 'From Gandhi? Surely not?'

'They admire him and love him, but,' Rajaji spread his hands, 'they do not feel that his ideals apply any more. They are certainly not the ones needed to create a modern, self-sufficient, industrialized country. That is the India of their dreams – while his is of villages, prayers at sunset, and spinning wheels. The Mahatma is truly a great soul, but he has not moved his philosophy with the reality of the times.'

Gradually, the sun was setting on the Raj. Sir Eric Miéville had left immediately after Independence; Sir Claude Auchinleck had completed his duties of supervising the division of the Indian Army by the end of November; and now it was time for Pug Ismay to depart.

'I don't think I'll be long in following you home,' said Mountbatten to him at his farewell drinks at Government House. The two men stood on the terrace overlooking the Mogul Gardens, now a riot of flowers in the more temperate weather of winter. 'It's time for the politicians to take over.' He paused. 'Not that I envy them.'

The two men fell silent. Far from at least quietening down for the winter months, and despite assurances given by Liaqat Ali Khan at a meeting in Delhi, Jinnah was becoming more confident in the powers of his own army officers, and a new military incentive by Pakistan had sparked off the Kashmiri crisis once again. To make matters worse, most of the Indian units there were cut off by road and could now only be supplied by air. Jinnah had not been convinced that the plebiscite to decide the future of the state would be impartially conducted and Ismay had suggested to Mountbatten that the United Nations should be approached to conduct the referendum under its auspices. Jinnah's actions now seemed to be a desperate gamble. Pakistan was heavily in debt, and its liquid assets stood at a mere million rupees. India still owed Pakistan 550 million in settlement of the original Partition Agreement, but it seemed unlikely that they would pay it while there was any chance of Jinnah's using the money to step up his claim to Kashmir by force.

There was also the question of the unity of the Congress Party.

'I agree that the signs are that Nehru and Patel are squaring up for a power struggle,' said Ismay when Mountbatten told him of Rajagopalachari's fears. 'But it's their own factions that are forcing them apart. In a sense, they still know that they need each other. Nehru's got the charisma and the flair for diplomacy; Patel's got his feet on the ground and keeps the party disciplined. But there's going to be an earthquake, you know.'

Mountbatten nodded. Already Acharya Kripalani had resigned his position as President of the Congress Party, complaining that neither of his two leaders sought to consult him any more.

'What you need to watch is what happens to Gandhi,' said Pug. 'He's proposed Narendra Dev to replace Kripalani, and Dev won't be so easy to push around. If Nehru and Patel accept him, it will mean that Gandhi is still a power in the land. If not . . .' He broke off, shrugged, and sipped his drink.

'It's a pity you can't stay, Pug,' said Mountbatten. 'I'm going to miss you. I couldn't have asked for a more honest, or unbiased advisor. And I don't know what I'm going to do without your sense of sanity, and your sense of humour.'

Ismay smiled warmly. 'I'll miss you too. It's been a privilege – apart from anything else, I enjoy working for a lucky man!'

Two days later Mountbatten received a note from Nehru informing him that the new President of the Congress Party would be Dr Rajendra Prasad. Mountbatten sat back at his desk, toying with the innocent-looking piece of paper and considering what effect this rebuff would be likely to have on Gandhi. The old order was indeed changing, he thought, and not just for the British in India.

The little brother and sister had managed to reach the camp at Panipat. Their goat had survived with them, and now they sat in a bewildered small group with the old Sikh on the dusty ground. The little boy watched the elegant English lady in her smart uniform walking towards them. To his surprise she stopped when she reached them, and said something. He didn't understand, but she looked friendly and tickled their goat Nala behind the ears. He looked at his sister who was shyly bringing her palms together and bowing a *namaste* to the elegant lady, who smiled and knelt down by his sister, picked her up, and gave her a kiss on the cheek before moving on. The little boy smiled to his sister. He felt they were safe at last.

Edwina put the little girl down and walked on, looking out among this new batch of refugees for any sign of illness or distress. She had finally settled down to enjoy her stay in England, and had adored her new baby grandson, but as soon as she was back in India she had had a meeting with Amrit Kaur, and thrown herself again into the work she loved so much.

A couple caught her eye. They were slightly apart from the main group. The man lay on his back, completely enveloped in a homespun cotton shawl, while his wife squatted by his head, looking down tenderly and fanning his face with an improvised fan made out of a piece of cardboard. She looked up anxiously at Edwina's approach.

Edwina had been struck by the man's stillness. Now she knelt by him, examining his face, feeling his chest, as her ADC reassured his wife.

Edwina leant back, and drew the shawl over the man's face. With a cry of anguish, his wife leant forward to pluck it away again, but Edwina caught her wrist.

'You mustn't touch him,' she said firmly, wishing that she could speak Hindi. She turned to Muriel Watson, who had come up behind her. 'It's smallpox,' she continued, urgently. 'They'll have to move the body at once. And I want all the people in this section examined!'

The map room had been rearranged and a small-scale map of Kashmir pinned to a board mounted on an easel. The hastily convened Defence Council meeting was in a state of uproar.

'We thought the invaders had been driven from the Vale of Kashmir, that we were in total control!' shouted Patel. 'Now, it seems that we are not!'

'Our garrison at Poonch is cut off except by air! Jhangar is under attack and the relief force was driven back,' added Baldev Singh.

The two Indians had just returned from a fact-finding mission to Kashmir, and the information they had received was shattering. Jinnah had moved a force of six thousand men in to attack Uri, a key town on the Muzaffarabad-Srinagar road, and every sign was that he would mount as big an offensive as he could afford, to gain as much of Kashmir as possible before the bitterly cold mountain winter finally brought all movement to a standstill.

'We must stop any more enemy reinforcements from getting into Kashmir,' said Nehru. He was distraught, cursing himself for complacency and vowing never again to treat Jinnah as anything but dangerous and untrustworthy.

'The only way to do that, Prime Minister, is by attacking bases inside Pakistan's borders,' pointed out General Lockhart. 'And that would be a formal act of war against Mr Jinnah.'

'And what is he doing against us?' Patel wanted to know. 'A short, sharp war might be the best thing in any case!'

'We'll settle it once and for all! It's Jinnah who is forcing the pace, not us,' added Baldev Singh.

Mountbatten was alarmed. He could see that this was hardly a time when an appeal for calm would be welcomed, but he had to make it. It received the rebuff he had expected. He then changed tack and pointed out that as things stood India had world opinion on her side, but an attack on Pakistan could easily reverse that. There were plenty of people in the world only too apt to see Pakistan in the role of David against India's Goliath.

'What does world opinion have to do with this?' growled Patel. 'It is *we* who are under attack! And I'll tell you another thing, Lord Louis – Jinnah can whistle for the rest of his money! I'm giving orders today that none of our financial agreements with Pakistan are to be carried out until he has called off his invasion.'

'Jinnah is already desperate. If you threaten to bankrupt Pakistan, you may drive him to stop at nothing! And the effect on India in world terms could be as disastrous as attacking his bases!'

'So,' said Nehru, violently, 'you would prefer us to give him the money to buy more weapons? Well, let me tell you, Governor General, we will not give Jinnah the means to buy one more bullet to shoot one more Indian soldier. Never! There is no other action we can take.' He leant back in his chair. The matter was closed.

Mountbatten considered what Ismay had advised before leaving for England, and decided in desperation to play this card now. Escalation of aggression in Kashmir could start a fire which might spread across a still highly inflammable subcontinent. He had at all costs to prevent that. 'Listen to me,' he said. 'There is one other course of action you can take. You can refer the whole matter to the United Nations in New York for a neutral commission to examine the facts and find a solution.' He looked at the angry faces across the table, and saw immediately that his appeal had fallen on deaf ears. Already, Nehru was on his feet.

'We have had over two hundred years of having our affairs settled by foreigners! Under what section of our Charter do we have to refer the Kashmir question to a third party?!'

The Governor General did not take up the argument again. He had hoped that they would have seen his invocation of the UN as an appeal to international law, but in their present mood they chose to interpret it as colonial intervention. All he could do now was pray that the idea at least of going to the UN would sink in, and that he would be able to reintroduce it when the ministers were in a calmer mood. And he knew that there was still one Indian who might be able to help him, and whose hold on the people was still strong, however weakened his hand in government might have become.

That evening, he sat quietly in his study talking things over with the Mahatma. Outside in the garden, fireflies hovered over the flowers on silent wings. The city was quieter than it had been, but still the sky was lit up here and there by the flames of a burning building, and now and then the silence was interrupted by the alarm bells of emergency vehicles, and the crackle of distant gunfire.

'Once conditions improved here, I had intended to visit Karachi,' said Gandhi, suddenly.

'Jinnah would never allow you into Pakistan!' Mountbatten was appalled at the idea. 'In any case, with tension running as high as it is, you would almost certainly be assassinated.'

Gandhi looked at him. 'My life cannot be shortened by one minute. It belongs to God.' His expression became sadder and more thoughtful. 'But perhaps you are right. I am barely able to help the situation here. The people no longer listen to me. They follow the example of their governments, and their governments regard one another with hatred and distrust . . . .' He paused again, but Mountbatten did not interrupt his line of thought. He knew Gandhi well enough by now to know that he was leading up to something, perhaps to a decision not yet fully formed in his own mind, but which he would surely reach if left alone to do so. 'Something must be done to bring back trust . . . . I wonder, Lord Louis, what is your opinion of this new decision to refuse to pay Pakistan the fifty-five *crores* of rupees that India owes her?'

'India has no right to withold it, and without it, Pakistan will be bankrupt. What will the Pakistanis do then?'

Gandhi did not need Mountbatten to elaborate. He nodded his head. 'I am in total agreement. From every point of view – legal, ethical, moral, political – not to send it would be dishonourable and unwise. It would be a pity for the Indian Government to start down such a path.'

Mountbatten was beginning to catch the line of Gandhi's thoughts, and trod as carefully as a cat. 'Nehru and Patel are determined. Nothing will change their minds.'

'And you tell me they will not take your advice about calling in the United Nations to settle Kashmir . . . .' Gandhi sighed. 'They are very, very misguided. They think they no longer need to listen to you, and they have long since ceased to listen to me . . . . For a long time I have felt helpless. Christmas and New Year came and went and still God remained silent . . . . But finally last night He spoke to me, and showed me the course to take.' Gandhi looked up again at Mountbatten and continued almost apologetically. 'With Him as my sole counsellor, I have decided from tomorrow morning to begin a fast unto death. It will end only if I am satisfied that there is a reunion of hearts in all communities, and when the debt to Pakistan is settled. It will be a fast not only to end violence, but for our honour.'

Mountbatten hardly dared breathe. He knew in any case that once Gandhi had taken a decision, it was useless to try to dissuade him from it. At once the Mahatma's announcement filled him with hope and dismay. If by his fast he could force the aims he sought to achieve, then all Mountbatten's prayers would be answered. If he died – well, Mountbatten reasoned, if he died, it would be because the people, including the leaders, had become indifferent to him. His death need not tear the country apart as it might have done only four months ago, in September. The risk was worth taking, and Mountbatten had never been a man to baulk at a risk.

'You are still very weak, Gandhiji. This time you may die.'

'That is in God's hands. Do not scold me.'

'On the contrary. I admire your courage and your convictions. And I believe you may succeed where everything else has failed.'

'That is as it may be. Oh, and I will talk to Jawaharlalji about the UN business. You know, he supported my nomination of Narendra Dev for the Congress Presidency. At least, at first. I think he is still my son.' There was a hint of his old mischief mixed in the old man's sad smile.

'What do he and Patel think of your decision to fast?'

The mischief became more pronounced. 'I really do not know. I haven't told them yet. They came to see me yesterday, but it was my day of silence.'

News of the fast spread through Delhi like a shock wave, but reactions to it were mixed. It was not only the RSSS who greeted it with impatient scorn, but many ordinary Hindus too, particularly those who had suffered the harsh trek from the Punjab. It had taken Gandhi three days and one hour to bring Calcutta round by threatening to die, but now the possibility of losing him softened fewer hearts. It was going to be a question of the stronger will, and it was going to be a test of how important a place Gandhi still had in people's hearts.

Yet if the people arguing fiercely in small groups by the entrance to Birla House were still undecided, the leaders who entered the building, who had fought by Gandhi's side for thirty years, and who now came to plead with him to save himself, were not. They came as penitent children to a father, but children who wanted to tell their Bapu that the actions which had incurred his grief were not wrong.

He lay prostrate on his *charpoy*, already weakened. Around him in the bare marble room stood an anxious group among whom were Nehru, Patel, the Muslim Congressman Maulana Azad, and other members of the Cabinet. At the head of the bed, Gandhi's attractive Christian doctor, his secretary's sister Sushila, stood watching over him. The brilliant young physician had turned down a post at a North American teaching hospital to care for the Mahatma, but she was only allowed to use Ayurvedic medicine upon him, and even this he did not permit under the conditions of his fast.

'Do not put us to this torture,' Nehru was saying, his face a mask of anguish. 'You know it is the one request we cannot grant.'

Patel, only six years Gandhi's junior, had been with him from the beginning and was equally moved, but, like Nehru, he remained firm. 'We're saving lives by not handing over the money. Soon Jinnah's invasion will fail because his raiders will run out of ammunition.'

'Bapu, it is a matter of national security!' pleaded Nehru.

Gandhi finally broke his silence. 'No – it is a matter of honour.'

Patel became angry in his frustration. His split with Gandhi was well known, and some vicious tongues were quick to state that the whole fast had been aimed at him. In his confusion he asked Gandhi if this were true.

'No, Vallabhbhaiji – it is aimed at India. You are not India, although I daresay you would like to be.'

The gentle reproof was not lost upon Patel. 'I am trying to deal in hard facts, not high-flown concepts of honour!' He stood four-square but tough, but his eyes had an embattled look. 'I have stated my position. Don't expect me to back down!'

Gandhi had painfully lifted himself up onto one elbow. He opened his eyes and looked searchingly at Patel. 'No . . . . . You are not the Sardar I once knew. I thought we were one. Now I realize that we are two.'

The fast had begun on the morning of 13 January 1948. Forty-eight hours later, Dr Sushila Nayyar, who made a daily analysis of Gandhi's urine to check his body's reaction to the constraint put upon it, was shocked to find that a process she had dreaded from the first had already started within him. The harsh regime of water and bicarbonate of soda, accompanied every day by a salt-water enema, was too much for the seventy-eight-year-old body which had not yet fully recovered form the fast undertaken in Calcutta.

'What is it?' Pyarelal asked his sister, noticing her worried look of preoccupation.

'I believe that Gandhiji has already used up his supply of carbohydrates.'

'What does that mean?'

'That his body will start to burn protein for energy. His kidneys will fail and he will no longer be able to dispose of fluid. When that happens it will be unlikely that he will recover.'

'How long . . . ?'

'Any ordinary man could not expect to live more than another thirty-six hours.'

The news was relayed urgently to the Secretariat and to Government House.

'We must go to him,' said Edwina, as a concerned Mountbatten told her what had happened. She had been sitting in the sunny arbour of the Mogul Gardens trying to distract herself with a book, but she had been unable to read more than half a page in an hour, and had not taken that in.

'I only wish we could,' Mountbatten told her.

'What do you mean?'

'It's protocol. I couldn't visit him on his birthday, remember? And now the rules must apply even more strictly.'

'Why?'

'This fast is not just to end the violence, it's to put pressure on the Government.'

She was gazing at him, her eyes blank with amazement. 'You do believe in what he is doing, don't you?'

'Of course I do.'

'But you won't help him!' She was trembling with anger. 'You won't even give him the comfort of knowing that you're with him – that you care! . . . You say it's protocol. Since when did that stop you doing something you wanted? Or is it only when it suits you?'

Mountbatten looked away from her, around the immaculate garden, glowing in the bright morning sunshine. A haven of peace, a never-never land laid out only half a mile from the misery Gandhi was giving his life to prevent.

When he turned back to his wife, he was able to meet the intensity of her look. 'You're right. So many are against him that he needs every grain of support he can get.' He stood up. 'To hell with the rules! We'll go and see him now.'

It was not far to the house on Albuquerque Road, and the permanent cluster of people round its gates parted in astonishment as the Governor General's Rolls drove past them and stopped by the main door.

Gandhi was lying propped up on his *charpoy* on the verandah outside his quarters, on the other side of the building. He was visibly much weaker, but he managed to nod and smile to the file of well-wishers who moved past him, each pausing to bow. Manu and Abha were squatting behind him. At his side, Amrit Kaur sat with Sushila, who now kept a permanent watch on him.

They looked round at a stir of excitement and Amrit Kaur was surprised and pleased to see the file of people break to either side to let Mountbatten and Edwina through, followed by Campbell-Johnson and a uniformed ADC.

Reaching the verandah, they bowed to Gandhi, placing their palms together, and he smiled delightedly, returning their bows.

'You will forgive me not rising, Your Excellencies,' he said, and they noticed at once that his voice was very weak.

'I would rather you saved your strength, Gandhiji,' Mountbatten said. He spoke loudly enough to be over-heard, and was glad to hear the murmur of appreciation at the public expression of his concern and his affectionate use of the diminutive. He gave his hand to Edwina and they sat on the verandah floor at the foot of the *charpoy*.

'You see what it takes to make the mountain come to Mohammed,' Gandhi said, and they smiled.

'How are you feeling, Gandhiji?' Edwina asked.

'Very well, I thank you.' He actually did feel better, after lying for a time in the sun, and the visit of the Governor General and Edwina was an unexpected honour,

315

a bonus, for it would make many in the Government take notice.

'How long must this continue?' Mountbatten asked.

'Until it is done,' Gandi told him, simply. 'I have laid down seven conditions which must be met, before I can consider breaking it. And there is the matter of the money.'

'Yes.'

Amrit Kaur could not hide her anxiety. 'It must be settled soon. Sushila says that already there are medical complications.'

'They fuss over me like mother hens,' Gandhi said, teasing.

'What complications?' Edwina asked.

'He let me examine him this morning,' Sushila told her. 'I found acetone bodies in the urine.'

'That is because I haven't enough faith in Rama,' Gandhi smiled.

'It does not concern Rama,' Sushila said. 'This is a chemical.'

'Acetone bodies . . .' Gandhi sighed. 'How little science knows. There is more in life than science and there is more in God than in chemistry.'

His voice was growing weaker. He has even less strength left than he pretends, Mountbatten thought. 'Well, we mustn't tire you,' he said. 'We'll say goodbye, Gandhiji. I am glad to see you in such good spirits.'

'Never better, Your Excellency,' Gandhi assured him. 'My only prayer is that I may be granted enough strength of soul that the temptation to live may not lead me to end this fast too hastily.' He smiled. 'Again, my thanks.'

Mountbatten helped Edwina up and they bowed. Sushila rose with them and walked back with them to their car. When they had gone, Gandhi slumped in exhaustion. Any conversation now drained his small reserves of energy.

Edwina could not conceal her distress any longer. 'He's even weaker than I thought he'd be by now,' she said.

'Yes, it's takiing effect faster than any of us expected,' Sushila told her. 'He's losing two pounds in weight a day.'

316

Mountbatten took Edwina's arm to steady her. 'Wouldn't it be an idea to issue medical bulletins, to let people know just how serious it is?'

Sushila nodded. 'Yes. Yes, I will see to that. Excuse me, Your Excellencies.' She hurried back.

Mountbatten could feel Edwina trembling, and knew what she was thinking. He himself no longer believed there was anything but the most slender chance of the Mahatma surviving. The only thing to do was pray that he did not die, and that he achieved at least some of his objectives.

Gandhi did not make it easy. Nothing would deflect him from his mission, but the demands he had laid upon his countrymen seemed almost impossible to fulfil. No matter what happened in the Punjab and Kashmir, he demanded that peace be restored unconditionally not only in Delhi but throughout the motherland. He demanded assurances of this not only from the leaders of all the religious communities, but from his fiercest enemies, the RSSS. Even more he asked. Muslims who had been driven out of their homes in Delhi and elsewhere to make room for Hindu refugees should have their property restored to them, and the Hindus should return to the camps. What he wanted seemed unrealistic, even cruel in its idealism. Yet he sincerely believed that the love that lay deep in every human soul would win through.

The night after the Mountbattens' visit, he lay asleep. Only a small nightlight partly illuminated the room. Manu and Abha heard the sound of muffled shouting in the road outside, coming closer, and sat up on their pallets on either side of him.

As the noise of the shouting grew louder, Gandhi woke too and his head lifted, listening. His secretary told him it was demonstrators, hundreds of them.

Gandhi smiled weakly, listening to the rhythmic chanting. 'What's that they're shouting?' he asked. His secretary did not answer. Gandhi smiled and persisted. 'I can't make it out. What is it?'

At last, his secretary told him, reluctantly, 'They're shouting . . . "Let Gandhi die."'

Pandit Nehru was surprised when Edwina was shown into his study. He had been working at his desk and was showing signs of great strain. 'It is some time since you last came to see me,' he smiled. 'Too long.'

Edwina was taut, under the same strain. 'Have you heard the latest bulletin?' she asked. 'Sushila called me only minutes ago. He's been losing weight every day. Now his weight's steady.'

Nehru was relieved. 'So he's getting better?'

'That's not what it means.' All at once he could see that she was nearly breaking down. She had to keep her voice under tight control as she went on. 'It means the liquid he's taking in is being retained by the body. His kidneys are giving up.' Nehru was staring at her. 'When is someone going to do something?'

He swung away from her to stand gazing out of the window.

'Are you all just going to let him die?'

Nehru was racked by warring emotions. Every day he went to see Gandhi and sit with him, and every day it had become harder to withstand the silent plea of his growing weakness. He could hold out no longer. 'We call him The Great Soul,' he said quietly, 'but we have forgotten what it means . . . . I don't care any more what use Jinnah makes of it. I am going to urge Patel and the Cabinet to send the money to Pakistan immediately.'

He expected Edwina to say something, to back him, to tell him that what he was doing was right. When she was still silent, he turned and saw that she was crying.

V.P. Menon brought Mountbatten the word in his study at Government House that the full fifty-five *crores* of rupees which India owed to Pakistan had been paid. 'So what was Gandhi's reaction?' Mountbatten asked.

'Apparently, he only nodded and said, "Now let's see what gesture Pakistan makes in return."'

'Is it enough to make him give up his fast?'

'He's had no response yet on the main issue, his seven-point demands. And on these, the groups he most wants to convince will never agree.'

'Why not?' Mountbatten asked.

'They are fanatics. Fiercely pro-Hindu and anti-Muslim.'

'They wouldn't want him to die, surely?'

'They might well,' Menon said, reluctantly. 'To pay him back for having those millions sent to Pakistan.'

Gandhi was speaking, his voice hoarse and faint. He lay on his *charpoy*, remaining conscious only by willpower. Patel sat brooding by the wall, isolated, watching him. Manu, Abha and Amrit Kaur crouched by the side of the *charpoy*, opposite from Nehru. They were bending down, trying to make out what he was saying.

Sushila knelt by his head. 'You must not speak, Bapu,' she told him. 'You must not say any more.' Her voice was breaking.

He shook his head very slightly as though to silence her. He needed every last ounce of strength to give his message to Jawaharlal. But there was a roaring in his ears, streaks of light flashed irregularly in front of his eyes, and to speak was so difficult, the greatest effort he had ever made. The telegram from Lahore in Pakistan had asked, 'How can we help to save Gandhi's life?' 'Tell them . . . treat everyone, Muslim, Hindu, Sikh, Christian, Parsi, Jew, as your brother . . . . Do not bother about what others may do . . . . Each of us should turn the searchlight inwards . . . and purify his or her own heart as much as possible . . . . And if you purify yourselves sufficiently – you will help India and shorten the length of my fast. Do not . . . fear for me. As a child, I dreamed of real friendship between religions. In the evening of my life, I shall jump like a child if that dream is fulfilled.'

His hoarse voice died away and Nehru leaned forward,

distressed. Manu cooled Gandhi's forehead with a damp cloth.

All day a crowd had been gathering and now filled the huge garden and all the spaces round the house. Many in the crowd were praying. Some were arguing in whispers. The indifference to Gandhi in the city, then the hostility, had given way to a deep anxiety as the realization grew that this time he might truly die. Not only in Delhi, but throughout the whole country, thousands of people had begun to pray for him, knowing that life without him would be a desert. Young people, students and schoolchildren marched through the streets carrying banners, 'Save Gandhi!', 'Brotherhood', 'Hindus, Muslims, Sikhs, Unite!'

In the room the sounds of the crowd had been blotted out by his hoarse voice, but now they could be heard again, and they were changing. A murmur of 'Gandhiji . . . Gandhiji . . .' was swelling like an incantation. The love Gandhi believed in was reaching out to him.

Nehru saw the others turning towards the door and looked round. Gandhi's secretary was coming in with a delegation of Hindus and Sikhs from the refugee camps. They had brought a declaration swearing to welcome any Muslims who returned to Delhi. The secretary had a telegram from the Untouchables of Bombay begging Gandhi to live. Nehru read it to him. 'They say your life belongs to them, Bapu.' Gandhi nodded faintly and tried to smile.

There was a stir of increased excitement, as Prasad arrived from the Peace Committee which had been formed. With emotion, he told Gandhi that the leaders of over a hundred organizations had signed a charter promising to work to bring back peace and brotherhood.

Nehru's eyes were wet. 'That's what you wanted, Bapuji!' he told him. 'You have what you wanted.'

There was a long silence. 'Have all . . . signed?' Gandhi whispered.

Prasad hesitated. 'All but two.'

'. . . Which two?'

'The RSSS and the Hindu Mahasabha.'

Gandhi's head lay back again and Nehru said urgently, 'You know they'll never sign – but you have all the others!'

'All . . . must sign,' Gandhi whispered.

Patel had started up and came to kneel by him, pleading. 'Bapu – please . . .' Gandhi shook his head.

Sushila came to kneel beside Nehru and said quietly, 'He could slip into a coma at any time now. It's almost too late.'

'Mahatmaji, please!' Prasad begged. 'The RSSS and the Mahasabha have said they will sign tomorrow.'

The chanting of the crowd outside had grown louder and louder as more had joined in. 'Gandhiji . . . Gandhiji . . .'

'Take something – just eat or drink something to see you through the night, Bapu,' Nehru said. He picked up the bowl of water into which Manu had squeezed a little lemon and held it to Gandhi's lips.

Gandhi shook his head weakly and smiled to him. His voice startled them by its strength. 'I cannot . . . not until all is agreed . . . I have never . . . felt so well. I am in the palm of God . . . .. If He has any further use for this frail body of mine . . . He will preserve it.'

The effort had been too much and his eyes closed.

Another night passed. Mountbatten and Edwina had to leave on an official visit to Bikaner which could not be postponed, but kept in touch almost hourly. Like the rest of India, they waited. Nehru had told them that the fast might end the next day, if the Mahasabha and the RSSS signed the declaration, but they were leaving it to the last moment, as long as they dared.

'But they *will* sign tomorrow?' Mountbatten asked.

'If he lasts the night,' Nehru said.

The next day the streets of Delhi were filled with Muslims, Hindus and Sikhs who had linked arms and formed peace brigades. It was a recreation of the miracle of Calcutta as they marched side by side, chanting, 'Hindu, Muslim, Sikh, *Ek Ho!*'

The crowd at the gate of Birla House had become a multitude which crammed itself into the gardens and spilled across Albuquerque Road. Most of the faithful were there to receive the grace of *darshan* by being in Gandhi's presence, but others wanted simply to watch the drama unfold as the leaders of all the religious communities approached the tiny immobile figure who lay crumpled on his *charpoy* against the wall of the plain marble room. With them were the High Commissioner for Pakistan, Husain Sahib, the Chief of the Delhi Police, and a representative of the Hindu extremist Mahasabha Party. The entire group represented the Peace Committee which Maulana Azad and Rajendra Prasad had put together, and it was Azad who spoke to the Mahatma on their behalf. He carried with him the signed documents of attestation Gandhi demanded, but as he spoke his brow was troubled. One key figure in the drama was still missing, and Gandhi would not end his fast without him.

Husain Sahib was returning the old man's faint gesture of greeting when there was a stir of excitement in the crowd outside. Newsmen and photographers whirled round, and flash-guns sent streaks of pale violet light across the room as Prasad hurriedly entered accompanied by a powerfully built Indian with dark, severe features. Some of the reporters looked at each other in disbelief. They had all heard of this man, and knew what he looked like, but few had ever actually seen him before.

Prasad led the man up to Gandhi's bed and knelt in front of it. 'This is Ganesh Dutt, who is the spokesman of the RSSS. He has signed the Peace Charter, and pledges that his organization will cease to use force to further its ends if you will only break your fast.'

The RSSS leader knelt by Prasad, the tears streaming down his tough, lined face as he held up his hands, palms pressed together, to Gandhi. After a long moment, and with a supreme physical effort, the Mahatma managed to raise himself sufficiently to take Dutt's hand in his.

As the camera lights flashed around him, Gandhi looked slowly round at the people in the room. He had remained unmoved at every appeal and had unflinchingly approached the very edge of death. If every last single demand of his had not been met, he would most surely have allowed himself to die. He was enough of a realist to know that there would still be pockets of extremists who would not associate themselves with the promises made in this room, and who would hate him the more for having extracted them, but the point was that he had won over the bulk of India. He had faught, he had pleaded, he had cajoled, he had finally used the ancient sanction of starvation – and he had won! But Gandhi was not a man to exult in personal triumph. It was the cause that mattered above all.

His look passed beyond the people in the room to embrace the sunshine outside, and the deep dusty green of the leaves of the pipal trees. There was total silence, except for his shallow, panted breathing.

'*Hé Ram*,' he whispered. 'God's will be done.'

The Mountbattens had returned that night to Government House from Bikaner. Tense, but exhilarated, still highly emotional, Nehru came to tell them the news.

'One by one, the leaders pledged themselves to carry out his wishes. He warned them that if they broke their word, his next fast would not end until he was dead.'

Mountbatten saw that his hands were unsteady and poured him a drink. 'What a remarkable man,' he said.

Nehru looked at the brandy which had been placed before him and pushed it a little further away. 'I felt so . . . ashamed, watching his agony,' he confessed. 'In the last two days, I had to join him in his fast.'

'Without telling anyone?' Edwina asked.

'It was something I needed to do,' he said. 'To do as he asked, and turn the searchlights on my inner self. It was . . . revealing, and frightening.' He looked at Mountbatten.

'I have been driven by circumstances. I regret bitterly any distance that has come between us.'

'It was as much of my making as yours,' Mountbatten answered sincerely. 'And I knew it couldn't last.' He glanced at Edwina. 'There has always been a bridge between us.'

'Yes.' The tension there had been between them was lifting. He was beginning to recover from the emotional strain of the last days and he picked up the glass, marvelling that his hand was again steady. He raised the glass to them in a gesture of friendship and smiled from one to the other.

'When you see Gandhiji again,' Mountbatten said, 'will you pass on some news from me, some extraordinary news?'

Nehru was intrigued. 'Certainly. What is it?'

'Something we would never have thought possible. Mohammed Ali Jinnah has asked me to extend his personal invitation to the Mahatma to visit Pakistan.'

# FOURTEEN

Gandhi was growing restless. It was twelve days since he had ended his fast and although he had resumed his regular evening prayer meetings almost immediately, he knew he was still not sufficiently recovered to begin his pilgrimage to the Punjab, and on to Karachi; and despite his fast, there was still much to be done in Delhi. He turned back to the heavy, brooding figure of Vallabhbhai Patel sitting opposite him. In the corners of the room, Manu and Abha sat meekly. Outside, he could hear the murmuring of the first early arrivals for that evening's prayer meeting. He sighed inwardly. It was proving a difficult interview.

As Gandhi and Patel resumed their conversation, Nathuram Vinayak Godse, the thirty-seven-year-old editor of a Hindu extremist newspaper in Poona, left the small Delhi hotel in which he had been staying for the last time. He had dressed carefully in an unassuming khaki bush-shirt and trousers. The small, flat, automatic pistol made almost no bulge in his sidepocket.

'There are no police outside,' Patel said, accusingly.

'I wouldn't have them. They wanted to search everyone who came in.'

'That's why I sent them!' said Patel, trying desperately to rein in his anger. 'As Home Minister I'm responsible for your safety. For God's sake, a bomb went off at your prayer meeting only a week ago.'

'It was a small bomb, and it harmed no one. One individual protestor. In any case, the police caught him, poor man.'

'Do you imagine he was the only one?' Gandhi merely smiled at him in reply. 'I'm not having you left without security!' Patel looked round the room. Apart from Manu and Abha, only his own daughter and Gandhi's secretary were in attendance. 'Where is your doctor?' he demanded.

'I have sent Sushila on to Karachi, to make arrangements for my visit.' Gandhi paused, and then continued, gently, 'But that is not why you have come to see me, Vallabhbhaiji.'

Patel sighed heavily, and, reaching into the deep pocket of his *kurta*, drew out an envelope which he handed to Gandhi. 'This is my letter of resignation from the Government. I wanted you to know first.'

Gandhi took the letter but did not open it. 'I was afraid of this,' he said quietly.

'It's just become impossible. For years, Jawaharlal and I made a good team . . .'

'And why not now?'

Patel made a gesture of impatience. 'Being in power has changed him. He wants to rule the roost, make all the decisions.'

'He needs you, as you need him. Talk to him.'

'It's too late for that, Bapu. You got me to take second place to him. I didn't even mind that. But now he's trying to squeeze me out, and if he thinks I'll stand for it – '

'Vallabhbhai, please,' Gandhi interrupted him quietly. Outside, he was dimly aware that the sound of voices had increased. 'You are hurt. You are angry. Don't make any decisions in anger. India needs you both.'

Manu and Abha had been exchanging glances for some time, and now they timidly rose and came towards him. 'It is time for my prayer meeting,' he said to Patel. 'After it, Jawaharlal will be here. Stay and talk to him with me, if you love me. It will be as it was in the old days. The three of us.' Gandhi smiled as he got up. 'You are supposed to be my watches,' he admonished Manu and Abha as he leant on their shoulders and walked slowly to the door. 'And now, see – you have let me be ten minutes late.'

Dusk was just settling on the garden, turning the greens of the leaves a shade deeper. Gandhi decided to save time by cutting across the lawn through the crowd. People stood aside to let him pass, bowing respectfully, as he mounted the four steps leading to the lawn and to the pavilion from where he conducted his meetings. As he reached the grass, he became aware of a stout young man in khaki who had stepped out from the crowd, and who now confronted him. The young man had his palms together and bowed deeply.

Gandhi placed his own palms together and returned the *namaste*, but the man still did not move back.

'Please,' said Manu. 'We are already late, and – '

She did not have an opportunity to finish her explanation. Nathuram Godse reached out with his left hand and brutally pushed her aside, exposing the black Biretta automatic concealed in his right.

Gandhi had already started to move forward, his hands still together, when he saw the gun. He watched the man's left hand come up again as Manu fell into the crowd. With appalling slowness, the two hands steadied the little gun not two feet from Gandhi's chest. The old man looked at its muzzle, and even as he understood, the gun erupted, still slowly, slowly, in bright bolts of orange and blue flame which briefly lit up the gathering dusk and which reminded the Mahatma of flashbulbs. Three small, hard hands caught him in the chest and started to push him backwards, and three tiny, spitting reports like firecrackers burst on his ears a moment later. He had lived with death for so long that it did nto surprise him.

'*Hé Ram*,' he sighed, feeling the palm of God close gently round him as he fell.

It had taken the Governor General's Rolls long, vital minutes to edge its way through the panicky, bewildered crowd which was already thronging Albuquerque Road, and drive into the forecourt of Birla House. Sitting in the back of the open car, Mountbatten was white and drawn, fighting to absorb the situation, to apprehend that it was real. In the forecourt, a babel of voices reached his ears. Next to him, Alan Campbell-Johnson looked about in consternation. 'Gandhi is dead.' 'No, he is alive.' 'He is dying.' 'Who was responsible?' The voices were muted, fearful, excited, exchanging pieces of information furtively, like contraband. Mountbatten too was looking about him, alert for any sign of trouble. Suddenly it came. A man standing near him in the crowd, his eyes wet with tears, called out in an anguished voice which cut through all other sound, 'It was a Muslim who did it!'

Tension ran through the crowd like a bushfire as the excited whispering started. In an instant Mountbatten was on his feet in the back of the car, rounding on the man who had raised the cry.

'You fool!' he thundered in a voice of the severest authority. 'Don't you know it was a Hindu?'

Silence fell upon the crowd, and the whispering diminished and died, to give way to a despairing silence. The Governor General fell back into his seat, reaching into his pocket to fetch out and light a very rare cigarette. Slowly, the driver managed to nudge the car forward to the entrance of the house.

'Are you sure the gunman was a Hindu, sir?' asked Campbell-Johnson quietly.

'No,' said Mountbatten sharply. 'I don't suppose anyone knows yet. But if I'd let them think it was a Muslim, there'd have been no stopping a massacre.'

The room the two Englishmen entered moments later was crowded with weeping people and heavy with the smell of incense. Gandhi lay on his straw pallet, his head on Manu's lap, his body covered in a white wollen shawl. Around him a dozen oil lamps burned in brass holders, and by him lay his few personal possessions, sandals, watch, spittoon, tin food bowl and battered copy of the *Bhagavad Gita*. Among the stooped and stricken figures in the room, Mountbatten recognized Amrit Kaur, Menon, members of the Cabinet. Indira Gandhi was scattering rose petals on the frail body. Near it her father sat with

Vallabhbhai Patel, the two men isolated in their unspeakable grief.

The Governor General approached, and accepted rose petals from Pyarelal to strew on the Mahatma in his turn. Having done so, he stood for a moment, head bent before the small pallet, listening to the prayers chanted by Abha and other disciples.

'Do we have any idea who did it?' Campbell-Johnson whispered to Menon.

'Yes – he didn't try to get away. A Brahmin – from an RSSS branch in Poona. He's been planning it since Partition.'

'How could they possibly blame Gandhiji for that?'

'These people cannot think – they can only hate. He says he'll give his reasons in court, but he's lucky to be alive. The Indian Air Force sergeant who tore the gun away from him would have shot him with it if the police hadn't arrived so promptly. As it was, they had trouble saving him from the crowd, who were ready to beat him to death.' Menon's voice faltered as he fought back tears. 'I suppose we should thank God there's been no communal violence as a result of this – yet.'

Mountbatten had knelt by Nehru, and after a few quiet words had taken him by the shoulders and helped him to rise.

'He's gone, Jawahar, but what he taught us must never be forgotten.' Nehru nodded, wiping away the tears. 'You must make sure the nation draws the right lesson from his death.' Mountbatten sustained his grip on his friend's shoulders, his voice gentle but firm. Everything hinged on the country being given the right leadership now.

'I suppose,' Nehru muttered, blankly.

'People are waiting for a lead from you. You must speak to them tonight. On radio.'

Nehru was immediately distressed. 'I can't! I can't think yet! I won't know what to say.'

'Think of him. You'll find the words,' Mountbatten assured him. He turned to Sardar Patel, still sitting on the floor and looking up at him with the open, hopeless eyes of a lost child. The Governor General reached down a hand and helped him to his feet. The two men stood mutely before him. He spoke just loud enough for them both to hear.

'The country needs you both, more than ever now. You know how much Gandhiji loved you both. At the last meeting I had with him he told me how worried he was that you, his greatest friends, were drifting apart. He longed more than anything to find a way to bring you together.' He paused for a moment to let his words sink in, one hand on each of their shoulders. 'If you wish to honour him, you could pay him no dearer tribute.'

Their differences melted by their tears, the two heirs of India embraced.

'The light has gone out of our lives, and there is darkness everywhere. I do not know what to tell you and how to say it. Our beloved leader, Bapu as we called him, the Father of the Nation, is no more. Perhaps I am wrong to say that. Nevertheless, we will not see him again as we have seen him for these many years. We will not run to him for advice and seek solace from him, and that is a terrible blow, not to me only, but to millions and millions in this country. And it is a little difficult to soften the blow by other advice that I or anyone else can give you.

'The light has gone out, I said, and yet I was wrong. For the light that shone in this country was no ordinary light. The light that has illuminated this country for these many years will illuminate this country for many more years; and a thousand years later, that light will still be seen in this country and the world will see it and it will give solace to innumerable hearts. For that light represented something more than the immediate present, it represented the living, the eternal truths, reminding us of the right path, drawing us from error, taking this ancient country to freedom.'

The Prime Minister had spoken without preparation on All-India Radio that night, but simply, from the heart.

Gandhi, in accordance with his wishes and in accordance with strict Hindu practice, would be cremated on one of the burning *ghats* on the River Jumna on the plain just beyond the city the following day. And a crowd was gathering to bid him farewell such as had never been seen in the memory of India.

It took the cortège five hours to cover the five miles from Birla House to the banks of the Jumna. The body was laid on a converted Dodge weapons carrier, painted white – the Hindu colour of mourning – its engine mute, pulled by a detachment of the Royal Indian Navy. Gandhi lay in a great bed of flowers, accompanied by three of his sons and by the bowed figure of Vallabhbhai Patel, who insisted on making the entire journey, his head exposed to the sun.

At the *ghats*, the press of the multitude was such that the Governor General, in formal blue dress uniform, caused his official party, which was placed near the pyre, to sit down in the dust to avoid the risk of being pushed forward into the fire. Gandhi's sons performed the final obsequies, and lit the great pyre, and a shout rose up from the crowd as the *ghee* and incense-steeped wood caught, and the smoke and flames stretched heavenward.

'Mahatma Gandhi has become immortal!'

Seated on the ground, dressed in a white coat and hat, Edwina was thinking of the little prayer he had taught her.

'Lead me from the Unreal to the Real,
'From Darkness into Light . . .'

As dawn broke over the Jumna the following morning, only one solitary figure remained by the still smouldering pyre. Pandit Nehru gazed long at the ashes he had watched over throughout the night. Now, he stooped and placed the delicate bouquet of pale roses he held in his hands on the blackened pyre.

'Bapuji,' he said in a voice no one else could have heard. 'Here are flowers. Today, at least, I can offer them to your bones and ashes . . .. Where shall I offer them tomorrow – and to whom?'

# FIFTEEN

The winter of 1948 gave way to spring, and the spring to early summer. Once more Delhi stretched out in the burning sun, but it was a Delhi in which the seeds of peace and cooperation between Muslim and Hindu Indian had taken root and were beginning to grow. The Kashmir question had been referred to the Security Council of the United Nations, but remained unsettled. United States' influence favoured Pakistan's claim, since the North Americans saw Jinnah as being less equivocally anti-Communist than Nehru, but this attitude in turn, and Britain's weak handling of the role of mediator at the UN, led to increasing anti-Western and anti-British feeling in Delhi. The Governor General, realizing that Britain and North America between them might easily drive India into the arms of Russia if they continued to take this line, stretched his constitutional powers to the limit, and managed to reverse the flow to the extent that by the end of March Nehru was able to admit that he was now reasonably happy with the way negotiations were going. Privately, Mountbatten felt that in the end Kashmir might be split in two. A final solution seemed remote, but at least the possibility of war had for the time being receded.

The Nizam of Hyderabad continued to play a game of cunning with the Indian Government, which left him precariously independent, and left them frustrated. Patel in particular was eager to invade the recalcitrant state, and in mid-March Mountbatten was furious to discover that secret plans had been drawn up for an invasion, code-named POLO. The fact that it was named after his favourite game not only stung him, but it associated the plan with him. He demanded an explanation of Nehru one afternoon in Nehru's book-lined study in York Road, but Nehru expressed extreme surprise at the Governor General's ignorance of POLO.

'Jawaharlal,' replied Mountbatten, keeping a tight rein on his temper, 'not only was I not consulted in the drawing up of this plan, to which I would never have agreed in any case, but it is my impression that your ministers are seriously considering putting it into operation. With the Kashmir question far from settled, and Jinnah still hungry at least for influence in Hyderabad, such an action will create the likelihood of war between your two countries at once! Why do you not see that?'

Nehru sniffed the rosebud in his buttonhole and did not quite look at him as he replied. 'My dear Dickie, nothing could be further from the truth. POLO is merely a contingency plan in the event of any aggressive action against the Hindus in Hyderabad by the Muslim extremist Razakhars.'

Mountbatten accepted this explanation, but sceptically. Three months later he flew to Dehra Dun, where Patel was convalescing after a severe heart attack, and showed him the terms of a deal with Hyderabad which paved the way for constitutional rule within the state and ultimate accession to India. It had taken the Governor General all the spring, and all the greatest powers of his diplomacy, patience and conciliation, to get all parties to agree to it. He was now himself exhausted and at the end of his own generous supply of stoicism.

Patel glanced through the document. 'This is far too generous,' he said, dismissively.

Mountbatten bit his lip. He had had enough. For the rest of the visit he talked only of idle topics and as soon as it was politely possible, he stood up to take his leave.

'You know, Lord Louis,' said Patel as he took his hand for the last time, 'India owes so much to you that you must not go away without some token of our gratitude.'

Mountbatten considered: 'Thank you, Mr Patel, but what might I ask for?'

'Anything you wish,' the powerful Indian shrugged.

In an instant, Mountbatten had taken the Hyderabad agreement from his briefcase again and held it out to Patel, together with his own fountain pen. After all, the Sardar could only refuse.

To his absolute amazement, Vallabhbhai Patel hesitated for only an instant before unscrewing the pen and signing the document, smiling wryly as he did so.

It was the Nizam himself who finally destroyed his chances by overplaying his hand. The old man demanded further alterations to the Agreement. By that time, Mountbatten had left, and India's patience was at an end. In August 1949 the Indian Army moved into Hyderabad and annexed the state. By then, Mohammed Ali Jinnah could no longer object: he was dead.

Alan Campbell-Johnson had finished his packing. In the morning he would board the train for Bombay with Fay and the children, on the first leg of their journey home to England. Now he sat with the Mountbattens on the terrace of Government House, enjoying a farewell drink.

'I'm sorry you won't be here for the final curtain,' said Edwina.

'It will feel very strange to miss it. But the phase-out plans were drawn up some time ago, so – ' he shrugged, leaving the sentence unfinished.

'Yes. Well, we'll be following you home very shortly,' said Mountbatten, sipping his Scotch and soda.

'Then it's back to the navy, sir?'

'That's right. Malta and the First Cruiser Squadron. That's not for publication yet, by the way.'

'Off the record, sir.' Campbell-Johnson finished his drink and stood up. 'And now, if you'll excuse me, I'd better run along. There're still a few loose ends to tie up.'

'Of course, Alan. We'll talk again later.'

They sat in silence for several minutes after Alan had gone. He stood and looked out over the garden, while she sat in her white wicker chair, leaning forward with her arms resting on her knees, thinking.

'Rajaji has already arrived back from Bengal,' said her husband. 'Once I've handed the Governor-Generalship over to him, our time will finally be over.' He was not sure himself whether he felt relief or regret at the prospect, but he was not a man to brood, or to look backwards. So Edwina's question was unexpected. 'Do we really have to go? So many people, our friends, the Government, they've all asked you to stay on.'

'Yes, my dear, but I'm more than ever convinced, certain, that now is the right time to leave, to hand the country over once and for all.'

'And besides, you want to get back to the navy,' she added, flatly.

'There's that. After all, if I'm ever to make Admiral of the Fleet, I can't leave it too long.' He smiled.

Her next words cut the air. 'And what about me?' He turned to her in surprise. 'My work doesn't matter, does it? Or my life.'

'Edwina – '

'I've given everything to this country, to my work here. And it's not finished. There's still so much to do. I can't just walk away from it.'

'You've taught others to carry on with it. And the rehabilitation plans for the refugees are going well. Look at the numbers who've been relocated already – why, the programme's one of the Government's top priorities!'

'You don't understand, do you? You never did!' she said, bitterly.

'Tell me,' he replied, quietly.

She stood up, moving away from him. 'You married me to be your consort, to run your home. And once that was enough. But in these last years, I've been coming awake. In Burma – and now here in India – I've found myself. I've given something, become someone, in my own right. How can I go back to England, to be a hostess and serve on

335

committees and make polite conversation? When I know that here I am needed?'

'. . . and loved,' said Mountbatten almost to himself. She turned to look at him. 'I've been thoughtless,' he continued. 'I've seen how much . . . being here has meant to you. Perhaps I didn't realize quite how much. But what can I do? It's time for me to go – my work is done. You are my wife. I can't leave you here.' He shrugged helplessly. 'We are a team. I need you with me, Edwina.'

She was about to reply but was interrupted as Pamela came onto the terrace from the house. 'There you are, Mummie. Muriel's waiting.'

'Oh – thank you, darling. I'll be there in a minute.'

Pamela had become aware of the tension and was troubled as she left, but the interruption had given Mountbatten enough time to collect himself.

'Where are you going?' he asked evenly.

'Just up to Panipat. To inspect the camp.' Edwina paused, wistfully. 'Poor Dickie. I'm spoiling your triumph.'

'I don't think of it like that.'

'No.' She moved a step closer to him. 'I suppose I'm being very unfair. You're right, of course.' She sighed. 'Staying on alone would be impossible. And after all, I'm used to moving around – I'm a navy wife. And what woman could ask for more than to be Countess Mountbatten of Burma?'

She left him quickly so that he would not see the tears.

It was a time of farewells. As it had been some time since Nehru had seen the Mountbattens, he was disappointed that the Governor General had come alone.

'I can only stay a moment,' said Mountbatten. 'I've just had a report from Karachi I thought you ought to hear. You remember how bad a cough Jinnah has?'

'Indeed.'

'I always just put it down to smoking. But it's tuberculosis of the lung.'

336

Nehru absorbed the news. 'There were always rumours – but no one believed them.'

'It's very advanced now. He only has months, less than a year to live. All through our negotiations, he must have known he was dying.' Mountbatten paused for a moment. 'I wonder if it would have made any difference, if I'd known.' Jinnah had always been the driving force behind the demand for Pakistan. If only they had been able to wait another year, two years . . . .

The Prime Minister shook his head. 'Probably not. There was no way we could have avoided Partition . . ..No way we could have avoided any of it.'

Mountbatten agreed. 'There's no point now in wondering . . . "if?"'

The two men had left the study and walked out onto the verandah together. 'It is odd how things turn out,' continued Nehru. 'I have never known such pain as on the day Gandhiji died. It seemed to me then as if the soul of India had died with him. And yet it was as if, overnight, we grew up . . . . His death seemed to bring us to our senses – or at least, closer to them. Our quarrels and our differences seemed so petty. Of course, it didn't settle our problems, far from it, but at least we have learnt that if we can only make the effort in his spirit, they can be solved.'

'And you need to do it on your own now. That's become clearer and clearer since January. It is high time for me to leave.'

Nehru did not reply immediately. He looked across the lawn, thinking. Even this tiny plot of India bore enduring memories of the last year, the talks with Edwina in the rose garden, the gate where the RSSS had set fire to the Muslim girl, this verandah, where so much of the work had been done. He looked at Mountbatten. It would be very lonely without him, but he was the last link with the British Empire. And he was right. India would not truly be free, until he had gone.

'We might not have many more opportunities to talk together alone,' he said.

'No,' smiled Mountbatten. 'From now on it will all be ceremonies and official speeches.'

Time . . . Time passed so quickly, Nehru thought. There was never enough, even for the most important things. 'I have seen very little of Edwina lately.'

'I know she's been hoping to see you, Jawahar, but she promised to make one last tour of the refugee camps.'

'Yes,' Nehru said, quietly. 'Those are the people she belongs to.'

Edwina walked slowly through the sprawling camp with Amrit Kaur, Muriel and Elizabeth. Her ADCs had given up trying to hold back the dense crowd of refugees which surrounded them.

She had meant to make a quick, impersonal visit, a last check on facilities and supplies, but the news of her leaving had been announced and people flocked to see her for one last time. They were not only from Panipat. They came by bus from the nearer camps. Many of those who had been relocated walked long distances to be here, some all night, some for many days. In the camps furthest away in the Punjab, the people pooled their few resources to buy a single train ticket, so that one at least could go to see her and say goodbye for them all.

The brief visit stretched into hours as she walked among them, talking, smiling, comforting, surrounded by an outpouring of love such as she had never known. People brought her small gifts, children gave her flowers, men and women knelt in the dust, weeping, some thanking her, blessing her, many begging her not to leave. She was moved to tears by the love and gratitude they showed for her. It was an ordeal, for she felt that really she had been able to do so little, compared to how much there was still to do, and that she was being forced to leave when she was still desperately needed.

The little boy and girl with the goat, whom she always looked for, had managed to struggle through to the front of the crowd. She spotted them and crouched to hug them

338

both. The little girl was crying, repeating the same words over and over. 'She is saying, "Please, don't go," Your Excellency,' the Indian ADC translated.

'Please tell her that I have to go,' Edwina said quietly. It was then that she realized that this could not be the end. Perhaps it would be too difficult for Dickie to return, but too much of her heart and mind was now involved in India for her to stay away for ever. 'But tell her that I will come back, as soon as I can, and whenever I am needed. I shall always be a part of India now.'

When she rose, word that she had promised to return was spreading through the crowd and people were cheering, applauding. Many were singing. She smiled to them and placed her palms together in the greeting of *namaste*.

The huge, glittering State Dining-room was filled to capacity. The entire Cabinet, and all the Mountbattens' dear friends in India, had gathered for this final farewell banquet. Amrit Kaur sat with Pamela; Maniben Patel with Indira and Ferooz Gandhi; Rajagopalachari and Prasad with Maulana Azad and V.P. Menon. At the centre, Mountbatten and Edwina, guests now in the vast palace where they had been hosts to India so often and for so long, sat with Jawaharlal Nehru. His farewell speech had begun. To Edwina, the occasion had taken on the unreality of a dream. Her heart and her mind were so involved, so much still remained to be done that she was unable to believe her role here was over, unable to accept that tomorrow they would board the York at Palam Airport to begin their journey home, that in three days she would be at Broadlands, six thousand miles away from the man who was speaking.

'You came here, sir,' Nehru was addressing Mountbatten, 'with a high reputation, but many a reputation has foundered in India. Yet your reputation has not foundered. That is a remarkable feat. Many of us learnt much from you. We gained confidence, and the lessons we learned will endure.' And now he turned to Edwina. She

339

dared not look at him. She glanced across at the impassive face of her husband, and lowered her eyes.

'The gods or some good fairy gave you beauty and high intelligence, and grace and charm and vitality. But they gave you something even rarer – the love of humanity, the healer's touch. Wherever you have gone, you have brought hope and encouragement. Is it surprising, therefore, that the people of India should love you, and should grieve that you are going?' His voice was steady. Only two people at the table knew how personally he meant what he was saying.

'You may have many gifts and presents,' Nehru continued, 'but there is nothing more real and precious than the love and affection of the people . . . . You have seen for yourselves, Sir and Madam, how that love and affection work. We do not look on this as a farewell. We shall remember you always.'

As he finished, he raised his glass for a toast, and the seventy people round the table rose, the wine glittering brightly in the light of the chandeliers.

The Governor General and his wife remained seated as the company stood to honour them. He smiled to her, and she returned his smile, trying not to cry. Reality, cruel reality, had returned at the end of the speech. They were leaving tomorrow.

The route to the airport, and Palam itself, was thronged with people who had poured into the city to say goodbye to the last Viceroy. As the huge open Rolls with its outriders in red and gold on their tall horses passed by the crowd, it took the final trace of the British Raj away with it. The ceremony would remain, and the panoply of state, but they could never be the same again. In the most triumphant Indian heart there was a tiny splinter of sadness at what was passing for ever.

Nehru waited with his Cabinet in the bright morning sunshine. They stood in a line by the steps that led up to the door of the aircraft. Suddenly a cry went up from the crowds by the airport gates.

'Mountbatten *ki jai*! Mountbatten *ki jai*!'

Nehru saw the sunlight glint on the bonnet of the Rolls as it slowly turned into the airfield. Mountbatten, resplendent in his white admiral's uniform, climbed out first and turned to help Edwina. She was wearing a simple cotton dress with an elegant chevron design. The Prime Minister walked forward to meet them.

With Nehru at their side, they said their final goodbyes to the line of waiting Ministers. The new Governor General, C.R. Rajagopalachari, Rajaji, in his immaculate white *kurta* and *dhoti*; V.P. Menon, sad and smiling; Sardar Patel, older and shrunken since his stroke, but as indomitable as ever, who took Mountbatten's hands in both his and could hardly speak at the moment of parting; Rajendra Prasad; Baldev Singh, the Defence Minister; Maulana Azad, the Education Minister; Amrit Kaur. Finally, the handshakes, the smiles, the exchanges of good wishes, were over.

'Mountbatten *ki jai*! Pandit Mountbatten *ki jai*!' the crowd roared.

He raised both hands to them, calling back, '*Jai Hind*!' and the cheers became deafening. Flowers were thrown to him, garlands and single blooms, and brightly coloured confetti which swirled in a light gust of wind. He could not help remembering his first arrival as Viceroy, the much smaller numbers and the muted applause. He was not proud of everything he had done since he came here, but he was proud of the trust and affection he had won from the great mass of the Indian people. He could not resist waving just once more, to hear again that unreserved, full-throated response. He doubted if, ever again in his life, he would hear such cheers for himself alone. Their lives, the lives of untold millions, had depended on the sureness of his hands on the reins and the quickness and agility of his mind. He must not forget his team. Together, they had achieved the impossible.

It was difficult to turn away from the crowd, hard to

give up a throne. He found himself thinking of his cousin and oldest friend, David, now Duke of Windsor. Edwina and he must visit him as soon as they got back. But he himself could never go into exile. He would always have to work. He would go on in the navy, serving his country whenever he was summoned, yet he knew that never again would it be at such a level – or for such high stakes.

Edwina saw that her husband had finished waving and was turning to shake hands with Nehru. Her heart seemed to fall away and for a moment she had to breathe deeply to steady herself. All through the journey from Government House a kaleidoscope of memories had travelled across her mind, distracting her from what she must face. Now the last moment had arrived. She became aware of Dickie waiting for her, and of Nehru, close to her, preparing to say goodbye.

Jawaharlal looked into her brown eyes, storing up his memory of them. He knew that no words which could pass between them would be of any use. Yet something must be said. He held her right hand in his, speaking formally because of the thousands of eyes which watched them.

'I shall not say goodbye, Your Excellency. I know that one day you will return. I shall pray for that day.'

Taking the fresh rosebud from his buttonhole, he kissed it, and gave it to her.

He watched her turn away to join her husband and mount the metal steps to the aeroplane. They paused briefly at the top and waved as the shouts and cheering of the crowd swelled. They entered the cabin, the steps were folded up and the door slammed shut behind them.

As the York taxied away, gathered speed and took off, Nehru found himself wishing that Gandhiji were with him, that he could hear again that wise, calm voice and that lifting, impish laughter. Then he would perhaps feel less lonely in the great task that awaited him. He turned and looked up to where the flag of his new nation flew proudly against the deep blue of the sky, and a verse from the ancient scriptures of India, the *Bhagavad Gita*, came into his mind.

'Thus in many ways men sacrifice, and in many ways they go to Brahman. Know that all sacrifice is holy work, and knowing this, thou shalt be free.'

Thoughtfully, he stood straight and walked towards the airport building.